The Daily Telegraph GUIDE TO PARENTING AND LAW

Aviva Golden

HarperCollins*Publishers*

HarperCollins*Publishers*
P.O. Box, Glasgow G4 0NB

First published 1998

Reprint 10 9 8 7 6 5 4 3 2 1 0

© 1998 Aviva Golden

ISBN 0 00 472142 X

A catalogue record for this book is available from the British Library

The Immunisation chart on p.88 is reproduced with the permission of the Health Education Authority.
The Child Restraints table on p.107 has been reproduced with permission from the Highway Code. (Crown copyright is reproduced with the permission of the Controller of Her Majesty's Stationery Office.)
The table on alcohol legislation appears with the permission of Alcohol Concern, Waterbridge House, 32-36 Loman St, London SE1 0EE.
The police forms on pp. 157-58 are reproduced with the permission of the Metropolitan Police Service.

All rights reserved. No part of this publication may be reproduced, stored in a retrieval system or transmitted, in any form or by any means, without the prior permission of the publisher.

This book is sold subject to the conditions that it shall not, by way of trade or otherwise, be lent, re-sold, hired out or otherwise circulated without the publisher's prior consent in any form of binding or cover other than that in which it is published and without a similar condition including this condition being imposed on the subsequent publisher.

Printed and bound in Great Britain by
Caledonian International Book Manufacturing Ltd, Glasgow G64

This book is dedicated to those who dedicate themselves to working in the voluntary sector and who provide information, support or advice to parents and their children. Their service to us all is inestimable.

CONTENTS

Contents	v
Acknowledgements	vii
Author's notes	ix
Introduction	xi
Part 1 – Starting a family	1
Chapter 1 – Expecting a baby	2
Chapter 2 – The birth	12
Chapter 3 – When you need help towards parenthood	17
Part 2 – Whose rights? Whose responsibilities?	28
Chapter 4 – Parental responsibilities	29
Chapter 5 – You want a divorce – What about the Children?	45
Chapter 6 – Coping in a commercial world	52
Part 3 – Other carers	60
Chapter 7 – Pre-school care	61
Chapter 8 – The extended family	70
Chapter 9 – When parenting fails	83
Part 4 – Minimizing risks	90
Chapter 10 – Your child's health	91
Chapter 11 – Your child's safety	105
Part 5 – Parental control and guidance	118
Chapter 12 – Knowing the rules	119
Part 6 – Education	
Ann Hand	138
Chapter 13 – Ensuring a suitable education	139
Part 7 – Crime	
Victor Gersten	163
Chapter 14 – In trouble with the law	164
Chapter 15 – Children as victims of crime	178
Directory of Organizations	189
Index	203

ACKNOWLEDGEMENTS

A book such as this cannot be written without the help and support of a wide range of people. I would like to stress how grateful I am for the interest and enthusiasm which I received from everyone I approached.

First and foremost I must acknowledge and thank the two persons who contributed directly to the book itself: Ann Hand, LLB (Hons) and Victor Gersten, solicitor, who are respectively responsible for Parts 6 and 7, which deal with the issues of *Education* and *Crime*. Their contributions add greatly to the book and are much appreciated.

In the preparation of Chapter 14, *In trouble with the law*, both Victor and I would like to thank, in particular, the help given to us by Police Sergeant Stephen Lewis of the Youth and Community Section, Metropolitan Police Service.

Jon Robins provided the in-depth legal and other research for Part 6 on *Parental Control and Guidance*, as well as assisting in assembling materials for Chapter 6: *Coping in a commercial world*. I hope that the resulting chapters reflect the care which he took and the involvement which he showed in the task which he undertook on my behalf.

The generosity of the directors of Context Ltd is also deeply appreciated. They allowed me to use Context's extensive databases for research purposes so that I had the use of their law libraries – quite literally – at my fingertips.

My publishers were enthusiastic from the beginning: Christopher Riches, publishing director and Edwin Moore, both of HarperCollins; Vicky Unwin, director of Telegraph Enterprises and Susannah Charlton, manager of Telegraph Books. I would like to thank them for the use I have made of some of the material from *Everyday Law*.

I know how much my editor, Monica Thorp, cared about this book. She brought to it her lively understanding and sympathy for its subject matter, as well as her assiduous attention to detail.

I would also like to thank the persons who answered queries relating to the diverse issues the book raises:

Dr Susan Dukes, GP, Dr John Festenstein, Consultant, and Lorraine Nolan, Health Visitor, for answering my queries on health-related issues.

Paul Bellringer, Director of GamCare, kindly responded to my queries on the intricacies of age-related gambling and fruit machines!

Celia Hampton, barrister and editor of *Financial Times Business Law Europe*, was always forthcoming with her expert help on European law issues.

Mr J M A Kilby, MA, LLB, Chairman, Legislation Panel, Society of Fellows of the Chartered Insurance Institute, was kind enough to answer in detail my queries relating to contracts of children, in particular contracts of insurance.

Jean Campbell, LLM, read the text through and provided useful pointers – legal, editorial, and intellectual, all the way through.

Jacky Carby, my administrative assistant, is a steadfast support and friend. Among her many tasks, Jacky became responsible for the presentation of the DIRECTORY at the end of the book.

Eileen O'Grady, barrister, as always, lent help and gave backing wherever she could.

I now turn to members of my own immediate family. Margaret Jacobson gave thought-provoking and searching commentary on the book as it was being written. Her early suggestions on topics – when the scope of the book was still being actively considered – have all be incorporated.

Hirsh Jacobson provided the background research to the entire range of subject matter of the book and was always at hand, both tirelessly and kindly, to dig up some revealing item or to answer a request.

I also must thank my three children who taught me so much about parenting. Finally, my husband gave me what I needed most – love, patience, and support.

Aviva Golden

AUTHOR'S NOTE

Disclaimer

Please note that the law in this book is applicable to England and Wales only. I have endeavoured to state the law as at the date of going to press. However, this only presents a snapshot of a moving image. With every day that passes the law undergoes significant changes both in the courts of law and in Parliament.

The text, and the examples which illustrate it, are there to give the reader guidance on general principles. They do not point to a specific outcome in any case and cannot be used as a substitution for a full consideration, by a trained legal advisor, of all the facts and the relevant law in any given situation. Therefore, as I cannot assume legal responsibility, readers should seek independent legal advice. Neither the author nor the publishers intend to render a professional legal service with this publication.

The Directories

At the end of the book you will find a DIRECTORY of relevant organizations listed under subject-matter headings. We have endeavoured to ensure that the names and addresses are correct at the time of going to press.

Readers are asked to note that some organizations require an annual membership; some organizations provide information but do not offer advice or handle complaints; some organizations respond to written queries only and cannot answer over the telephone; many of them have publications for sale while a few organizations offer library and other resources.

If any organization would like to be considered for inclusion in future editions of the book, please write to the Reference Department, HarperCollins Publishers, P.O. Box, Glasgow G4 0NB.

Aviva Golden
January 1998

INTRODUCTION

In general, parents love and wish to do the best for their children. Pride and devotion and joy are all part of parenting; so are hard work and strenuous endeavour. Our children's successes become our triumphs and their unhappiness generates our own heartache.

Today, parenting issues receive unprecedented attention, and much advice is offered to parents and to all those who play a part in bringing up children. Whatever values and approach parents may have in caring for their children, however, there is a basic legal framework within which we all have to operate. The law regards the fundamental task, and overwhelming purpose, of parenthood as the duty to care for our children. Parents are expected to safeguard the physical, moral, and emotional welfare of their children and to recognise that these responsibilities decline as children grow up – as Lord Denning said, parental authority 'starts with the right to control and ends with little more than advice'.

As the complexity of society increases so legal involvement in parenting grows, whether it be in relation to fertility treatments, the changing nature of family structures, the provision of child care, school selection, or ensuring that our children are safe while doing a paper round or baby-sitting for a neighbour. However, the law must strike a balance between taking measures in the interest of children and their parents and at the same time not intruding too far into the family and its intimacies. We all quite rightly regard our family life as our own private arena.

In examining the multi-faceted role that the law plays in parenting, it became apparent that there was scope for a book which would deal with wide-ranging information for parents, carers, and others involved in bringing up children. In 15 chapters, this book covers a multitude of topics and takes parents through them from the very beginnings of their child's life to the onset of adulthood.

The book examines the inter-relationship of law and medicine in the sections on pregnancy, childbirth and fertility treatments. It deals with parental responsibilities and examines the legal implications of the parents' status (for example, if they are married to each other or not) as well as their relationship to their children. Important issues such as discipline, religious upbringing, change of name, nationality, and application for passports are all dealt with as part of parental responsibilities. Divorce and maintenance are also examined, as is the very concept of parenthood itself where, for example, a man denies that a child is his. We look at the 'extended family' such as the stepfamily and foster caring because it is now recognized – both in fact and in law – that children of today may encounter more than one home environment in the course of their childhood. Education is at the top of most parents' agenda and the education chapter pays special attention to parental participation. An effort is made to keep parents abreast of the law on education even though it is undergoing such rapid change.

As we shall see, the law's role can be one of support for parents in, for example, laying down regulations on safety matters, such as insisting on safe toys, clothing, or car seats for toddlers. It gives rights to parents and their children who are caught in a fraught situation, such as occurs when a child becomes involved with the criminal law. Sometimes the law restrains parents: in issues of health, for instance, a child may be entitled to opt for confidential medical treatment without involving adults. The law attempts to regulate moral and social behaviour particularly in the spheres of under-age sex, drinking and gambling, and it endeavours to protect the vulnerable against the drug scene. We must also not forget that the law can intervene compulsorily in family life if a situation is reached where a child is likely to suffer significant harm because parenting has failed.

All these topics, and many, many others are examined together with everyday examples and careful advice. You will find checklists for choosing a childminder and for ensuring greater peace of mind if you send your child on an activity holiday. The text does not gloss over some of the areas where the law is unclear or unsatisfactory and you will also be told when you should seek professional legal advice. Referral is made throughout the book to organizations in the voluntary sector which are listed at the end in a DIRECTORY, according to subject matter, and which offer support, information or advice to parents. Their role cannot be overstressed in their readiness to assist in every facet of child-rearing – from dealing with the stress of a crying baby at night to coping with the trauma of bereavement.

The book is clearly focused on the reader's needs. The beginning of each chapter boldly states the issues which you will find in that chapter so you do not have to wade through text in order to find the particular topic which you require. The text is free of legal jargon but is full of topicality. Headline news finds its place along with the law!

Vivid examples are also used to bring the law home to you in a most direct and accessible manner. What happens if your child is hit by another pupil as he reaches the school gate? Are you answerable if your 17-year-old son gets into debt? What is your legal position if you find drugs in your house? Who, if anyone, is responsible if a child complains in court that his parents neglected him and that the local authority should have taken him into care? Have the rules governing adoption changed? What should you do if you receive a phone call from your local police station that your child is accused of shoplifting but he says that he simply forgot to pay? What remedies are available if your ex-husband or former partner is molesting you or your child? Can you stop your teenage child from listening to an adult chatline? These are but an indication of the problems which are dealt with. We all know that they can and do crop up in everday life.

The law – in relation to parenting – can make us acutely aware of the difficulties, stresses and hazards of family life. However, it makes us equally aware of the need for legal structures so that we are able to establish those areas in which the law has a vital role to play in ensuring (or endeavouring to ensure) the wellbeing of children, their parents, and through them, our society at large.

PART 1
STARTING A FAMILY

In the first three chapters we take up some of the topics mentioned in the Introduction. We examine the interaction between law and parenthood – not only from the moment of a child's birth, but even before. Among other matters, we examine the legal aspects in the relationship between medicine, pregnancy, and childbirth. While, above all, the physical wellbeing of children and their parents is the paramount consideration, other pressing questions are raised by this legal intervention.

For example, through the mechanism of the law, society has sought to regulate the techniques which assist infertile couples to have children. The consequences of successful treatment can also be subject to legal control. Legislation determines the parental link in certain cases – in other words, it is the law that decides the basic question of who is the father or mother of a child born as a result of fertility treatment or a surrogacy arrangement.

The debate in these areas is not likely to cease even though legislation endeavours to decide the issues. Pressure groups will continue to seek changes to the law for ethical, social, moral, or medical reasons.

The law itself – in any event – has to keep pace not only with constantly-evolving social patterns in our family relationships, but with scientific advances which generate ever more new challenges in the very creation of life itself.

In these chapters we look at

- Pregnancy
- Childbirth
- Infertility
- Adoption
- Surrogacy.

CHAPTER 1
EXPECTING A BABY

This chapter is divided into sections A, B and C, which deal respectively with the help available from the State, responsibility if something goes wrong, and antenatal screening.

A. HELP FROM THE STATE

The State helps pregnant mothers by providing health education, free antenatal care, and financial support in the form of benefits.

While it is beyond the scope of this book to enter into details of all the benefits which are available, the following outline is an indication of their scope.

MEETING MEDICAL NEEDS

Free NHS prescriptions

To claim free prescriptions during pregnancy you must get form FEW 8 from your doctor, midwife, or health visitor. The form must be forwarded to your health authority. You will then receive an exemption certificate. You must fill in the back of the prescription before you hand it to the pharmacist.

You are entitled to free prescriptions for the duration of your pregnancy and for 12 months after your baby's birth.

Free NHS dental treatment

Any course of NHS dental treatment which starts while you are pregnant or during the 12 months after your baby is born is available free of charge.

You go to a dentist who practises privately. You tell him that you are pregnant. You wonder whether you are then entitled to free treatment.

Only the NHS provides free dental treatment during the course of your pregnancy and for a year after your baby is born. A private dentist is still entitled to his fees.

Supplements to diet

Free milk and vitamins are available for pregnant women and for children under the age of five where the mother is on income support.

For maternity benefits in employment see immediately below. A very useful leaflet is available from the Benefits Agency: *Babies and Benefits – guide to babies and benefits for expectant and new mothers* (Leaflet FBA 8).

RIGHTS AT WORK

Antenatal care

If you are pregnant you are entitled to reasonable time off work to attend appointments for antenatal care. The term 'care' is quite broadly defined and includes

- appointments with doctor or midwife
- relaxation classes
- parenting classes.

You acquire this right immediately. You are also entitled to be paid at your appropriate hourly rate for time off work.

You have told your employer that you have seen your doctor and he has confirmed that you are pregnant. You now wish to make an appointment during working hours for another medical examination. Your employer asks you to confirm that you are pregnant.

Your employer is entitled to see your doctor's certificate. He would also be entitled to see your appointment card if he asks for it.

Dangers to health in employment

While pregnant women cannot be discriminated against in employment, a situation can arise where the work itself can pose a problem to a pregnant woman's health. The position is covered by health and safety regulations intended to protect women who are pregnant or who have given birth within the past six months. Working conditions which could harm a pregnant woman are, for example, exposure to certain chemicals and noise, extremes of temperature, and handling of loads.

You are a librarian in a library and have to carry heavy books. You became pregnant three months ago and you fear a miscarriage. Your doctor advises you against lifting weights. You wonder what your position is in law.

First you must inform your employer in writing that you are pregnant and give him a certificate of pregnancy from your doctor or midwife to that effect. Your employer would have to conduct an investigation into the risk and establish whether it is significant. Your working conditions might be altered to suit you if this can be arranged.

If you have to give up your present work, the conditions outlined below must be satisfied.

Giving up work

You might have to give up a particular job during pregnancy if the reason for doing so is to protect your health.

However:
(a) the risk to the foetus must be clear
(b) you should be offered suitable alternative employment on the same terms
(c) if there is no suitable employment you should be compensated for all financial loss if you have to stop working (in other words, you should be given paid leave)
(d) you should be entitled to reinstatement after the baby is born.

If your employers do not co-operate the onus is on them to show why they are unable to do so.

In the first instance, you are advised to approach your personnel, or trade union, officer or your local Citizens Advice Bureau.

Do note: From 1 January 1996, all employers must provide facilities which will enable pregnant women and nursing mothers to rest.

The Benefits Agency issues a leaflet: *Pregnancy Related Illness* (Leaflet NI 200). This leaflet lists common problems which might relate to pregnancy (although the list is not exhaustive). It should be used to seek professional guidance where there is a continuing dispute between an employer and a pregnant employee.

Part 1 — Starting a family

Maternity leave

Do remember: to claim for the rights below, you will need a maternity certificate (form MAT B1) which you will receive from your doctor or midwife in the 26th week of pregnancy.

The basic right

All women are entitled to a basic 14-week maternity leave period.

Leave can begin at any time within 11 weeks of the confinement date (expected week of confinement (or EWC).

Further rights

For a woman who has worked for two years with the same employer full time, there is the right to an additional period of absence, making 40 weeks in total.

Allowances

Statutory Maternity Pay (SMP)

If you are pregnant you may be able to get this weekly payment from your employer if

(a) you have been in the same employment without a break for at least 26 weeks up to and including the 15th week before the week your baby is due, and
(b) your average weekly earnings were at least £62 per week.

For the first six weeks you will earn 90 per cent of your average pay. After that you will get the basic rate of SMP which as from April 1997 is £55.70 per week.

Must you return to work to claim your allowance?

You are pregnant and have been with the same employer for the past six years. You have been earning approximately £150 per week so you qualify on both the grounds outlined above.

You wish to apply for SMP but have decided that you do not intend to return to your job after your baby is born.

You do not have to intend to resume working to apply for SMP. However if you return to work but for a different employer, you cannot claim from your former boss.

Maternity Allowance

This is a weekly allowance for women who do not qualify for SMP, either because they have changed jobs so that they do not qualify for the two-year period, or because they have left work. It could equally be because they are self-employed.

Do remember: There is a National Insurance payment stipulation.

You have been a self-employed businesswoman for some years. You are pregnant but do not qualify for SMP.

You can claim a maternity allowance provided you have paid National Insurance contributions for at least 26 weeks out of 66 weeks before the EWC.

Unfair dismissal

If the principal reason for dismissing an employee is the fact that she is pregnant, the dismissal is automatically deemed to be unfair.

You are pregnant and have told your employer that you intend leaving work 8 weeks before the baby is due. You have only been with the firm for six months. You have since received a letter from him stating that you will shortly be made redundant. When you requested reasons for your redundancy, you were told that you did not satisfy the minimum service requirement for your request.

You are entitled to full written reasons if you are dismissed at any time during pregnancy. There is no minimum service requirement for this stipulation.

Further, your employer is not allowed to decide to make you redundant because it is inconvenient for him that you are pregnant and will be taking maternity leave. If he has made that a factor, then your dismissal is automatically unfair.

Returning to work

(a) Right to resume employment

After 14 weeks' maternity leave – irrespective of length of service or hours or work – you have the right to return to your work. You may also have a right to return after maternity leave of 29 weeks provided that you have worked for two continuous years.

(b) Same work

You should be able to return to the job (or its equivalent) in which you were employed under your original contract of employment and on terms and conditions not less favourable than before you were absent on maternity leave.

(c) Notified date of return

A woman must give notice in writing to her employer of her intention to return to work at least 21 days before the day on which she intends to return. The process of exercising the right to return to work is complete once the appropriate notice has been given.

Ann wants to return to work after her baby's birth but is not sure of the exact date on which she wishes to return. Her 14-week statutory maternity leave period is due to expire within 21 days.

Giving notice does not oblige Ann to return to work. She is, however, keeping her options open. Notice is very important because all the other rights to which Ann is entitled follow on from it. However, rights are not lost if Ann is unable to return to work because she is temporarily ill on the specific day she had arranged to return.

Position of the father at work

Note that a father-to-be is not entitled by statute to time off work, e.g. to attend parenting classes, unless the terms of his employment allow for it under a private contract with his employer. However, this situation may change now that the UK has signed up to the Social Policy Agreement annexed to the Maastricht Treaty. A draft Directive has been adopted on parental leave which would provide for leave for both parents for family reasons. It stipulates a minimum of three months' unpaid leave, as well as a right to take time off work for urgent family reasons, without being in breach of contract.

The Agreement has been called 'an important contribution to the promotion of real equality in the labour market . . . and the . . . better reconciliation of work and family life . . .'.

B. WHO IS RESPONSIBLE IF SOMETHING GOES WRONG?

Broadly speaking, most women who are expecting a baby will wish to do the best that they can to ensure that their baby will be born well and healthy. To encourage them in this endeavour, the State provides, as we see above, free health care, and other benefits. It is a self-evident fact that the physical well-being of a pregnant woman can have a direct effect on her baby's health.

TAKING CARE OR TAKING RISKS?

Despite the effect of a pregnant woman's health on that of her unborn child, English law cannot compel a mother to adopt a healthy lifestyle, for example by avoiding drug or alcohol abuse or by stopping smoking. She can only be urged to take care of herself.

If she does harm her child because of excess, and her baby is born handicapped as a result, the child has absolutely no rights against her in law. In other words, the mother has legal immunity from being sued by her child.

A pregnant woman also cannot be forced to attend an antenatal clinic. The only exception would be where a woman is detained under the Mental Health legislation where consent of a patient is not required for any 'treatment of a mental disorder'. There have been cases where pregnant women who did not want to accept medical help for a condition in pregnancy were treated under these provisions. (For further questions of a woman's 'competence' to decide on management of labour, see Chapter 2, *The birth*, p.13).

Reckless driving

Jane drives recklessly while pregnant and she has an accident. Her baby is born seriously handicapped as a result.

In these circumstances, legislation allows Jane to be sued by the child as this is seen as a matter for the insurers. She has no immunity in this case.

Injury to the baby through the fault of others

Medical negligence

A mother is entitled to antenatal medical care from the moment she knows she is pregnant. If the care which she receives is negligent and harms the baby then she is entitled to sue on the child's behalf.

In general it is not easy to prove that a baby's handicap has arisen through negligent treatment of the mother as a result of medical advice during the course of pregnancy. As with all negligence claims, the problem lies in proving cause and effect, in particular that it was the negligent medical treatment which caused the baby's subsequent handicap.

Susan consulted her GP because she was having acute backache and was unable to sleep as a result. She had no reason to suspect that she was pregnant and nor did her doctor. He prescribed a strong sleeping tranquilliser. In fact, she was pregnant. Her baby was born with a handicap. She suspects the drug caused the deformity.

Susan would have to prove first, on a balance of probabilities, that the doctor was negligent in not establishing her pregnancy. She then has to prove that he should have known that the drug was likely to cause harm to her unborn child.

Legal liability

The dangers inherent in prescribing drugs for pregnant women became tragically clear after a number of children were born with deformities as a result of their mothers having been prescribed thalidomide. As a result of the public outcry, Parliament was jolted into passing the Congenital Disabilities (Civil Liability) Act. In essence, the Act provides that children born disabled, as a result of someone else's fault, have a remedy in law.

Chapter 1 — Expecting a baby

Note: The negligence must have occurred before their birth.

Under the Act, parents have a right to sue on their child's behalf if a doctor's treatment of the pregnant mother is negligent – not only by prescribing drugs but in any other way – provided it can be shown that the baby was born deformed as a result of the negligence.

If there is negligence in a case of assisted conception which leads to disability, an action for negligence can also follow (this is further discussed in Chapter 3, section *IVF – The 'test-tube' baby*, p.19).

Negligent treatment administered even prior to conception can lead to liability.

A woman is given a blood transfusion which renders her rhesus incompatible with her husband. She is not warned of the danger of conceiving. Some months later she falls pregnant and the baby thereafter is born severely disabled.

In a similar case, the mother received damages on behalf of her handicapped child.

Note: A mother cannot be liable to her child if she takes an unsuitable drug during her pregnancy against the advice of the doctors, and the child is born disabled. In such a case, her child can sue neither the mother nor the doctors.

Violence to the mother

Obviously if the mother is harmed by another person, her unborn child can be harmed too. There is no immunity for the father equivalent to that for the pregnant mother. If he harms his pregnant partner and that harm results in a disability to their child, the child can sue him.

C. ANTENATAL SCREENING

PRE-EXISTING CONDITIONS

Pregnant women now have several tests as a matter of routine. Pre-natal diagnosis is being used more and more as screening allows the presence of certain diseases and abnormalities to be established within a few months of conception.

The legal implications of these new techniques are far-reaching. All advances create their own dilemmas, both for society as a whole and for parents who find themselves in a situation where critical decisions have to be made.

A pregnant mother will be told at an antenatal appointment which blood tests are required during the course of her pregnancy and what they are for. Some women do refuse the tests as they do not want to know of the risk of any abnormality. The doctor would note in the records that the tests were offered and refused.

No specific consent forms need to be signed for a blood test. An HIV test would be offered where the mother's history (or that of her partner) indicates that this is advisable.

Amniocentesis test

An amniocentesis test is offered for women over 35. The test is intended, in particular, to detect a chromosomal abnormality which indicates Down's Syndrome. The risk is age-related.

An amniocentesis test would also be offered where previous blood tests showed a higher than usual risk of foetal abnormality – irrespective of age.

The amniocentesis test can bring on a miscarriage – the risk is put at about 1 per cent.

The legal position is as follows:

Part 1 — Starting a family

1. Under the law, the mother must consent to the test and it must be 'informed consent' i.e. she must be aware of the risk that the test entails.
2. Where this or other tests reveal a 'serious handicap' the mother would be entitled to have an abortion (see p.9).
3. However, a woman should not be subjected to pressure to have an abortion although doctors might try to persuade her to terminate the pregnancy.
4. Where a test is not given to a woman over 35 the medical team may be liable for negligence.

Failure to give the test

In a recent case, a doctor told a thirty-five-year-old woman that she did not need an amniocentesis test as she risked aborting what was probably a perfectly healthy foetus. (In fact the procedure carries a one per cent risk of miscarriage.) Her baby was born with Down's Syndrome and the mother sued for negligence. She was awarded £300,000 compensation.

Pre-pregnancy screening

The problems of identifying faulty genes can arise even before conception if either partner has a family predisposition to a particular disease.

Inherited single-gene diseases are found in an extremely small percentage of the population. However, within the family at risk, there might be a high percentage of carriers, or potential carriers, of the gene.

International Treaties governing genetic testing

1. *The Convention on Human Rights and Biomedicine*
   This is a new Treaty that was signed on 1 April 1997 by some member states of the European Community. Article 1 provides that the Convention is intended to protect and guarantee rights, integrity and fundamental freedoms with regard to the application of biology and medicine.

   Tests which are predictive of genetic disease may only be performed subject to appropriate genetic counselling, and intervention can only be undertaken for therapeutic and related purposes.

2. *The Draft International Convention on the Human Genome*
   The genome project is intended to identify and define the function of all the genes (some 100,000) in every cell in the human body.

   Member States must take effective measures

   (a) to ensure that pressure based on these findings is not brought upon any parent of an unborn child for a pregnancy to be terminated;
   (b) to forbid as a ground for encouraging termination of pregnancy alleged congenital or gene-related deficiencies based on any preconceived 'standard of normality';
   (c) to forbid as a ground for encouraging termination of pregnancy genetic predisposition to illness which may be likely to occur in later life;
   (d) to impose no financial or social consequences on persons who refuse to undergo operations advised for genetic reasons.

   It also 'encourages' complete confidentiality of human genome information. Moreover, persons should have the right to choose whether or not to be given such genetic information.

Note of warning: the insurance industry has issued a code of practice which deals with test information. It requires that existing test results should be given if insurers ask relevant questions.

Genetic screening and fathers

For the would-be father, advice on diet, smoking and alcohol is available and should be followed.

In addition, in our present context, the problems raised by genetic counselling apply to men as they do to women.

1. In certain instances, it might be the father who is carrying the defective gene and not the mother.
2. A man may have an illness which can also affect the child.
3. Where a foetus is found to be abnormal, the father's wishes about whether to have the child should also be taken into account as both parents may have to face a lifetime of caring for their handicapped child. (However, see *Fathers and abortion*, p.11 below.)

Rubella (German measles)

If a woman falls ill with Rubella during the early months of pregnancy, her child could be born severely disabled. Women therefore ought to be screened for immunity to Rubella before becoming pregnant. If the test proves negative, they are entitled to a vaccination. They are advised not to try for a pregnancy until three months thereafter.

If Rubella is contracted during the course of pregnancy, an abortion is advised.

TERMINATION

A mother must receive proper advice on the options available to her if tests do prove positive or if a routine ultra-sound scan shows an abnormality such as spina bifida.

In deciding whether or not to proceed with an abortion, mothers are entitled to all the information available so as to make a free and informed choice. They should not be put under any pressure to have an abortion if it is against their wishes, although it would seem that with scarce NHS resources, and the cost of caring for a handicapped child, pressure is sometimes being brought to bear for an abortion as the alternative which parents should choose. One must remember too that the pressure may be applied when the mother is vulnerable both because of her pregnancy and because of fear of what the future may bring.

Thus enormous problems are raised. The Abortion Act refers to a 'serious handicap' but cannot, of course, define it. What is a serious handicap? Each case depends so much on the individual views of parents and their doctors.

Prolonging life

A further issue is that if a handicapped baby is born alive, doctors now have a vast array of advanced technological facilities at their disposal to prolong an infant's life.

> Mrs A, who is pregnant, has been told that her baby may be born with a severe handicap. She refuses an abortion and wants to be assured that her baby will be given every chance to survive.
>
> Generally speaking, doctors are under a duty to provide all the medical services at their disposal.

Two cases which considered this issue decided that above all the doctors had to determine what would be in the best interests of the child. Even given the fullest possible weight to human kind's desire to survive, it might not be in the interest of the child 'to subject it to treatment which will cause increased suffering and produce no commensurate benefit. . .'.

Should doctors or parents decide the issue?

The guidelines laid down by the courts appear to be as follows:

1. Doctors cannot hasten the death of a handicapped baby.
2. They are not obliged to resort to artificial feeding and other methods to prolong life.
3. Treatment should 'allow . . . life to come to an end peacefully and with dignity. . . .'
4. Any decision should be based on the best interests of the child alone.
5. The wishes of parents are not conclusive.

Parents might not agree, and might wish to see their child's life preserved at all costs. Thus it is the courts which have had to decide these issues where parents and doctors have disagreed.

Do remember: Each case is different and will be decided upon its own particular set of circumstances.

Abortion Act 1967

Until the Act most abortions were performed illegally. Not only was the woman's health put at risk but doctors, who might have acted out of genuine concern because the mother's health was in danger, found that they themselves were in jeopardy from the law and could face prosecution.

The Act allows for a lawful abortion under the following conditions:

1. Two registered doctors must decide that an abortion is necessary on the grounds that continuance of pregnancy would involve a risk greater than would exist if the pregnancy were terminated,

    (a) to the life of the pregnant woman or
    (b) of injury to her physical or mental health or
    (c) to the physical or mental health of her existing family.

2. Alternatively they might decide that there is a substantial risk that if the child were born it would suffer from such physical or mental abnormalities as to be seriously handicapped.

Note: the doctors are entitled to take into account the mother's environment in assessing the risk either to her or to her existing children. In light of all these factors, it is generally accepted that abortion is easily available.

Must there always be two doctors involved?

You are pregnant but have found yourself in a life-threatening situation because you have developed cancer. You understand that you need the opinion of two doctors.

Under exceptional circumstances, where an abortion is immediately necessary to save the life of the woman, or to prevent grave or permanent injury to her health, a single doctor can act alone.

Time Limits

Under the Abortion Act the time limit for lawful abortion on grounds of risk to the mother is 24 weeks since conception.

However under the Human Fertilization and Embryology Act, there are no time limits where

(a) the abortion is necessary to prevent grave permanent injury to the physical or mental health of the mother;
(b) a continued pregnancy threatens the mother's life; or

(c) there is a substantial risk that if the child is born it would suffer from such physical or mental abnormalities as to be seriously handicapped.

In other words, abortion in these circumstances may be performed right up to birth.

Selective reduction of the number of foetuses

Where there is likely to be a multiple birth, whether as a result of fertility drugs or for any other reason, selective reduction is lawful on the same grounds as those which apply for terminating the whole pregnancy.

'Morning after' pill

The 'morning after' pill would appear to give no clear dividing line between abortion and contraception. However, the pill is available on prescription.

Fathers and abortion

The father of an unborn child has no say in law in a decision on an abortion.

> *Your partner is pregnant but says that she does not want the child. She feels that she has good legal grounds for an abortion. You are desperately keen to have a baby and wish to take steps to prevent a termination. What can you do?*

> As the law stands at present, you would not be able to stop the abortion provided your girlfriend can fulfil the legal/medical grounds for terminating her pregnancy.

Do note: The same rule applies irrespective of whether the couple are married or not.

CHAPTER 2
THE BIRTH

This chapter deals with issues relating to the baby's birth. Part A deals with the medical/legal aspects and Part B with the formalities of registering a birth.

A. THE LAW GOVERNING THE MEDICAL ASPECTS

HOME OR HOSPITAL?

Home birth

You can have your baby at home and you are legally entitled to do so. You will have to sign form EC24 which is a contract for care with your GP or the hospital team in charge. A midwife will then contact you.

If your doctor is not prepared to treat you you could write to the Nursing Officer, Midwifery section, c/o your local district health authority.

You were unhappy giving birth to your first baby in hospital. You want to have a home birth. Your GP has advised against it. You wonder what the criteria, if any, are for advising against a home birth.

A home birth is not advised for women who might be at risk of developing problems during labour. Women in this category are those

(a) whose previous pregnancy and labour developed complications;

(b) who are 35 or over.

High-risk women are still safer in hospital.

Hospital births are also advised for women expecting their first baby.

Even where there are factors predisposing to problems, a mother can still opt to have her baby at home. The midwife will try to explain that it would be in the best interests of mother and baby to go into hospital. The midwife is in the position that although her advice may not be taken, she is still responsible for mother and child.

Should complications arise in home labour thereafter, the midwife can call in an emergency obstetric team.

Who can 'attend' in childbirth?

Except in a case of emergency, it is a criminal offence for a person other than a registered midwife or a registered medical practitioner to 'attend a woman in childbirth'. The offence is punishable with a fine. Any person means any person including a husband! However, a husband or partner can be present at the birth – the word 'attend' in this context should be taken to mean 'deliver'.

A MOTHER'S RIGHTS

The NHS has issued a Patients' Charter on Maternity Services, available from the Health Information Service: Tel. 0800 665544.

Chapter 2 — The birth

Much has been done to make childbirth safer for the majority of women. Doctors and midwives are there to assist and, in the normal course of events, their assistance is appreciated.

However, the courts have been much troubled recently by the question of consent of the mother to various procedures – even taken in her best interests. When a mother goes into labour, what is she consenting to? There have to be some routine procedures which can go ahead without specific consent, but where is the line to be drawn?

Certain procedures, for example the giving of an epidural injection to relieve pain, are explained to the mother during the course of her pregnancy by doctor and anaesthetist. The consent of the client is then documented – as would be any refusal. There is no specific consent form for routine matters.

Management of labour – consent and competence

However, the question of consent has recently arisen in a number of cases where the medical team have advised a Caesarean birth and the mother has opposed one.

In 1994-95, about 15 per cent of deliveries were by Caesarean section; more than half of these were emergencies. In the decade between 1985 and 1994-95, the Caesarean rate increased from 10.4 per cent to 15.5 per cent.

In one case a mother was suffering from high blood pressure (pre-eclampsia). She did not wish the baby to be induced and refused obstetric intervention. She was sectioned under the Mental Health Act for her own protection and for the protection of her unborn child and a Caesarean operation was then performed against her wishes.

There have been other such cases. A recent test case was heard in the Court of Appeal where a mother took the Health Authority to court to challenge the doctors' powers as well as those of the judges.

She had refused to have a Caesarean because of a needle phobia. The Health Authority obtained a declaration from the High Court that it would be lawful for a consultant gynaecologist to perform the operation. The Court of Appeal confirmed the declaration on the ground that the mother had not been 'competent' to decide at that particular juncture because her fear of needles had overridden her reason.

However, in the judgment, the appeal court endeavoured to lay down guidelines while acknowledging that each case presented its own problems in deciding on 'competence'. The judgment states the following:

(a) that every person is presumed to have the capacity to consent to or to refuse medical treatment unless and until that presumption is shown to be wrong;
(b) that a competent woman who has the capacity to decide may – for religious reasons, other reasons, for rational or irrational reasons, or for no reason at all – choose to refuse medical intervention, even though the consequences could be her death, or the serious handicap or death of her baby;
(c) the court cannot take the interests of the unborn child into account even if those interests are put at risk because of the mother's refusal to have medical intervention where the mother is competent to decide the issue.

Thus for a decision to be taken against the mother's will, the doctors would have to show to the court that the mother suffered from some mental impairment or mental disfunctioning which rendered her incapable of deciding whether to consent or to refuse treatment. Panic or irrationality in themselves did not amount to incompetence but might be symptoms or evidence of it.

Negligence

Note: under the general law of negligence, there can never be consent to the negligent treatment of either mother or child.

Note also: a child sues by a 'next friend' – generally this is his or her parent. Court proceedings involving claims by children are discussed in Part 4, *Minimizing Risks*.

PREMATURE BIRTH – WHAT ARE THE PARENTS' RIGHTS?

Some sort of balance must be struck between the pain of prolonged life and the finality of death in severe cases of prematurity. One in fourteen children is said to be born prematurely. The parents' views are always to be considered but are never in law conclusive as to their child's fate.

In one case a doctor concluded that a baby girl was too premature to live and took no steps to save her life. The parents insisted upon a fatal accidents inquiry which decided that doctors can override parents' wishes where, in their medical judgment, the baby has no survival prospects.

The guidelines appear to be that babies with a birthweight of over 500 grams should be put into intensive care, although in each case the circumstances will vary with medical assessment of all the factors. Statistics appear to show that very premature babies – if they survive – may suffer from major disability in later life.

In the DIRECTORY are names of organizations which provide assistance in cases of stillbirth, neonatal deaths and miscarriages.

POST-NATAL CARE

Under the Patients' Charter, every mother can expect a visit from the Health Visitor within two weeks of the birth. The welfare of the mother and baby then becomes the Health Visitor's responsibility. The role of the Health Visitor is further discussed in Chapter 10, *Your child's health*, p.92.

Post-natal depression

Many women suffer from post-natal blues. Post-natal depression is a term which indicates a state which goes beyond feeling rather low and unable to cope properly. The health visitor will make a judgment on a sliding scale in order to assess the severity of the depression. She will also consider other factors in the household in addition to the mother's state of mind.

> *You have recently given birth to your first child. You found it difficult to bond with her from the beginning. Lack of sleep and the baby's fretfulness are beginning to prey seriously on your nerves. You find that you are crying all the time and want to run away from home. You have spoken to your GP and felt him to be unsympathetic. You wonder what help your health visitor can provide.*

She may put you in touch with outreach or parenting groups to prevent social isolation. If she feels that your mental state has gone beyond her remit, she may wish to refer you to a community psychiatric nurse or request your consent to approach your GP.

If she felt that either you or the baby were in danger she would approach your GP even without consent.

There are mother and baby units where mothers and babies can stay to tide them over the worst stages of post-natal depression.

Chapter 2 — The birth

Psychotic state

These preventative measures are taken because it is recognized that a newly delivered mother can succumb to a psychotic state in which she can harm herself or her baby. Infanticide is the killing of a child by its mother within 12 months of birth while the balance of her mind is disturbed. In the chapter on *Children as victims of crime*, infanticide is further discussed (see Chapter 15, p.179).

B. FORMALITIES

NOTIFYING THE BIRTH

A notice of every birth must be given by a person in attendance at the birth, such as the doctor or midwife, to the district officer of health within 36 hours.

Registering the birth

The birth of every child must be registered within 42 days with the Registrar of Births and Deaths of the sub-district in which the birth took place. The Registrar may go to an 'outpost' office such as a local library or community centre where you can have the birth registered. It may be possible to register the birth before you leave hospital.

Married parents

Where parents are married, it is usually the father or mother who registers the birth.

Arrangements can be made to register a child even if you are no longer in the district in which the birth took place.

You leave the district where your baby was born. Do you need to go back to it in order to register the birth?

The answer is 'no'. You need not return to the district in person. You could go to any registrar of births in England and Wales to give details. The mother or father, as well as the registrar, must sign a declaration, which is then sent to the registrar of the sub-district where the birth took place.

Unmarried parents

For fathers and mothers who are not married to each other, the procedures are as follows.

If the father wishes his name to appear on the birth certificate, then either

(a) the father and mother must attend together at the Registrar's office;
(b) if the father cannot attend, he must make a statutory declaration of paternity. This a pro-forma form which must be completed in the presence of a solicitor and must be produced to the registrar. The mother must make her own declaration at the same time that he is the father;
or
(c) if the father attends the office, the mother can make a statutory declaration, also on a pro-forma form and completed in a solicitor's presence, acknowledging the father's paternity. The father must give this declaration to the Registrar. He must then make his own declaration at the same time;
or

d) where mother and father have entered into a Parental Responsibility Agreement (see Chapter 4, p.30) or there is an appropriate court order, this must be produced to the Registrar.

You fell pregnant and the father abandoned you. You have since given birth to a little girl. You do not wish to include any details of her father on the birth certificate.

No details need be given of the unmarried father if the mother so wishes. (For the father's on-going liability to support the child, see Chapter 4, p.34.)

Among other information to be supplied to the Registrar are

- the date and place of the baby's birth
- the sex of the child
- the baby's name (see also Chapter 4, section on *Naming a child*, p.38).

Birth Certificates

In all cases, after the birth is registered, a short birth certificate is issued free of charge. This short certificate is sufficient for most requirements but a complete copy of the register entry can be purchased – as a full birth certificate – if need be. Additional copies of the short certificate can also be purchased at any time.

Note: if natural parents subsequently marry, their children are legitimated and can be re-registered as such.

For the situation of registering a birth under a surrogacy arrangement, see Chapter 3, p.26).

NHS card

Your baby will need an NHS card to register with a doctor. When you register your baby's birth the registrar will give you form FP 58 . Fill it in and send it your doctor. You will then receive an NHS card with your baby's number on it.

CHAPTER 3
WHEN YOU NEED HELP TOWARDS PARENTHOOD

There has been the most extraordinary progress in medical science in helping infertile couples who would have remained childless even a few years ago, to have children of their own. It is estimated that as many as one in six couples seek advice and assistance in dealing with problems of infertility.

At the same time, these undoubted advances have brought in their wake serious legal and ethical issues. In such a difficult area, the law must try to reach some sort of consensus of society's view of the issues. There is no doubt that these developments in the field of bio-medicine and fertility treatment have forced us to reconsider some of our most familiar patterns of human relationships. The treatments impinge on our private concerns, as well as society's view as a whole on family life. The treatments can overcome age – a woman of 63 recently gave birth as the surrogate mother to her own daughter's child – and even death itself where the frozen sperm or eggs of a deceased man or woman can be used today to conceive a future generation.

Until the advent of fertility treatments, adoption was the only alternative for childless couples who wished to start a family. Adoption patterns have changed over the years; for example about half the present number of adoptions involve the step-parents of the child, and the age of the children has risen steadily. At present, adoption placements and procedures are the subject of two inspection reports issued by the Department of Health – *For Children's Sake*, Parts 1 and 2.

Some childless couples enter into surrogacy agreements which are also discussed below. The vexed questions posed by surrogacy are currently under government review.

This chapter is divided into sections A, B and C, which deal with *fertility treatments*, *adoption* and *surrogacy* respectively.

A. FERTILITY TREATMENTS

THE LEGISLATION

Because reproductive science is developing in so revolutionary a way, and society at large feels so intense an interest in the issues and dilemmas which are being raised, the need for regulation by law was soon recognized. The Human Fertilization and Embryology Act was passed in 1990 as a result. The Act set up a supervisory body, the Human Fertilization and Embryology Authority, whose function is

(a) to regulate and license reproductive medicine;
(b) to regulate and license research in the field;
(c) to establish the status of parents and of the children born as a result of new techniques;
(d) to 'outlaw' research and/or techniques which are felt to be unacceptable in our society.
 Its role is also to protect
 (i) patients
 (ii) doctors

(iii) children born as a result of treatment
(iv) anonymous donors who might not want to have unexpected parenthood imposed upon them.

The Human Fertilisation and Embryology Authority has numerous publications available for those seeking advice and clarification both on the medical techniques involved in and the legal implications of accepting fertility treatment.

The *Patients' Guide*, issued by the HF&EA contains a list of all the clinics available and the type of treatment which each clinic provides (see the DIRECTORY for these and other addresses).

All clinics which provide fertility treatment must be licensed by the Authority and operate according to its Code of Practice which is also available on application. The Patients' Guide publishes the success rates for the various clinics and treatments.

PROCEDURES

There are many procedures, all subject to the Code of Practice issued by the Authority. This specifies that licensed treatment can only be given with consent in writing.

The welfare of the child is to be taken into account so that an assessment must
- try to establish risks to the child's future well-being
- try to gauge the commitment of would-be parents to bringing up a child.

It also specifies that persons seeking treatment must be given proper information and be offered counselling.

There are a number of treatments available. If treatment is successful, the legal implications depend, among other matters, on whether or not the couple are married to each other, on whether or not the mother's own eggs are used, and on whether her partner's or a donor's sperm is used.

Note: you are strenuously advised to seek legal assistance and counselling if you are uncertain of the legal implications of the outcome of successful treatment.

Consent

A woman has to give written consent to treatment. She can consent to all stages of the treatment or to certain stages only. Before consenting to treatment, she must be given a suitable opportunity to receive proper counselling about the implications of what is being proposed.

A man must also give written consent to the proposed course of treatment.

If he is married to the woman, his consent will make him the legal father of the child even though the child was conceived with donor sperm.

If he is not married to his partner but they have both consented together to receiving treatment then he too will be considered in law as the father of the child.

The issue of whether consent must always be given in writing both for the removal of genetic material and for its subsequent storage and use is the subject of a government consultation exercise set up in September 1997.

RELATIONSHIPS

Both parents providing genetic material

Provided a woman's own eggs are used, together with her partner's sperm, the genetic status

Chapter 3 — When you need help towards parenthood

of their child is exactly the same as in any other case of genetic parentage. If the parents are married to each other, they both have parental responsibility for their child. If they are not married to each other, the father must acquire parental responsibility either with the mother's consent or by court order.

A man's sperm can be stored by freezing, and difficulties could arise where a woman would wish for

(a) a post-death conception
or
(b) a post-divorce baby (i.e. where the divorce precedes conception).

Cases such as these have arisen and the law in this regard – as well as the legal implications of the removal, use and storage of frozen eggs – is to be reviewed.

IVF – The 'test-tube' baby

You are unable to conceive because, although you ovulate normally, for physiological reasons fertilization cannot take place.

By using IVF, you have a chance of having your own child.

Sperm and eggs are mixed in a culture dish (*in vitro*) outside your body. Between one and three of the resulting embryos are then transferred into your womb.

The embryos are screened for normal development. If there is negligence in a case of assisted conception and your baby is born disabled as a result of the doctors' fault, then you have a remedy in law under the Congenital Disabilities (Civil Liability) Act.

Although IVF is generally used when the mother has difficulty in conceiving, it can also be used when one partner may have a defective gene and the parents wish to ensure their baby's health.

Note: Donated eggs may also be used because the mother has none, so her partner's sperm is used to fertilize a donor's eggs. The birth mother is the legal mother of the resulting child.

Insemination by donor sperm

Donor insemination is a treatment used when the male is infertile. It is now an established fact that levels of male fertility are declining so treatments relating to insemination by donor, rather than by the woman's partner, are likely to become more frequent.

Who is the father of a child by donor insemination?

Married parents

Tests have shown that you are infertile. Your wife suggests that donor sperm be used. You wonder whether that will affect your status as father of the child.

If your wife seeks treatment with donor sperm, you will be the legal father of any resultant child provided that you can show that you consented to the treatment. Consent should be in writing.

In effect, this is an extension in a modern medical context of the traditional presumption of legitimacy, i.e. that the husband is the father of any child born to his wife during their marriage.

Unmarried parents

Under the Human Fertilization and Embryology Act, a man not married to his partner, who has agreed to her receiving artificial insemination because he is not fertile, will be regarded in law as the father of the child provided that the couple are treated together in a licensed clinic.

A judge has described this as 'a unique provision'. It is the only provision in English law whereby an unmarried partner acquires parenthood along with the mother though he is not the genetic father. Not even an adoption order can be made in favour of two people unless they are married; nor can a parental order relating to a child born to a surrogate mother be made other than in favour of a married couple (see p.26).

By being given non-genetic paternity, an unmarried man acquires substantial obligations of fatherhood towards the child – in particular, he at once acquires an obligation to provide financial support for the child (or children) throughout their years of dependence.

However, he does not enjoy the rights and powers of parental responsibility as is the case with a man married to the child's mother. He can, though, acquire parental responsibility with the mother's formal agreement. Alternatively, without her agreement, he has the right to seek to persuade a court to grant him parental responsibility.

Note of warning: In the above circumstances, before a man acts in such a way as to acquire non-genetic paternity under the Act he should have been warned of the consequences and given a full opportunity to make an informed choice.

The Code of Practice identifies the information which has to be given to the couple before treatment is provided – in particular, who will be the child's parent or parents under the Act.

The legal consequences of fertility treatment on parenthood

The complicated issues of parenthood can be summed up as follows:

(i) *Married parents*
Where the sperm is taken from the father and the eggs from the mother, their baby is in the same position with regard to status as any other. Both parents have parental responsibility.

If sperm is taken from a donor, the woman's husband will be the legal father of a child born as a result of the treatment unless

(a) they are separated;
(b) he did not consent to the treatment (consent or refusal should be in writing).

(ii) *Unmarried parents*
(a) Where the father is not married to the mother but the embryo is conceived from his sperm and his partner's eggs, he is in law the child's father. He would have to take the same steps to acquire all the rights, duties and powers comprising parental responsibility as any other unmarried father. He would be liable for maintenance in any event.

Jack agreed with Jill that they should have fertility treatment together. They had been living together for two years but were unable to conceive. He donated his sperm at a clinic where it was stored. Jill became pregnant some time thereafter. Jack and Jill separated before the child was born. Jill sought financial support which Jack refused.

The biological father of a child will be treated in law as the child's father where he has given effective consent and the parents have together received treatment. As Jack fulfilled both these conditions and had never withdrawn his consent to treatment, he is liable for maintenance.

(b) Where the woman and man are not married to each other and sperm from a donor is used, provided that her partner has given written acknowledgement that (1) they are being treated together, and (2) donated sperm is being used, then the woman receiving treatment and her male partner will be the legal parents of any resulting child. Her partner will still have to take steps to acquire parental responsibility.

Centres must try to obtain the written acknowledgement of the man both that they are being treated together and that donated sperm is being used.

Chapter 3 — When you need help towards parenthood

Do Note: This is not an exhaustive statement of the law and couples are strenuously advised to seek proper assistance in all cases to establish their legal position as would-be parents.

Donation – position of donor

Donors are screened for HIV, as well as for genetic disorders.

Sperm donation

A sperm donor will not have any legal relationship or obligations to any child born as a result of his donation. The child also has no claims upon him.

Egg donation

In the case of egg donation, the law states that it is the birth mother who is the legal mother of the child.

There is no prohibition on the use of close relatives as donors, but the HFEA is likely to discourage it because of concern about problems of identity for the child and potential conflict between 'mothers'.

Counselling

The Act requires that a patient or donor must have 'a suitable opportunity to receive proper counselling about the implications of taking the proposed steps.' All relevant information must be provided.

Confidentiality for donors

The clinic specifies that all donors must provide certain information such as name and date of birth. Other non-identifying information, such as eye and hair colour, and occupation, is also held on a register. The record is confidential.

It also records children born as a result of fertility treatments. Donors and patients are allowed to access their own records to check for accuracy.

A child's right to establish his or her parental background

The position in law is that the HFEA has a duty to provide information to anyone over the age of 18 who asks whether they were born as a result of treatment using donated eggs or sperm. They must have been given a suitable opportunity to receive proper counselling about the implications of complying with their inquiry. The identity of the donor is kept anonymous.

Persons aged 16 or over are entitled to establish whether the person he or she proposes to marry might be a relative as a result of donated eggs or sperm.

The legal position may change in that further information could be required to be given by law in the future. However, that information could not be given retrospectively, so a sperm donor today will remain anonymous even if the legislative requirements about the degree of anonymity change at a later date.

Is there a 'right' to infertility treatment?

Two questions arise here:

(a) the availability of treatment under the NHS
(b) whether the would-be parent must be a suitable candidate for parenthood.

Age and gender restrictions

Legislation does not exclude any category of woman from being considered for treatment. However, the welfare of the child has to be taken into account before a woman is given fertility treatment (and this includes the need of that child for a father). The duty to take into account the child's welfare is a pre-condition for a treatment licence for the clinic.

Each clinic follows its own practice regarding the question of an upper age limit for women or whether single women should receive fertility treatment provided that the child's welfare has been considered. The importance of there being a stable and supportive environment for the child is also stressed.

Co-parenting

In the ever-changing patterns of social behaviour, certain families have opted to co-parent. In other words, they share parenting, in heterosexual or other households. Co-parenting is most commonly associated with lesbian partnerships where one partner may have had a child from a previous union or has been artificially inseminated so that both partners can bring up 'their' child. Co-parenting, in the absence of legal arrangements such as a Parental Responsibility Agreement, is completely informal.

B. ADOPTION

Adoption is the total and legal transfer of a child from the birth parent(s) to other parent(s). It is intended to terminate the child's existing legal relationship and to give all the rights, duties and powers of parental responsibility to the adopting parents.

Adoption procedures are strictly controlled by legislation and the child's new status is given formal recognition by the court. A new birth certificate is entered into the register in place of the child's original birth certificate.

Adopting parents are carefully vetted by an adoption agency (in the voluntary sector) or the local authority acting as an adoption agency. There are many more parents wishing to adopt children than there are children available for them to adopt.

Adopting parents are usually

- childless couples or
- step-parents or
- a natural parent, such as the unmarried father of a child.

There were 5,962 orders for adoption made in 1996. Of these, about 50 per cent were step-parent adoptions. Only 253 involved babies under 12 months. The majority of children were already in the care of the local authority, and only one in four were birth-parent referrals. Over 62% of children were aged 6 or older.

(See the DIRECTORY for organizations which give information or advice on adoption issues.)

Where there is a complete severance of all ties between children and natural parents, the child's new family is expected to take their place, as well as the place of other relatives.

You are unmarried and have given full agreement to the adoption of your baby girl aged three months. However, your mother, the child's grandmother, wishes to maintain contact with the child. What is her position?

A natural grandmother would have to obtain the permission of the court [i.e. 'leave of court'] to make application for a contact order and would have to persuade the court that it would be in the child's best interests for contact to be maintained. The court would also take into account the views and feelings of the adopting parents.

Chapter 3 — When you need help towards parenthood

Do Note: Even though the law intends adoption to sever all former ties, this may not be practicable for many adopted children, as the majority are aged 6 or over at the time of adoption, and links with their birth parents are already forged.

THE PROCEDURES

By law, local social services authorities and other adoption agencies must

(a) give first consideration to the child;
(b) pay attention to the natural parents' concern for religious upbringing.

They are under a statutory duty to set up adoption panels which, by law, must now consist of three lay persons (in addition to social workers and health professionals). Where practical one of them should be an adoptive parent or an adopted person.

Recent changes

During the course of 1997 other changes were introduced into the procedures for selecting adoptive parents.

1. Couples must be told when their application is being considered by an adoption panel.
2. They will receive a copy of their assessment report, which goes before the panel, and must be given a chance to respond to it, in writing.

Jane and John have applied to adopt a child. They have been told that the agency is refusing their application. They want to take further action.

The agency has to notify them in writing that they do not consider them suitable. They must receive written reasons together with a copy of the recommendation of the adoption panel if different. Jane and John are then entitled to make their views known within 28 days. The adoption agency can then refer the matter back to the panel for further consideration.

Conflicts of interest

In cases of adoption, the natural parent(s) must consent voluntarily. Regulations require the local authority to 'work in partnership with birth families to meet their needs arising from the adoption of their children.' This responsibility is not limited in time.

Conflicts do arise between a local authority, which has a child in care and wishes to free it for adoption, and the child's natural parent(s) who oppose this. The court thus becomes the final arbiter in disputes where the natural parents – usually an unmarried mother – refuse to agree to an adoption.

An adoption agency can submit that the parents are 'unreasonably withholding their consent' and ask the court to override the parents' wishes.

These are some of the most difficult and painful cases which a court has to deal with. The guidelines at present are that the court must view the case in terms of whether a 'reasonable' parent would see that adoption is in the long-term best interests of the child.

However, the prospect of a child being reunited with his or her birth parents can play a critical part in the court's decision.

Adoptions from abroad

In this country a couple who wish to adopt a child from another country are advised to go through the proper channels for inter-country adoptions.

At present, the preliminary, official process for an adoption from abroad involves the following:

- the local social services department
- the Department of Health
- the Home Office and
- the British embassy of the country where the child is located.

The procedures are intended to protect the interests of both would-be parents and their prospective adopted child. In 1995/96 there were 155 applications to adopt children from abroad processed by the Department of Health.

Re-establishing contact – child and natural parents

(a) Access to birth records

At the age of 18 adopted children now have access to their original birth records so that they can establish their original parentage.

There are limitations:

(a) for adoption before 1975, counselling is obligatory;
(b) information against the public interest can be withheld where, for example, there are genuine fears that the applicant might harm his birth parents.

See the DIRECTORY for organizations that give counselling and advice on re-establishing contact with your natural parents.

(b) Adoption Contact Register

Relatives of a child who has been adopted can record their details in a register if they wish to resume contact. These details will then be passed on provided that the adopted person – in turn – has indicated that he or she wishes to resume contact.

Changing adoption patterns

Unmarried mothers now receive state support to bring up their babies. The stigma which attached to having children out of wedlock has also largely gone.

Termination of unwanted pregnancies is also generally available. As a result fewer and fewer babies are placed by their mothers for adoption soon after birth. And, as we have seen, about half the annual number of adoptions now take place between children and their step-parents.

Thus the concept of a total legal severance of ties between adopted children and their natural parents is no longer always apposite. The law of adoption, therefore, is likely to be reformed.

Age limits

While there is nothing in law setting an age limit, in practice many agencies have not allowed adoptive parents over 35 to join waiting lists. This has been seen as unfair when birth mothers today are often over that age. The rationale is that

(a) there is generally a long wait for babies;
(b) birth parents, who are entitled to have a say on prospective adoptive parents, generally prefer younger couples to bring up their child.

Gay couples

Gay couples are in the same position as cohabiting couples. Only people who are married can adopt

Chapter 3 — When you need help towards parenthood

as a couple. Others must apply as a single adopter – whether gay or not. According to a recent decision there is no fundamental objection in principle to an application for adoption of a child by a homosexual who wished to bring him up together with his male partner. The prospective adopter had to be treated as an individual and not as a member of a class. At the same time the first consideration has to be given to the need to safeguard and promote the child's welfare.

Issues relating to sexual orientation, lifestyle, race, religion or other characteristics of the parties involved have to be taken into account, but they cannot prevail over the most fundamental principle of ensuring the child's best interests.

Do remember: married step-parents are favoured over cohabitees by adoption panels for fully-fledged adoption, so the law still favours marriage.

However, an adoption order has been made in favour of a co-habiting couple in a 20-year stable relationship on the application of only one partner.

Passing on information to adoptive parents and child

Under the law the adoption agency must provide the adopters with such information about the child as they consider appropriate. However, the range and scope of the information appears to differ from one authority to another. Adopters are advised that they can pass on the information to the child at a time which they consider is appropriate but no later than the child's 18th birthday.

Questions relating to a child's physical and emotional health should be covered during the period when the child is being placed for adoption. It is known as a review (see immediately below).

Review

New regulations require adoption agencies to carry out a review when a child is placed for adoption, including regular examination and assessment by a doctor. The agency must consider an appropriate course of action, in light of the review, for additional care or treatment.

Post-adoption services

Older children tend to have closer ties with their birth families. Part 2 of *For Children's Sake* stresses that the changing nature of adoption – involving greater openness, older children and more contact with birth families – can entail greater demands on adoptive parents, birth parents and children alike. Local authorities are called upon to provide counselling and support both before and after the making of an adoption order to all the parties involved.

C. SURROGACY

Of all the options available to a couple unable to have a baby, surrogacy is perhaps the one which has raised the most legal and ethical dilemmas.

Surrogacy can be defined as one set of parents 'commissioning' another woman to carry a child for them. The agreement must be made before the woman carries the child and it is essentially an arrangement that the mother will hand over the baby at birth.

She can either be implanted with the embryo of the couple – thereby having no genetic material of her own involved in the baby – or be inseminated by the sperm of the commissioning father so that she contributes part of the genetic material to the child.

THE LEGISLATION

Legal private arrangements

Private arrangements are not outlawed and the carrying mother can receive expenses.

However private arrangements are controlled by statute and in particular by a Code of Practice laid down by the Human Fertilization and Embryology Authority. (It is interesting that in this context, new legal terms are in use: 'commissioning couple' , 'carrying mother' and 'surrogate parents'. Even a new form of legal order, as a procedure for acquiring parental responsibility, has been used to deal with such cases: a 'parental order', see below.)

There have been instances where a baby was born to a surrogate mother after normal sexual intercourse with the commissioning father. The HF&E Act 1990 insists on artificial insemination with the husband's sperm and disallows what could be viewed as an adulterous act.

Commercial surrogacy

In this country, commercial surrogacy arrangements are banned and indeed are made a criminal offence. Commercial arrangements include taking part in any negotiations with a view to the making of a surrogacy arrangement on a commercial basis, or the advertising, compiling of information or contracting for commercial surrogacy services.

Enforcing a surrogacy arrangement

Legislation specifically and unambiguously states that a surrogacy arrangement cannot be enforced as a contract, in a court of law. It is not enforceable by either the commissioning couple (where, for example, the carrying mother refuses to hand over the baby) or by the carrying mother (where the commissioning couple refuses to take on the child because, for example, the baby is born handicapped).

In a recent case, the mother refused to hand over the baby to the commissioning parents. There were also allegations of large sums of money having changed hands. As a result, an independent inquiry has been set up to review the legislation on surrogacy and to assess whether there is a need to change the law to meet public concern.

Obtaining a 'parental order' for a baby born to a surrogate mother

> *You and your husband entered into a surrogacy arrangement with a woman who has three children of her own. She is agreeable to the handing over of the child soon after birth.*

You can obtain a modified form of an adoption order known as a 'parental order' from the court.

At present the Code of Practice insists upon the following:

1. The child must be genetically related to at least one of the commissioning couple;
2. The surrogate parent(s) must have consented to the making of the parental order no earlier than six weeks after the birth of the child;
3. The commissioning couple must be married to each other;
4. They must have applied for an order within six months of the child's birth;
5. The only money to change hands must be for expenses;
6. The child must be living with the commissioning couple domiciled in the UK.

Do note: This is not an exhaustive statement of the law and counselling and legal advice should always be sought.

Registering a birth by a surrogate mother

Until a parental order has been obtained by the commissioning couple, the surrogate parents (birth mother and her partner/husband) are the legal parents of the child.

The surrogate mother must register the birth in the normal way.

Her husband or partner would normally be registered as the father.

Once a parental order has been granted to the commissioning couple by a court, there will be an entry in a separate Parental Order Register re-registering the child. This will be cross-referenced with the entry in the Register of Births.

The public will not be able to make a link between these entries.

Obtaining records by the child involved

Due to surgery, your mother was not able to carry a pregnancy to full term. Your parents told you in your teens that you were born as a result of a private surrogate arrangement. You would like to find out more about your surrogate mother.

Once you become an adult you should be able to gain access, after being offered counselling, to your original birth certificate.

PART 2
WHOSE RIGHTS? WHOSE RESPONSIBILITIES?

Family relationships, as well as attitudes towards children, have undergone truly dramatic changes in the second half of the twentieth century. As a result the legal approach to parent/child relationships has also changed.

To bring the law relating to children more in line with modern views, the Children Act was passed in 1989. Until then, the law had spoken of 'parental rights' – now it refers to 'parental responsibilities'. This is more than a mere change of terms; it reflects a distinct shift in perception of the relationship between parent and child. The concept of 'rights' over your son or daughter is quite a different one from that of 'responsibility' for them.

The Act was also intended to make uniform the multiplicity of laws governing the legal position of parents and children and to ensure, as far as possible, that the voice of the child would also be heard above the clamour when adults are in conflict.

Other landmark legislation has been passed to reflect changing attitudes. The Child Support Acts also marked a fundamental turning-point in social policy. The intention behind them was to shift the burden of maintaining children of single-parent families from the State on to absent parents, generally absent fathers.

Then in 1996, yet another contentious and significant Act was passed – the Family Law Act. It is an attempt to bring the law of divorce up to date while, at the same time, bolstering the institution of marriage.

In these three chapters we examine the nature and extent of parental responsibilities, the position of parents and children in divorce proceedings, and the parents' legal obligations in bringing up children in a commercial world. The topics covered are:

- Defining parental responsibilities
- Who can exercise them
- Paternity issues
- Duty to maintain children
- Names, emigration, nationality and passports
- Issues relating to protection, discipline and religion
- Divorce proceedings
- Domestic violence
- Children, contracts, and money
- Children and work

CHAPTER 4
PARENTAL RESPONSIBILITIES

This chapter deals with the topic of parental responsibilities. Section A discusses the parents' role in exercising responsibility for their child; section B deals with paternity issues; section C covers maintenance issues; section D examines question of status; and section E outlines other parenting issues such as disciplining your child.

A. EXERCISING PARENTAL RESPONSIBILITIES – THE LEGAL VIEW

A QUESTION OF DEFINITION

In order to enable parents to carry out their parenting role, the law grants them 'parental responsibility'. This means that the law entrusts to them 'all the rights, duties, powers, responsibilities and authority' which parents have in relation to their children.

Thus it is of crucial significance to examine who has parental responsibility in law. We will see that this is determined – to a large extent – by the relationship in law of the parents to each other. The parent–child relationship becomes the focus of concern in those cases where a father denies paternity.

Once we know who, in fact, has parental responsibility, we can then concentrate on the exercise of these parenting 'rights, duties, powers, responsibilities and authority.'

Do remember: Parental responsibility can be shared. This would appear to be an acceptance of the fact – built into the law itself – that children of today can lead lives in more than one family relationship – for example, when they live in stepfamilies.

[Parental responsibility issues concerning the appointment of guardians are discussed in Chapter 8, *The extended family*, p.79; the duty placed upon parents to ensure a proper education for their children is covered in detail in Chapter 13; the role of the social services in taking children at risk into local authority care is dealt with in Chapter 9, *When parenting fails*.]

Parental responsibilities – who exercises them?

Married parents

Where the parents of a child are married to each other, the mother and father have equal parental responsibility from the moment that their baby is born. Even if they subsequently divorce, so that their child lives with only one of them, both parents still have continuing responsibility for their child.

Parents who are not married to each other

In the case of parents who are not married to each other, the mother is entitled to all parental responsibilities in law from the moment of birth. The parents themselves or the courts can decide, however, that parental responsibilities should be shared between father and mother.

(a) Position of the mother

Thus the law still draws a very clear distinction between the parental responsibility of parents who are married to each other and those who are not.

If the mother is not married to the child's father, the law gives all parental responsibility to her at the birth of the child. The father's position may not be irrevocable, however (see *Position of the father*, section c below).

Further there is no obligation for an unmarried mother to register the father's name on the birth certificate if she does not wish to. That part of the register can be left blank.

(b) Position of the child

As far as the child is concerned, the law has moved steadily in the direction of equalizing the status of a legitimate and an illegitimate child. The stigma has been removed as far as illegitimate children's own rights in law are concerned. For example, if a parent of an illegitimate child dies and does not leave a will, the child can inherit under the laws of intestacy.

(c) Position of the father

The position of a father who is not married to his child's mother is different from that of a father married to the mother. However, his position has been strengthened by recent legislation as well as by the attitude of the courts. The Government has put forward proposals giving unmarried fathers the same rights and parental responsibilities as married men.

The courses now open to a father who is not married to his child's mother are as follows:

- he can acquire parental responsibility with the mother's consent, by undertaking what is known as a Parental Responsibility Agreement
- if the mother does not consent, he can apply to court and ask for a Parental Responsibility Order so that he then has a right to be involved in all major matters concerning his child
- he can apply for a Residence Order which is an order determining the person with whom the child is to live. This order automatically carries with it parental responsibility if the court orders that his child should live with him.

So although the position of an unmarried father has improved under the Act, he still does not have the same status in law as a married father unless his partner agrees or he takes steps to acquire it.

Acting with the mother's consent

If an unmarried mother agrees, parental responsibility can now be shared by both parents.

Your girlfriend has just given birth to your first child. You have been living together for some years and have a happy, stable relationship. Although you are not married, you would like your legal relationship with your child to approximate to that of a married father as much as possible. What can you do?

You can sign a Parental Responsibility Agreement with your partner's consent. This Agreement remains binding even if the relationship with your girlfriend subsequently breaks down.

Procedure for a Parental Responsibility Agreement

The Agreement has to be on a prescribed form (obtainable from Law Stationers). The form must include details of both parents, who must declare that the two of them agree that the father should have parental responsibility, which will thus be shared by both parents.

The form must be signed by each parent in the presence of a witness, who must be a JP, a justice's clerk or an authorized court official. The mother must bring along the child's full birth certificate, plus evidence of her identity showing a photograph and signature (e.g. a passport).

The father will also need evidence of his identity showing photograph and signature. The Agreement is legally binding on both mother and father so it is essential to get advice from either a solicitor or another adviser before signing.

The Agreement must then be filed with two copies at the Principal Registry of the Family Division of the High Court, Somerset House, Strand, London WC2R 1LP. The Agreement is then recorded and a copy sent to each parent.

Do note: The Agreement is not effective until it has been received and recorded at the Principal Registry of the Family Division.

If the mother does not consent: The Parental Responsibility Order

A father who is not married to the mother of his child, and who wants to be involved in the child's upbringing even though the mother refuses to sign a Parental Responsibility Agreement, can apply to court for a Parental Responsibility Order.

The court's duty is to act in the child's best interest. Generally speaking, a child's interest is best served by the involvement of both natural parents unless there are very strong contra-indications such as fear of violence or abuse.

On a father's application to the court for an order for parental responsibility, the court will weigh his commitment to the child and the child's attachment to him. If the court is satisfied, an order in his favour may be made – even against a mother's objection.

Do remember: No two cases are the same. It is difficult to predict how the court will weigh a father's application. So in all cases, do seek legal advice.

When parental responsibility ends

Parents who have parental responsibility for their child cannot give up that responsibility unilaterally for as long as the child is a minor – even if one of the parents no longer lives in the child's home.

A child becomes legally an adult at the age of 18. At that age parental responsibility formally ceases. Many court orders last until a child is 16 or 17. However, if a child is in further, full-time education, a parent can be called upon to support him or her beyond the age of 18.

Apart from the 18-year threshold, parental responsibility will also cease
- when a minor marries
- when a minor is serving in the armed forces
- by court order.

Sharing of parental responsibility

One of the interesting and important aspects of parental responsibility is that the law allows you to share it.

> *Your daughter and her husband split up in acrimonious circumstances. You offered to look after your granddaughter and her parents agreed that she live with you. You are concerned to establish your status in law as you have to make arrangements for your granddaughter's admission to a local school.*

You can obtain permission from the court to apply for a residence order. This order will determine the person with whom the child is to live. A residence order automatically carries parental responsibility with it, which you would thus share with the child's parents.

If you explain the position to the school authorities, and show them the court order if they ask to see it, you should be able to go ahead with the admission procedures.

B. PATERNITY

DECIDING PATERNITY ISSUES

Where a couple is married, there is a legal 'presumption' that the husband is the father of the child.

Note: A presumption in law has binding force unless and until proved otherwise.

The presumption that the husband is the father of the child is extended to cases where the parents married after the child's birth.

There is also a presumption where the father's name appears on the birth certificate irrespective of marriage.

If a mother asserts that a certain man is the father of her child and he is therefore liable to maintain her child, this assertion may have to be proved. Blood tests, which were used in the past, can be inconclusive. DNA 'fingerprinting' which is used today, on the other hand, has made proving the truthfulness or otherwise of an assertion of paternity much more certain.

DNA testing

The courts will not order a test

- to satisfy a suspicion of adultery; or
- where it would be against the child's best interests.

The child's interests

The courts have a duty to protect the child and a test will not be ordered if it is against the child's interests. However, as a general rule the court will regard it as in a child's interests that his or her father should be known.

> You had a relationship with a married woman who was living apart from her husband. You are convinced that you are the father of her child born at that time.
>
> She has since refused to consent to a Parental Responsibility Agreement and refused to let you have any contact with the child. She has also returned to her husband and says that he is in fact the child's father. You are very anxious to establish the true position. The mother has adamantly refused to consent to blood tests for either herself or the child.

In a similar case, the Court of Appeal ruled that every child had the right to know the truth unless his welfare justified a cover-up. The court ordered the blood tests despite the mother's unwillingness and stated that if the truth could be established with certainty, a refusal to produce certainty would justify the inference that she was hiding the truth.

Retrospective testing

The courts will order a DNA test to take advantage of genetic fingerprinting even though an earlier blood test proved inconclusive.

> You are a married man. A child was born to a woman friend of yours in 1985. She alleged that you were the father of her child and that you were liable to pay maintenance – a claim which you strenuously denied. You took a blood test which proved inconclusive. The mother's claim against you was dismissed. She has now sought to reopen the case and asked the court to order a DNA test. You want to know whether she is entitled to reopen the case.

The answer is 'yes'. There is no rule against retrospective DNA fingerprinting. And if you refuse to take another test, the court might draw the inference against you that you are the father, just from your refusal.

Where one party refuses

Where both parties agree to DNA testing, there is no problem. However, where someone refuses a test, the courts can direct a DNA test in any civil proceeding.

> *Some three years ago, you had a relationship with a young woman. At the time that you separated, she gave you no hint that she was pregnant. Since then you have received a note from her stating that she will be seeking maintenance from you for her child.*
>
> *You are convinced that it is not your child. You feel that to undergo a DNA test is not fair in the circumstances.*

Your refusal to undergo the test may not be in your interests as it could be used as an inference against you.

The courts will not direct a test on a baby because the father has a suspicion of adultery.

DNA testing and Child Support

Legislation has placed a duty on every 'absent' parent to maintain his or her child. Generally the duty to maintain is on the father – irrespective of whether or not he was married to the mother and irrespective of whether or not he has parental responsibility for that child.

Today a mother will apply to the Child Support Agency [the CSA] for child support. She will have to give the name of the father except in certain cases where to do so could lead to harm. If the man whose name is given [the 'putative' father] denies parentage, a court can be asked to determine the paternity issue. If a man refuses to have a test, the court can draw inferences against him from his refusal. Thus DNA testing has acquired particular significance in relation to child support.

Under the Child Support Act 1995, there is the power to recoup the cost of the fees for the DNA test from the person established by the test to be the father.

The CSA will interview both the mother and the alleged absent father in order to decide whether there is sufficient evidence to show that he is indeed the father and thus liable for maintenance.

If parentage cannot be decided by the interview(s) the CSA can suggest that both parents undertake a DNA test which can be done by a company with which the Agency has a contract.

(a) Refusal to take the test

If the father refuses the CSA's request for a blood test, the Agency can take the matter to court, which can direct a test. If the father still refuses the test, which he is entitled to do in law, the courts will usually draw their own conclusions. The courts have stated that where a man is in a position to establish, once and for all, the parentage of a child and he refuses to submit himself to a DNA test, the inference that he is indeed the child's father would be 'virtually inescapable'. Medical or religious grounds may be accepted by the court where the test is refused.

(b) Procedure for taking the test

Blood samples are taken of both parents and the child. The doctor who takes the samples will require, in every case, two passport-sized photos each of mother, father and child. The doctor will sign the photos to confirm the identities of the person(s) who are present to give the samples.

If the test is proved negative, the fee will be refunded to the person who was alleged to be the father.

A leaflet is issued by CSA which sets out requirements regarding registration forms, etc. (Leaflet no 2090).

All information is treated in confidence except where it is necessary to provide evidence to a court of law.

C. CHILD SUPPORT ACTS – THE BASIC ASSUMPTIONS

DUTY TO MAINTAIN

As we see above, the duty to maintain children financially does not depend upon the marital status of the parents. This duty applies whether parents are married, whether they have been married and are now divorced, or whether they have never been married at all.

In cases of broken homes, maintenance used to be imposed by the courts of law although in practice the State often had to bear the cost.

The Child Support legislation changed the whole approach to child maintenance. Until the Acts were passed, the courts acted as the collectors of children's maintenance. However, the task of assessment and collection was then given to the Child Support Agency, run by the Department of Social Security with centres throughout the country.

Assessment of maintenance

Under the Child Support Act 1991, each parent of a 'qualifying child' is responsible for maintaining him or her. A qualifying child has one or both parents absent from home. The Act stipulates how maintenance is to be assessed and also allows for appeals against assessment. Even if an unmarried father has no parental responsibility for his child, he still has a legal duty to maintain the child.

(i) *The 'qualifying child'*
A child qualifies for maintenance under the Child Support Act if one of its parents does not live at home – in other words if he or she has an absent parent. A 'child' must be under 16, or under 19 in full-time education.

(ii) *The absent parent*
An 'absent parent' is the one who does not live with the child at home. The status of an absent parent does not depend on whether the parents are married.

(iii) *The person with care*
This term applies to the person who has the daily care of the child. Although the absent parent is usually the father and the person with care is usually the mother, this need not always be the case. In either event the same rules apply.

(iv) *Wide ambit of the Act*
The Act was originally intended to apply to families on social security benefits. However, it has now been extended to apply to all families which have a qualifying child. This means that all new claims for maintenance from April 1993 are dealt with by the CSA.

Parents – other than those on income support or family credit – can still make their own arrangements but cannot bind themselves by private agreement to dispense with the services of the CSA.

When you and your husband got divorced, you reached a private agreement for the maintenance for your son, in an amicable divorce settlement. You would like to vary the amount payable. Your husband says that having reached an agreement, you are not now able to turn to the CSA.

A private agreement cannot exclude the right subsequently to apply for a maintenance assessment through the CSA.

However, your husband could ask the court to uphold the maintenance agreement. If the court agrees with him, it would effectively dispense with the services of the CSA.

The Act applies where both parents are normally resident in the UK. The courts will deal with cases where an absent parent or a person with care lives abroad. (For other matters still dealt with by the courts, see p.36 below.)

(v) *How the assessment is made*
Lone parents on social security benefits are sent an application form automatically.

They have to fill in the form and, in particular, supply information so that an absent parent can be identified and traced. Refusal to supply the information will have to be justified by showing good reason – such as fear of violence. The CSA would have to decide that you or any of your children would be 'at risk of harm or undue distress' if you were to co-operate.

According to statistics issued by the CSA in December 1997, a consistent 30 per cent of 'parents with care' who claim means-tested benefit and are required to co-operate with the Agency have claimed 'good cause' not to divulge the necessary information. The figures now suggest an increase to 70 per cent.

Not all those making this claim are accepted as having good cause although all cases require consideration.

If the information is incomplete, the CSA might ask you for an interview. A child support officer is entrusted with the task of making the assessment.

(vi) *How the assessment is calculated*
The assessment is calculated according to a formula which takes into account

- the maintenance needed for the children
- the income available to each parent after their own personal expenses have been set off against their net income
- the assessable income then left after the set-off. It is from that assessable income that the maintenance requirement is taken.

(vii) *Element of maintenance for carer*
The assessment includes an amount for the person who has care of the child based on income support rates. This particular provision has caused a great deal of resentment as it is seen as an 'adult' maintenance payment.

(viii) *Criticism of the Act*
The original Act evoked a great deal of public outcry. The application of the formula was seen as too rigid and it was felt that

- long-standing agreements between ex-partners were being overturned
- fathers who started second families, bought second homes etc., were finding themselves unable to finance commitments made before the Act came into force
- caring fathers were being penalized as 'soft targets' while feckless fathers, who are more difficult to track down, were not being dealt with.

The Child Support Act 1995

This Act was intended to

- remedy certain criticism of the original Act

- provide for a more flexible interpretation of it
- give greater discretion to those administering the formula for assessing maintenance.

To achieve these goals, the 1995 Act introduced the concept of the 'departure direction'.

Departure direction

This enables either the person with care or the absent parent to apply to the Secretary of State for a 'departure direction' [i.e. an instruction to depart from the normal rules]. The applicant must show that it is 'just and equitable' to give the departure direction, which can lead to an increase or decrease in the amount of child support maintenance.

The direction will be given in three situations:

(a) where the applicant has 'special expenses' which could not have been taken into account when the original assessment was made;
(b) where there is a court order or agreement transferring property as a result of which maintenance payable for children is less;
(c) where a parent artificially reduces his or her income.

Guidelines to a departure direction

'Special expenses' include expenses of travelling to work; costs of maintaining contact; costs of supporting another child in a new family; debts incurred in the previous relationship.

Note of warning: these guidelines and the examples are not intended to be exhaustive.

With regard to transfers of capital assets, the Act is yet another attempt to deal with the question of the transfer of the family home in settlement of all financial claims including child maintenance. These settlements will be examined in a departure direction to establish whether the effect of the transfer has been 'properly reflected' in the current assessment.

Remember: if you are refused a departure direction, you can appeal to a child support appeal tribunal.

Matters still dealt with by the courts

The following matters are outside the scope of the Child Support Acts:

(a) maintenance for step-children;
(b) children who are too old to be qualifying children (i.e. who are over 19 and in full-time education or training);
(c) maintenance to be paid in addition to what has been assessed by the CSA;
(d) maintenance to meet related expenses of a child's education;
(e) expenses associated with caring for a disabled child; the court can make an order for this to supplement the CSA's assessment.

Issues of confidentiality

Before the CSA will disclose your name and address, it requires your written consent. There are exceptions to maintaining confidentiality – for example, if you appeal against an assessment, the appeal letter as well as the basis for the Child Support Officer's assessment will be sent to your ex-spouse or former partner.

Appeals

Once an assessment is made, there is an automatic review every two years.

Reviews and appeals – when an assessment may be varied

(a) 'Change of circumstances' review

You are an absent parent. Since an assessment was made for maintenance you have been made redundant.

Apart from the periodic review, the Child Support Act provides for a 'change of circumstances review' which you can apply for if there is a change which affects the amount of maintenance you should pay.

In addition there are several layers of appeal built in to the system of child support maintenance. They are outlined below.

(b) Section 18 review

If either the parent with care or the absent parent is not satisfied with a Child Support Officer's decision because they think it is wrong – not because their circumstances have changed – he or she can apply for a review under section 18 of the Child Support Act.

You have 28 days from the time of the decision to apply for a section 18 review.

Another Child Support Officer will then conduct the review to establish whether the decision was made on the basis of facts which were incorrect or insufficient or whether it was wrong in law.

If you are dissatisfied by the decision of the second CSO, for example if they decide

(a) that there is no need for a review, or
(b) maintenance was reassessed but in a way with which you disagree,

you can appeal to a Child Support Appeal Tribunal (CSAT).

(c) Reduced benefit direction

You are a lone mother, living with your young daughter. You are refusing to give to the CSA the information which they require, because it is against your principles to have dealings with your former partner.

If a CSO decides that you are not co-operating and you have no good reason for non-co-operation, then your other benefits, such as Income Support or Family Credit, may be reduced. You can appeal against this direction to a Child Support Appeal Tribunal as well.

(d) Child Support Appeal Tribunals (CSAT)

The Tribunal comprises three people, of whom one (the Chairman) is legally qualified. You may present evidence yourself or ask someone to appeal on your behalf. However, you will have to pay the costs yourself if you use a lawyer.

Procedure for an appeal is set out in a 40-page leaflet issued by the CSA: *A Guide to Reviews and Appeals* (leaflet no. 2006). Do pay particular heed to time limits and the need for careful documentation.

(e) Appeal to the Child Support Commissioner

An appeal, on a point of law only, can be made to the Commissioner (for example, that the regulations were not properly applied or understood). You would have to receive permission [i.e. 'leave'] to appeal from either the Chairman of the Tribunal or from the Commissioner.

Caution: you cannot appeal merely because you

- do not approve of the decision which was reached or
- do not agree with the facts on which the decision was reached.

Part 2 — Whose rights? Whose responsibilities?

Legal Aid

If your income and savings fall below the threshold limits set by the Legal Aid Board, you may be able to get help from a lawyer in preparation for an appeal before a Tribunal, e.g. in preparing your case, or possibly getting a barrister's opinion.

Note of warning: You will have to pay the costs yourself if you use a lawyer to present your case before a CSAT.

D. A CHILD'S STATUS – QUESTIONS OF NAMES, EMIGRATION, NATIONALITY AND PASSPORTS

NAMING A CHILD

As parents, you give your child both forename, usually for life, and surname. The custom, although not the law, in the case of married parents, is that the child is given the father's surname. The names are registered at the time of the registration of the baby's birth. If the parents are married to each other, both names must be registered. An unmarried mother does not have to include the name of the child's father when registering the birth.

(a) Can you change your child's name?

Changing a name on a birth certificate:

(a) *Forename*: if you wish to change your child's forename, this can be done within 12 months of the original registration, either on production of a baptismal certificate under the new name or on a form available from the registrar.

(b) *Surname:* in the case of married parents, once the child's name has been registered, neither father nor mother can change it without the consent of the other. Over the years, the courts came to feel that the unilateral change of a child's name, for example to the name of a step-parent, was a serious matter.

Under the Children Act 1989, a child's name cannot be changed without the consent of persons who have parental responsibility for the child – usually both mother and father.

If one of the persons with parental responsibility withholds consent, application will have to be made to court to give its consent. The court will scrutinize such an application very carefully indeed to see if it is in the child's best interests.

You divorced your husband in December 1991 when your little girl was three and she came to live with you under a residence order from the court. The child has very regular contact with her father. You recently remarried and changed your name to that of your second husband. You are now expecting another baby. You would like your daughter to have the same surname as yourself as you think it will be easier for her to integrate into her new family. Can you do so at will?

Under the Children Act, as we have seen, you cannot change your daughter's surname to that of your second husband without her father's consent or the consent of the court. That was an automatic condition attached to the fact that the court allowed her to live with you under the residence order.

You thus have two choices. You could discuss it with her father and seek to persuade him that it is in your daughter's best interest to have the same name as her half-brother or sister. You can assure him that you do not wish to take this step in order to sever the relationship or weaken the links between him and his child.

If you cannot persuade him, you could apply to court for permission for the name change but you may find it difficult to persuade a judge that your reasons are sufficient.

In a recent case, the Court of Appeal held that adolescent children should keep their father's name though they wished to use their stepfather's name.

(b) Who must consent to a change of name?

Under the Children Act persons with parental responsibility for a child must consent in writing to any change of surname of the child. If that cannot be obtained, consent of the court must be granted. The long-term interests of the child are always the court's primary consideration.

Your 14-year old son by a former relationship lives with you. You have recently married and want to change your son's surname to that of his stepfather. His natural father has not seen his son for many years and his consent is, in any event, unnecessary as he never assumed parental responsibility for the boy. However, your son, who is entering into a rebellious phase, objects to the change of name plan. Can you insist?

The answer is 'no'. Under the Children Act 1989, a child of 'sufficient understanding' is entitled to object to a change of name. He can even seek the court's assistance in prohibiting you from taking such a step.

An unmarried mother's right to determine the surname

A mother who is not married to the father of her child has a duty by law to register the birth herself. The father's surname can only be entered with her co-operation and consent.

Accordingly, an unmarried mother has the right to determine the surname of her child – except in extreme cases where she makes a manifestly absurd choice.

You had a relationship with a divorcee, Mrs Jones. She had two children from her former marriage, Ann and Stephen Jones. She gave birth to your son, Joseph. Soon afterwards, your relationship broke down. Your son is called Joseph Jones. You would like him to have your surname which is Smith. You apply to court to have him registered as Joseph Smith. You do not see why your son should go through life with the surname of a man who divorced his mother before you had even met her.

A similar case was heard recently before the Court of Appeal. The appeal court held that

(a) it had power to order that a child should be known by his father's surname rather than that of the mother in which the child had been registered;
(b) any change of a child's surname was a profound and not merely a formal issue whatever the age of the child;
(c) any dispute over a surname had to be decided by a court and could not be made unilaterally;
(d) Jones was the name of Joseph's half-brother and sister and it was a logical choice for Mrs Jones to have made. It was not alien merely because it was also the name of her former husband.

The court therefore turned down Mr Smith's application to have his son bear his own surname.

Emigration, nationality and passport matters

Parents can decide together to take the child out of the UK. However, a parent's right to act alone is limited. Where a child lives with one parent under a residence order, that parent can take a child abroad for a period of up to one month; for a longer period, every person with parental responsibility must give written consent. If they refuse, consent of the court must be obtained.

The question of abduction is dealt with in Chapter 15, p.183.

Warning note: In dealing with issues of status, immigration and nationality, you are always advised to seek legal advice as the law is technical and the issues at stake so fundamental.

(a) Emigration

You have recently married for the second time and your new husband is Canadian. You would like to settle in Canada with him, taking your two children by your first marriage. Their father objects. What can you do?

If you cannot get the father's written consent, you would have to apply to court for an order to settle this specific issue (a 'specific issue order'). The court would weigh the advantages to the children of a new life against the fact that they would lose touch with their natural father. The views of older children would also be taken into account.

(b) A child's nationality

A child born in the UK is automatically a British citizen provided that at the time of the birth one or both of the parents is a British citizen or is settled in the UK without time limit restriction. This applies where the parents are married.

Where the parents are unmarried, only the mother's nationality or settled status is relevant with regard to the child's nationality under English law.

To bring your child into the UK

If you child was born outside the UK, you must show that

- you are settled in the UK with no time limit on your stay; and
- you have proper accommodation where you can all live without seeking housing under the homeless legislation or other benefits such as income support;
- you are the child's parent (this includes a parent of a child born out of wedlock).

The child must be under 18 and not leading an independent life.

For further information and leaflets, do contact the Immigration and Nationality Department (see DIRECTORY). Do also take heed of the *Warning note* above.

Child's passport

Married parents

Your child can be included on both parents' passports and can travel abroad with either parent. If the parents divorce, unless there is concern for the child's safety, a child can go abroad for up to one month with either parent on his or her passport.

In all cases, a child over the age of 16 must have his or her own passport.

A passport can be issued for a child in his own name at any age; this would be necessary if, for example, you work abroad but your child is being educated in the UK. A parent must consent on the application form for a passport for a child under the age of 18.

Passports are generally granted to children with the consent of either parent.

Unmarried parents

If the parents have not been married to each other, consent for issuing a child's passport should be given by the mother unless the father has a parental responsibility agreement or order.

Objections to the issue of a passport

An objector can ask the Passport Agency not to grant a passport if a court in the UK has issued

(a) a prohibited steps order;
(b) an order that the child's removal is contrary to the child's wishes;
(c) a residence order in favour of the objector.

Apart from a court order, the Passport Agency can consider an objection from

1. the mother – if the parents of the child have not been married to each other and the father has not been given parental responsibility
2. the police – where there is fear of the child being abducted.

The UK Passport Agency has issued a leaflet entitled *Passports for Children and Young People*, dealing with the most common passport enquiries on requirements for children of married and unmarried parents. See DIRECTORY.

E. OTHER RESPONSIBILITIES

Parental responsibilities are not defined in the legislation of England and Wales. They have been inelegantly described – as far as the law is concerned – as a 'ragbag' of duties which parents owe to their children. Some are outlined below. Despite the move away from parental 'rights' to an emphasis on 'responsibilities', these duties nonetheless can convey old-fashioned authority – e.g. the authority to discipline your child.

Duty to protect

There is a duty to protect a child from harm. This duty is enforced with criminal sanctions, i.e. you can be sent to prison. A child under 16 is not to be ill-treated, neglected or abandoned, under the Children Act 1933. This law is now 60 years old; there are calls to reform it.

A parent is guilty of neglect if he or she fails to provide a child with adequate food, clothing, medical aid and lodging.

The 'home alone' case of a mother who left her two-year-old daughter alone when she went to work is an extreme example of neglect or abandonment under this heading.

It is also a criminal offence for anyone over the age of 16 to allow a young child in a room with an unguarded open fire or any other heating appliance which causes a serious injury to the child.

The 16-year-old threshold for the right to protection under the 1933 Act would seem to indicate that a parent can lawfully turn his child out of the family home at that age.

Consenting to marriage

- Marriages of children under 16 are not allowed at all.
- Marriage of minors between the ages of 16 and 18 need parental consent.
- Over-18-year-olds are free to marry without parental consent.
  A marriage where one of the persons is under the age of 16 is absolutely void.

Who must consent to the marriage of a child aged 16 to 18?

1. the parents or
2. the guardian or
3. the court.

You are 17 and wish to get married. You live with your mother, who divorced your father when you were ten. She is quite agreeable to your proposed marriage. You received occasional visits from your father for the first couple of years after your parents' divorce, but he has been out of touch with you since. Do you need his permission too?

The law on this issue is not clear; if your mother has sole parental responsibility for you only her consent would be necessary. If your father and mother have joint parental responsibility then you might have to seek your father's permission.

In any event, you could apply to a magistrates' court to dispense with your father's consent.

Keeping discipline

Parents generally insist on certain behaviour from their children, although in some families discipline will be much stricter than in others. The law states that parents can inflict 'lawful' punishment. The question, of course, is what is 'lawful'? It is important to note in this context how much society as a whole has moved away from accepting corporal punishment as the answer to a recalcitrant child. However, it has not been outlawed.

In one case, a father was reported to the police after disciplining his children with a leather belt. Their PE teacher noticed bruises on the boys' legs and reported the matter to the headmaster. The social services were called in and they, in turn, alerted the police.

The father was charged with assault. He claimed that he was legally allowed to punish his children. The court agreed that there was no law which prevented him from 'reasonably chastising' them.

You have recently remarried and there is a running conflict between your teenage daughter and her stepfather. He has lost his temper with her frequently and has lately begun to hit her too. She states that she will not be punished or hurt in this way and is going to complain to the police.

If excessive force is used against a child by a parent or someone in the role of a parent, the child may invoke the criminal law of assault. It is all a matter of degree.

The government is to clarify the law on parental discipline following a case where a 12-year-old boy was repeatedly beaten by his stepfather who was charged with causing actual bodily harm. The court here acquitted him on the ground that he was using 'lawful correction' and 'reasonable chastisement'. The boy applied to the European Commission on Human Rights which found that he had been subjected to degrading punishment in contravention of the Human Rights Convention. A Bill is presently before Parliament to incorporate the Human Rights Convention into English law.

As a result of this case, the government issued a press release which stated that cruel behaviour had nothing to do with parents who exert discipline by smacking their children when they misbehave. The law would have to reflect the finding of the Commission's report without 'getting in the way of normal family life'.

Do remember: there are various organizations and Help Lines available to contact – for parents, step-parents, and children who need assistance if there is a fraught situation (see DIRECTORY). Many of the organizations issue leaflets on parenting and stress, to help overcome situations where a parent feels driven to resort to physical action to deal with a recalcitrant child.

A parent's 'right' to punish his or her child cannot be passed on to another member of the family. In one case an older brother administered a beating to his younger brother and claimed that he did so on their father's behalf. The courts held that this was unlawful.

It is also unlawful for a teacher to administer corporal punishment in a state school. 'Degrading and inhuman' punishment is outlawed in all schools.

It is only too clear that children are vulnerable to violence or abuse wherever they are.

Cases have occurred where children who have been taken into care, on the grounds of need or of being at risk – in other words, some of the most vulnerable of all children –have been subjected to unlawful punishments such as 'pindown' in local authority homes.

Medical treatment

The general rule is that parents are entitled to give consent to medical treatment for their children up to the age of 16. A child over the age of 16 can consent to any surgical, medical or dental treatment without his or her parents' permission.

Children below the age of 16 who are 'competent' to do so, that is have sufficient maturity and understanding, are entitled in law to seek medical treatment and can give their consent to receiving it. However, delicate and difficult problems have arisen and the issues are discussed in greater detail in Chapter 10, *Your child's health*, section B.

Choosing religious upbringing

Parents are generally said to have the 'power' to determine their child's religious upbringing. Indeed such a right would seem to be self-evident along with all the other incidentals of parenthood.

In today's pluralistic, secular society, parents may choose to bring their children up as non-believers.

There is a general requirement under the Education Acts that schools must provide religious education.

As far as the law is concerned, religion as an issue in a child's upbringing also arises

- in cases of adoption
- in cases of fostering
- where there is conflict between the parents.

Although the courts have intervened where they feel that a child may be brainwashed by an undesirable set of beliefs, in general it is not the duty of the courts to sit in moral judgment on people's religious beliefs.

You discover that your ex-husband is taking your six-year old daughter to meetings of a revivalist sect on the weekends that he has access to her. You are very unhappy about it as you fear that the child is being indoctrinated with the sect's beliefs. You have talked to him about the problem but to no avail. He stoutly maintains that there is freedom of religion in this country. What can you do?

You would want to avoid the child becoming embroiled in a conflict in court over religion between two estranged parents, although the courts have taken such matters up in the past. You might try to arrange for her father to have contact on days other than those on which meetings are being held.

If it were to go to court, you could seek a 'specific issue order' that the child should be brought up in your own religion – but you would have to persuade the judge that such an order would be better than no order at all and was in the child's best interests.

Alternatively, you could apply for an order which would prohibit her father from taking your daughter to the meetings (a 'prohibited steps order'). Again the court would weigh up the issues very carefully in your daughter's interests before making any order at all. See Chapter 5, p.46.

Where certain sects have been outlawed for dubious practices and beliefs, the courts will take a stronger view in protecting children against them.

CHAPTER 5
YOU WANT A DIVORCE – WHAT ABOUT THE CHILDREN?

The emphasis of much of the recent discussion on divorce reform has been, paradoxically enough, to try to bolster the institution of marriage. A stable and secure family is seen as the best way of safeguarding the welfare of children of the marriage. A Press Notice issued by the Lord Chancellor's department in November 1997 stresses that the family is the fundamental social unit in our society because of its capacity for providing a strong basis for care and learning. The government, it added, was 'acutely aware' of the potentially damaging effect on children of divorce and family breakdown.

Accordingly, much of the debate and resulting legislation has been concerned to try to ensure that parents endeavour to continue to live together. Where they nonetheless have reached a fundamental parting of their ways, the law is then concerned to minimize ensuing bitterness and to make arrangements so parents should maintain continuing responsibility for their children.

Thus both parents are still expected to take an active role in bringing up their children despite separation or divorce.

However, the law can only help couples to help themselves. It can only try to assist them in reaching an amicable agreement on the future of their children's well-being. To this end, there has been a marked trend towards mediating such agreements over recent years. This trend has now become entrenched in legislation. The Family Law Act, which was passed in 1996, has introduced a new dimension into divorce procedure by making available mediation services for couples whose marriage has irretrievably broken down.

The DIRECTORY at the end of the chapter has an extensive list of organizations which exist to help parents and children in situations of family conflict.

The Lord Chancellor's Department issues a set of three leaflets on obtaining a divorce. Leaflet 3 is entitled *Children and divorce* and it clearly sets out the procedures to be followed.

In this chapter, section A deals with current procedures for divorce; section B deals with changes to be introduced by the new Family Law Act; and section C deals with seeking help in a situation of domestic violence.

A. PROCEDURES FOR DIVORCE – THE EXISTING LAW

PRINCIPLES INVOLVED IN OVERSEEING THE WELFARE OF CHILDREN

The prevailing attitude of the law is that personal issues are not really meant for litigation, particularly as far as children are concerned.

However, today one child in four is expected to experience parental divorce. In fact, the UK has the highest divorce rate in Europe. Great concern is expressed therefore on how to limit the damage that a divorce might have upon children. The question of how the divorce is 'managed' from the children's point of view then becomes crucial.

Thus, if children are involved in any proceedings before the courts, the courts are under a duty to consider arrangements for them. A range of duties and powers are available to assist in determining their future well-being.

The following guiding principles are laid down by the Children Act 1989.

(a) The welfare of the child will be 'the paramount consideration' in decisions on the child's future.
(b) Any delay in deciding that future will be considered prejudicial to the child.
(c) The court must pay regard to a principle known as the 'non-intervention principle'. In other words it should only make an order on behalf of a child when it is sure that a court order would be more helpful than no order at all.

Orders available to the court under the Children Act 1989

Residence order: an order which decides with whom the child should live. Most importantly, a residence order also gives parental responsibility to those (e.g. a relative) who have the child living with them but who are not necessarily the child's parents This means that parental responsibility can be split amongst several people.

Contact order: an order to the person with whom the child lives to allow visits from the person named in the order or to allow other contact (e.g. by letter or telephone). This would apply most frequently in cases where a father lives away from his child but wishes to maintain contact.

Prohibited steps order: an order which prohibits certain steps being taken in relation to the child without consent of the court (e.g. taking a child abroad on a permanent basis).

Specific issue order: an order which decides a specific question which has arisen in connection with the child's upbringing (e.g. whether or not to have medical treatment, or to change schools).

Do remember: The court can issue any order in a child's interest – not necessarily the order which was applied for. The orders last until a child turns 16.

The court's checklist

In order to decide whether an order would be justified, the court must consider the following checklist:

(a) the wishes and feelings of the child;
(b) the child's physical and emotional needs;
(c) the likely effect on the child of any change in his or her circumstances;
(d) the child's sex, background, and characteristics which the court considers relevant;
(e) any harm which the child has suffered or is at risk of suffering;
(f) how capable each of his parents or any other person is of meeting the child's needs;
(g) the range of powers available to the court under the Children Act 1989.

Who can obtain an order?

Any person with parental responsibility can apply for an order – i.e. parents or guardians. So can any person with a residence order in their favour (for example, grandparents who have the child living with them under a residence order). An unmarried father can apply for an order even if he does not have parental responsibility. He can also apply for a parental responsibility order even if he is not allowed contact with the child.

Take note: No single order is dependent on another and each application is dealt with as a separate issue. At the same time the court will weigh all the circumstances to establish which order would be the most suitable to meet the child's needs. Indeed, the court can issue an order regarding the children's future even where the parents have made no application for one at all.

Chapter 5 — You want a divorce — what about the children?

The most suitable order

In all cases, the court can make any order which it feels is best for the child. In other words, even if you apply to court for a particular order, you may find that the court makes some other order on your child's behalf.

You apply to court for a specific issue order that your child should go to the boarding school which you attended as a young boy.

The court may think it best for the child to issue a prohibited steps order that the child cannot be removed from his present day-school because of the school's proximity to his extended family.

Children themselves can apply to court for permission for an order to be made in their favour. Their views and feelings must be taken into account in any event. See below.

WHO ARE THE ORDERS FOR?

The orders relate to a 'child of the family' and includes anyone brought up as a family member. This feature is particularly important today where there are so many step-families involving children from previous relationships.

When your husband married you, he was a widower and was living with his young son, then aged six. You lived with your husband for four years, during which time you cared for, and looked after, his son. You and your husband have now separated. You quite understand that the boy should remain with his father but you would like to continue seeing him even though you have left the family home. However, your husband is hurt and angry and he refuses you any contact with the child. Is there anything you can do?

Contact orders under the Act are made in relation to a 'child of the family'. It includes any child who has been treated by both husband and wife as a child of the family and clearly includes your stepson in your case. You would have to persuade the court that it is in the child's interest to make an order so that you continue to keep in touch with him. (For assistance in these cases, see under DIRECTORY.)

Family assistance orders

A probation officer or local authority social worker can be appointed by the court to advise, assist, and befriend any parent or guardian of the child, or any other person with whom the child lives, or with whom the child has contact.

A family assistance order can also apply to a child in need of assistance. However, these orders will only be made in exceptional circumstances.

Your wife has suddenly left you and your two children and has gone to live abroad with another man. You are in a great deal of distress but want to make all possible endeavours to keep the children at home with you and not have to put them into care.

It would seem that a family assistance order might help you in your circumstances. However, these orders are intended as a short term help only. An appointment only lasts for six months.

Which parent?

There are factors which the courts have applied in the past to settle the contentious and painful issue of whether children should live with their mother or father. Although the Act is intended to transform the nature of family proceedings, some of the factors will, no doubt, still apply. The court must consider

- the personality and character of each parent;
- the desirability of a mother caring for young children;
- the need to preserve stability in a child's life and provide continuity of care;
- the need to keep brothers and sisters together.

See also matters which will concern the court under the new Family Law Act – *Weighing up the children's future*, p.50.

No delay

Until October 1991, a divorce could not be made final until the court had considered arrangements for children of the marriage.

Today under the Children Act, delay is seen as harmful to a child's welfare. The court must only postpone the decree if it needs time for further consideration in the interests of the child.

It will also impose a timetable on proceedings so that parents and children have issues decided as speedily as possible. Children's futures are not to be kept hanging in the balance while others wrangle over them. Despite the Act's good intentions, however, delay has continued to be an increasing matter for concern in proceedings involving children.

The court's view

The child's welfare is the paramount consideration.

> *Your estranged partner has insisted that you should not have personal contact with your child. You have accepted the situation for the time being in the hope that her quite irrational antipathy to your presence will dissipate with time. However, you would like to send the child cards and presents and receive some photographs. Your partner has refused, saying that she cannot be made to do anything against her wishes.*

The courts are most unlikely to heed her wishes in this regard. They have stressed that parents who look after their children on a day-to-day basis should not think that the more intransigent, unreasonable and uncooperative they are the more likely they are to get their own way.

Where parents are separated and the child is in the care of one of them, it is almost always in the child's interests to have contact with the other parent.

Listening to a child's views

In trying to gauge a child's feelings and wishes the law regards developmental age as more significant in this context than his or her chronological age.

In a landmark decision, the House of Lords stated that in reality children become increasingly independent as they grow older.

Parental authority dwindles correspondingly so that the law does not recognize that there is any rule of absolute parental authority until a fixed age. Indeed parental rights are recognized in law only as long as they are needed for the protection of the child. Such parental rights have to yield to the rights of children to make their own decisions when they reach a sufficient understanding and intelligence to be capable of making up their own minds.

As we have seen, a most important feature of the Children Act is its emphasis on giving children their own voices, and this is not age-dependent. Rather, the court's duty is to pay heed to the views of children provided that they have sufficient understanding and maturity to grasp the issues at stake. Thus although parents still have responsibility for their children, a young person of sufficient understanding can put his or her views to the court in matters which affect their welfare or well-being. For example, they can ask the court to decide that

- an absent father should visit them

Chapter 5 — You want a divorce — what about the children?

- a parent should pay for their full-time education over the age of 18
- contact with their natural parents by adopted children should be resumed
- a move into a boyfriend's family should be allowed, because life at home is so intolerable
- they should not have to leave the country.

All these instances have been heard in the courts recently.

Do take heed: children can apply to court themselves. To do so, they need permission ['leave'] of the court to make application for an order. Leave will only be granted if the court is sure that the child has sufficient understanding of the issues involved.

To obtain leave, children must have a solicitor prepared to act on their behalf and apply for legal aid if needed.

Children are now assessed for legal aid in their own right.

B. DIVORCE PROCEDURES – THE NEW LAW

FAMILY LAW ACT 1996

The Family Law Act was passed in 1996 amid a storm of controversy. The proponents of the 1996 Act felt that new measures were urgently needed to

- stem the rising tide of divorce
- reduce the bitterness in divorce proceedings
- reduce the cost to the taxpayer of marital breakdown.

Hopes were also placed on the Act that it would bolster marriage as an institution by introducing numerous procedural changes so that husband and wife would not be hurried into divorce proceedings. In particular, it insists upon time for 'reflection and consideration'.

The Act draws a clear distinction between reconciliation, which is intended to support the marriage, and mediation, which is intended to make the parting easier.

Information on counselling and marriage support services are to be given to all those who are thinking of getting a divorce, at an initial information session. However, if attempts at reconciliation fail, then couples can take advantage of the services of a trained mediator to sort out their affairs, including arrangements for any children of the marriage. The costs of mediation can be met by legal aid depending on the parties' financial circumstances.

Present legislation – position of parents and children

Until the relevant provisions of the Family Law Act are brought into force (expected to be in 1999), proceedings involving children are still governed by existing legislation.

Under the present system, when parents file for divorce, they have to supply the court with details of the 'children of the family' i.e. children who are either under 16, or under 18 (if in full-time education). Children who are adopted are included, as are stepchildren who have lived as part of the family unit.

The court needs to know where the children will live, who they will live with, contact arrangements and so forth.

The court will then decide – in the light of the arrangements – whether it should make any orders under the Children Act concerning the children. It might, for example, decide to vary the children's living arrangements and make a residence order in favour of the father rather than the mother.

Do note: It is not usual for the court to alter the arrangements which the parents themselves have made, although it has the power to do so. It can also call for additional evidence or, if the facts warrant more serious action, order that the child be taken into local authority care.

The Family Law Act – procedural structure

The Act sets out a procedural structure for divorce which will apply once the Act comes into force. This is as follows:

(a) *The information meeting:* these meetings must be attended by one or both parties to a divorce. The information will cover such matters as

- counselling and support services
- the welfare, feelings and wishes of the children and how they might be helped to cope with the divorce.

(b) *Statement of marital breakdown:* this can be made three months after the information meeting.

(c) *A period of time for reflection and consideration:* in families where there are children under 16, the period is extended to fifteen months instead of nine months.

(d) *Mediation:* this will be proposed after the statement is received by the court. In particular it is also intended to enable the parties to reach amicable arrangements for the children.

(e) The court must then consider whether – in the light of the arrangements proposed for the children by the parties – it should exercise any of the orders under the Children Act.

Weighing up the children's future

The court must have particular regard, on the evidence before it, to the following:

(a) the wishes and feelings of the child in the light of his or her age and understanding;

(b) the conduct of the parties in relation to the child's upbringing;

(c) the general principle that the welfare of the child will be best served by having regular contact with members of his family and a continuing relationship to his parents;

(d) any risk to the child in deciding on the person with whom he or she is to live.

Reminder: These provisions of the new Act are expected to come into force in 1999.

Financial provision

For parents applying for a divorce today, the usual route for maintenance will be via the Child Support Agency. These matters have been discussed in Chapter 4.

However, the courts are very concerned to see that children of a marriage have a roof over their heads, and can order transfer of property – generally the matrimonial home –to the wife if she has the children living with her. The order can be for an outright transfer or for a period: for example, until the youngest child reaches the age of 18.

C. DOMESTIC VIOLENCE AND THE FAMILY LAW ACT – POSITION OF PARENTS AND CHILDREN

The question of how best to assist victims of domestic violence, together with the unsatisfactory and complicated law governing their protection, led to new measures which were incorporated into the Family Law Act 1996.

The provisions concerning domestic violence, which set out a single set of legal remedies, came into force on 1 October 1997. They provide for two orders – an occupation order and a non-molestation order.

Chapter 5 — You want a divorce — what about the children?

If you wish to obtain an order, do seek legal or other advice. The provisions have not yet been tested in the courts, and they break new ground insofar as they extend to a wider range of people who can now apply for the court's assistance.

Occupation Order

This is a new order which decides who can occupy the family home. The court can also order another person to leave the home.

The court will take into account all the circumstances of the case including the housing needs of the children, as well as the nature of the parties' relationship, and the likely effect of an order (or refusing to give an order) on the health, safety and well-being of any child.

Non-molestation order

This is an order which prevents a person from molesting another person or child living in the same household.

Further, where the court wants to take emergency action to protect a child, a suspected abuser can be removed from the home under a non-molestation order.

A child of under 16 can apply for an order with the court's permission [i.e. with 'leave' of the court]. The court will assess whether the child has sufficient understanding to make the application.

Further discussion on non-molestation orders will be found in Chapter 8, *The extended family*, p.73, and Chapter 15, *Children as victims of crime*, p.182.

Contact centres

Contact centres are available to enable estranged parents to meet their children in a neutral atmosphere. There are 158 such centres, and information on their locations can be obtained from the Network of Access and Child Contact Centres (see DIRECTORY). The Network also assists persons who wish to set up a centre in their own area.

CHAPTER 6
COPING IN A
COMMERCIAL WORLD

In this chapter we examine the laws relating to parent–child rights and responsibilities in dealing with money matters, as well as the complicated rules governing the employment of children under 16.

Section A deals with contracts involving children; section B looks briefly at tax issues; section C covers insurance matters; and section D covers children and work.

A. CONTRACTS

THE GENERAL RULE – NO BINDING AGREEMENTS

Generally speaking, the rule is that children under 18 are not bound by contracts which they make. The law is concerned to protect children from their own inexperience which may lead them into contracts on unfavourable terms. For example a child may be tempted into buying an expensive item of electronic equipment on hire-purchase without properly understanding the full extent of such a commitment.

On the other hand this rule can be unfair to adults. Children may not give their true age if asked. They may run up bills to purchase goods which they then proceed to use but do not pay for, or they may sell the goods to someone else and then pocket the proceeds.

It is also clear that in today's world, young people under 18 may earn large sums of money in, for example, advertising, fashion, sports, or the music world.

The law relating to the contracts of 'minors' [under-18-year-olds] reflects this dilemma. Many of the cases date from the nineteenth century when quite different social attitudes prevailed. A few types of contract are binding in law while others are not. Ten years ago an Act had to be passed to deal with the particular situations where children have kept, or have sold on, goods which they have not paid for.

With regard to the work children are permitted to do, the government has announced a review to enable it to update the law and to set national limits. The existing law is dealt with below.

Although the general rule is that minor children cannot be bound by contracts into which they have entered, there are certain exceptions to the rule.

When a contract can be enforced against a child

Children under 18 are contractually bound if they enter into certain contracts.

(a) Contracts for 'necessaries'

Certain goods are considered in law to be 'necessaries', for example food, clothing, and a roof over one's head. These are the basics. Contracts for necessaries are valid even if entered into by minors, e.g. if a 17-year-old, in full time employment or education, lives away from home in

Chapter 6 — Coping in a commercial world

a rented room, he or she will be liable for the rent.

However, the law recognizes that children have other needs apart from the basics; for example, the term 'necessaries' has been interpreted to include education, or legal or medical services.

Your 17-year-old son, John, rides a bicycle. Unfortunately he has an accident and knocks over a pedestrian. The man threatens to sue John for having been negligent. John consults a solicitor.

John has entered into a binding contract with his solicitor as legal advice is clearly necessary in the circumstances. However, the law would insist that the solicitor's fees should be reasonable.

Not all goods which can be 'necessaries' – such as clothing – would count as such if they were very extravagant for the child in question, e.g. designer-label goods. Also the contract would not be binding if a child already had a plentiful supply of those particular goods. The purchases would not then be necessaries.

In both these cases, a shopkeeper who sold to an under-18-year-old would either have no redress or his redress would be to seek return of the goods via the Minors Contracts Act. He cannot seek money payment unless those particular goods have been sold by the minor and the money represents the sale proceeds.

So, for example, if a 17-year-old apprentice buys a designer suit for £600 on credit, and does not pay the shopkeeper, he can be ordered by the court to return the suit. He can only be ordered to pay £600 to the shopkeeper if he has sold the suit and still has the proceeds in his pocket. However, if he has spent the money, the shopkeeper cannot ask him – nor the court order him – to hand over other funds he may have in a bank or savings account.

(b) Contracts for employment

These contracts are binding on a child provided they are to his benefit 'on the whole'. It has been held for a long time that minors may bind themselves by a contract of apprenticeship or of service, since it is to their advantage that they should acquire the means of earning a livelihood. Such a contract must be substantially to their advantage, looked at as a whole, even though some of the terms might be disadvantageous. These principles have been applied to contracts between young boxers and the Board of Boxing Control, an underage entertainer and his agent, and an underage author and his publisher.

Contracts of work are regulated by various legislative provisions in an endeavour to ensure that children are not unduly exploited. This is dealt with in more detail in section D.

(c) Other contracts

If a child buys a watch, for example, and pays for it in cash, there are two points to note:
1. the shopkeeper is bound by the contract;
2. the child cannot ask for his money back unless either
   - he never received the watch or
   - it was defective.

However, in those cases an adult also would be entitled to the return of his money.

Parents' liability for their children's debts

Your 15-year-old daughter persuaded an aerobics teacher to become her 'personal fitness trainer'. You were not aware of the arrangement. Your daughter had assured the teacher that you would meet the bills.

Parents are not liable for their children's debts. There are exceptions where it can be shown that, in some way, either

- the child acted as agent for her parent, i.e. you instructed the child to run up the bill; or
- the parent confirmed the agreement [i.e. 'ratified' the arrangement].

If, for example, the aerobics instructor had telephoned you to discuss fees for your daughter's training, and you had said 'Send the account to me', you would have ratified your daughter's agreement and become liable on it.

Parents can also be liable on a guarantee even though the child is not bound by the original debt (see below).

Must a child return goods for which he has not paid?

The Minors' Contracts Act 1987 is aimed at a situation where a minor has acquired something on credit and refuses to pay. While the child is entitled to refuse to pay, the court can make him return the purchase.

Guaranteeing a child's debts

If a child makes a contract – for example, borrows money or buys something on credit – and the person dealing with him realizes he is a minor, he may ask for a guarantee from an adult. The adult is then liable on the debt although the child is not bound by the loan.

> *Your 17-year-old son has ambitions to be a singer in a band. He buys expensive recording equipment after raising a loan from the bank. The bank manager insists that you guarantee the loan. Your son then decides that he has not got the talent, loses interest in the project, and refuses to repay the bank loan.*

Even though the bank cannot enforce the loan against your son because he was a minor when the contract was made, it nonetheless can enforce it against you under the Minors' Contracts Act, section 2.

Parent-child agreements

A parent has no right in the property of his or her children of any age. Thus parents have no claim on a child's wages.

Even an arrangement by which a child agrees to pay a weekly sum for board and lodging is unlikely to be a binding agreement on the grounds that there was no intention to create a legal relationship between parent and child.

B. TAXING MATTERS

Tax law discriminates between income which a child under 18 earns and income which he or she receives by way of 'gift' from a parent.

Earned income

> *Jean, who is 17, has left school and is now working part-time in a typing pool. She is earning above the taxable threshold.*

She is entitled to full personal allowances against her income.

Gifts

If you make a gift to your child of certain investments which bring in an annual income which is paid direct to the child, that payment will be treated as your income, not that of your child.

> *As a 17th birthday present, Sam's father gives Sam certain shares which bring in an income of £1,000 p.a.*

The income is treated for tax purposes not as Sam's but as his father's.

C. CONTRACTS OF INSURANCE

In general, anything of value which became the property of your child would go on your household insurance policy. This would be the case, for example, if you bought an expensive computer which was installed in your child's room. Similarly if your 17-year-old son or daughter took out a provisional licence and started learning to drive your car, you would inform your car insurers and pay any additional premium which might be required.

Do note: third party liability insurance is compulsory by law for motor cars and motor cycles for drivers of any age. Thus even if a 17-year-old took out a policy, he or she would be bound to pay for cover.

3.1 Life insurance

Other problems arise with life insurance.

(a) life policies do not count as 'necessaries';
(b) as a parent you may want to insure the life of your child.

You can only take out valid insurance to cover an eventuality where you stand to lose financially. This is known as your 'insurable interest'. The law assumes that you have an insurable interest in your own life and that of your spouse, but you cannot insure the lives of others you care for – even your own child.

The situation may be different, however, if your children are giving you financial support. As you would stand to lose financially on their death, you do have an 'insurable' interest' which means that you can take out insurance on their lives.

Travel insurance

Your two children, aged 16 and 17 respectively, have been given Euro-rail travel passes as Christmas gifts by their grandparents. They want to travel extensively on the continent. You wonder whether they can take out travel insurance.

It would seem, in such a case, that travel cover might count as a 'necessary' so as to be legally binding. In any event, once the premium on the travel insurance was paid, the insurer would have to pay out on a valid claim.

Advertising

Although children live in a commercial world, they are nonetheless to be protected against certain kinds of advertisement which might lead them into all sorts of temptation. The subject is discussed in greater detail in Chapter 12, p.130.

D. CHILDREN AND WORK

SCHOOL-LEAVING AGE

As from 1 September 1997, arrangements are in place for a single school-leaving date. This is the last Friday in June in the school year in which a child reaches the age of 16. Until then, some 16-year-olds could legally have left school before the end of the school year, depending on their birth date.

This date is binding on all children and their parents. The intention is to ensure that the education of children continues at least until the summer in which the child completes 11 years of compulsory education.

Do note: in the eyes of the law, anyone who is not over compulsory school age is a 'child' for the purposes of all rules and regulations concerned with the employment of children and young persons.

Your child cannot work full time until compulsory school-leaving age is reached.

Work and the under-18s

Under 13

A child under the age of 13 may not work at all.

13- and 14-year-olds

Your child can take a part-time job once he or she is 13 years old.

But there are restrictions on the number of hours and the kinds of job your child can do. The main restrictions are against work

- before the close of school hours on any school day
- before 7 in the morning or after 7 in the evening
- for more than two hours on any school day
- for more than two hours on Sunday
- in a job which requires children to lift, carry or move anything likely to injure them
- for more than four hours a day during school holidays (maximum 20–24 hours per week depending on locality)
- for more than four hours on a Saturday.

15- and 16-year-olds

Restrictions against working are for more than

- two hours a day outside school hours
- eight hours on a Saturday
- two hours on a Sunday
- eight hours a day in school holidays (with a maximum of 30–35 hours per week)

Also a child under 16 cannot work in any industrial undertaking, factory or mine or on board ship.

The restriction on not working before 7 a.m. or after 7 p.m. also applies to under-16-year-olds. **Most important:** each local authority has its own bye-laws so that there will be specific laws relating to the area in which you live.

Other restrictions

Your child cannot work

- in a fairground or amusement arcade
- at a theatre, dance hall, cinema, or disco
- in or on any racecourse or track.

See also *Health and safety* below.

Employment card

You must check with your local authority education department, which has the power to make

Chapter 6 — Coping in a commercial world 57

further restrictions. It will issue an *employment card* or *employment certificate* which will tell you what work your child can do and the hours (s)he may work.

The certificate has to be signed by both the employer and the parent. A medical certificate also has to be completed certifying that the child is fit and healthy.

Looking after your child's welfare

Unfortunately, many of these rules which are in force are not being applied; for example, children who work before the start of school do tend to begin their jobs earlier than 7 a.m.

Almost all jobs require a child to have a work permit but only 10 per cent of child workers have one.

Registration with the local authority is essential to your child's welfare, because local education authorities are responsible for registering employers and issuing permits or certificates for each young person in part-time employment. Education welfare officers or employment officers are responsible for policing their bye-laws and other legislation. Education Welfare Officers can serve a notice on a parent or an employer if they feel that the work is hindering the child from getting the full benefit of education. It is an offence if you fail to comply with the notice.

Note: Parents should always check whether an employer is registered with the local education authority. In that way, they can ascertain that their child is being employed legally, is being properly protected, and is not being exploited.

You are 15 years old and have a part-time job after school assisting with the filing in a small local firm. The hours are far longer than you had expected, as you are required to finish certain jobs before the end of the day.

An education welfare officer can serve notice on either your parent or your employer that you should give up your job if it is detrimental to your education or welfare.

Work experience

Different rules apply for the employment of children in the last year of compulsory schooling in work-experience schemes. However, such placements must be approved by law by the local education authority and they are usually arranged through the child's school. If you have any questions regarding your children's placement in a work experience scheme, you must apply to their school.

16- to18-year-olds

Once minors have reached compulsory school-leaving age and the date for school leaving has been passed (see above), they can enter full-time employment.

Restrictions on working nightshift and number of hours have been repealed.

There is also no minimum wage in force at present.

After a child's 16th birthday, he or she should pay National Insurance whether in part-time or full-time work.

It is outside the scope of this book to deal with benefits; however unemployed 16- or 17-year-olds may be entitled to Jobseeker's Allowance in certain circumstances, so do go to your local Careers Service Office or Jobcentre for advice. The availability of income support is also subject to certain conditions which are subject to change, so do apply to your social security office for advice.

Health and safety

The Health and Safety (Young Persons) Regulations 1997 govern the safety of young people in work. They apply to 16- to18-year-olds.

There are exemptions for domestic and family work, e.g. where a child helps her mother in a bed-and-breakfast enterprise in their own home.

The Regulations require employers to make an assessment 'in relation to risks to the health and safety of young persons'. The assessment is to take into account the following:

- the inexperience, lack of awareness of risks, and immaturity of young people
- the work place
- any work equipment
- the organization of tasks
- health and safety training; and
- the nature, degree and duration of exposure to physical, biological and chemical materials.

Parents should be supplied with 'comprehensible and relevant' information concerning the risks to health and safety and preventative measures affecting their children.

Your daughter, who is 17, has just been taken on full-time in a small printing and photocopy shop. Her breathing seems to be affected by some of the chemicals used in the various processes.

You should check whether an assessment has been carried out and, if so, ask that it be reviewed in the light of your daughter's reaction. An employer is required to reduce a risk to the lowest level that is reasonably practicable for a young person under the age of 18.

Further, as a parent, you should know that the regulations require that no young people should be employed for work that is

- beyond their physical or psychological capacity
- harmful because of exposure to toxic or carcinogenic agents or radiation
- involves risk of accidents to which young people may be vulnerable
- involves risk to health from cold/heat, noise or vibration.

Take note: The Metropolitan Police, Youth Crime Prevention, has issued a *Streetwise guide to earning money*. It contains useful advice on reading job ads, gives work tips, and has a 'Paper Round Code'. It is intended to enable children to earn money safely while being alert to any problems or dangers that they may encounter.

Child performers and models

There are various rules and regulations intended to protect the welfare of children who take part in entertainments of different kinds, or who are used as child models. Unfortunately the law which governs these activities is very out of date – the primary law is the Children and Young Persons Act which was passed in 1933. Much has happened since then!

The need for a licence

Children cannot take part in certain performances except under a local authority licence. The rules are detailed and cover premises and whether the performance is to be broadcast, or to be shown live. Work can take place in theatres, photographic studios, and locations near or far from home. Where work takes place away from home, a licence will not be issued by the local authority unless it is satisfied about accommodation, travel arrangements, working conditions etc.

If children are to stay in hostels, for instance, security arrangements also have to be checked.

Local authorities will also keep close contact with schools and will not issue a licence unless the local education authority has given clearance that the child's education will not be jeopardized.

A child takes part if (s)he 'performs' or takes part in the preparation. No licence is needed if the performance is given under arrangements made by a school – for example where a school orchestra goes on tour (see the Education Act 1996).

Exemptions to the need for a licence

Children under the age of 16 can work for four licence-free days every six months – provided that the work is out of school hours.

The need for a chaperone

All children must be supervised throughout the duration of the licence. They will be interviewed by the police and vetted by the local education authority. They ensure that there are suitable rest periods, adequate food for the children etc.

Under-14s

There are restrictions on the grant of performance licences in respect of children under 14. A licence cannot be granted unless

- you declare that the part cannot be taken except by such a child; or
- the licensing is for dancing in a ballet/musical.
  Four licence-free days are allowed per year.

Review of child employment law

A Department of Health press release in December 1997 announced a review of legislation designed to protect children from work exploitation. The review will report to the Minister of Health by the end of 1998 and will look at rules restricting the hours and work children are allowed to do. It will also cover health and safety, and deal with children's welfare and development.

Current regulations will be updated to set clear national rules and national work time limits will be set.

The law will also be extended to give greater protection to children in sport and advertising, including modelling.

PART 3
OTHER CARERS

The task of parenting can fall on others, for a variety of reasons. Apart from major trauma such as death or divorce, there may be other stresses in a family which mean that a child has to leave home for a while to be cared for by someone else.

However, among pre-school children by far the greatest need for care is not related to extreme, or even unusual, circumstances. Women now enter the workforce in ever-increasing numbers and children must be looked after in their parents' absence. Friends and relatives often help out – about two out of three parents rely on them to take care of their children while they are at work. Otherwise care and responsibility for the child may be taken over by a professional childminder or a live-in or daily nanny, or the child may be sent to a day nursery. All these options are examined in turn. In these cases, caring is shared on a daily basis rather than devolved on someone else for a period of time. Chapter 7 looks at *Pre-school care*.

As we see throughout this book, children can encounter more than one experience of family relationships. For example, they may experience their family life in a 'reconstituted' household together with step-parents. They may live with other relatives such as grandparents or may, by force of circumstance, be separated from them. They may need the care of foster parents. All these situations are examined in Chapter 8: *The extended family*.

Finally, the task of parenting can also devolve on others by force of law. If parents fail to take care of their child and the law regards the child's welfare as being at risk, other authorities will step in to take care of the child. The circumstances in which a child can be taken into care are examined in Chapter 9.

In Chapter 7 we look at
- Pre-school care.

In Chapter 8 we look at the *extended family*, including
- Step-parenting
- Grandparenting
- Parenting and bereavement
- Children as carers
- Fostering.

In Chapter 9 we look at the position *when parenting fails*:
- Taken into care
- Wardship.

(Adoption has been dealt with in Chapter 3, see section B, pp.22–5.)

CHAPTER 7
PRE-SCHOOL CARE

In September 1997, for the first time ever, more than half the members of the workforce were women. By the year 2000, it is estimated that they will constitute 65 per cent of all new employees. There is an ever-growing need, therefore, to ensure that proper day care is available for their children.

However, according to current statistics, there is only one registered childcare place for every nine children aged under eight years. Furthermore, available services are unevenly distributed throughout the country with rural areas being particularly poorly served.

About four out of ten parents of children under five use a formal, paid-for arrangement for regular childcare. Under two per cent have childcare provided by the firms for which they work although some employers are beginning to allow for more flexible working practices including job-share and part-time working. (For information on the Social Chapter and parental leave, see Chapter One, section on *Position of the father at work*, p.5.)

Of course, it is not only availability of places for pre-school childcare that matters – the quality of that care must also be of paramount concern.

In this chapter, section A covers the legal aspects of childminders; section B deals with private nannies; and section C examines the rules relating to the various day care centres and other types of care available.

A. CHILDMINDING

Informal childminding has always existed. In extended families children are cared for by aunts, grandparents, older sisters, when the mother is otherwise pre-occupied.

Outside family and friends, however, by far the largest source of care for working parents is some form of formal, paid-for childminding. Formal childminding is regulated by law.

THE LEGAL REQUIREMENTS

Under the Children Act, any person who looks after more than one child under the age of eight, in his or her own home for payment, for more than two hours per day on a regular basis, must, by law, be registered as a childminder.

Do note: by law, a single childminder is not allowed to care for more than three children under five and a further three children under the age of eight.

Certain local authorities might impose additional limitations, e.g. on the number of babies under 12 months who can be cared for.

> *Your childminder has two toddlers of her own and wants to take in your two young children (one aged 12 months and the other two and a half years). She says that she doesn't think that the restriction on numbers would include her own children.*

The restriction on three children under the age of five is absolute and includes a childminder's own children aged five or under.

Searching for a childminder

Your first steps in searching for a childminder must be to

- contact your local authority and
- ask for their list of registered childminders.

Do remember: the local authority checks every would-be childminder's home for safety and hygiene.

Police and social services record checks are also carried out on the childminder, as well as on all persons over the age of 16 living in the house.

Local authorities might also insist on insurance cover.

The childminder's home will then be inspected annually to ensure that standards are kept up.

Choosing your childminder

1. To make sure that a prospective childminder is registered with the local authority, ask to see the registration certificate. Make sure that this is the current one.
2. Find out whether the childminder
    (a) is a member of the National Childminding Association
    (b) has attended a childminding training course
    (c) has insurance cover (ask to see the certificate)
    (d) has passed a first aid course.
3. Then you must carry out your own research once you have a list of childminders.

The National Child Minding Association has over 50,000 childminder members and acts as a support network to promote quality and to improve the status and conditions for childminders, their charges, and their parents. It offers information, training facilities, and insurance policies for its members (see DIRECTORY).

Note of warning: The mere fact that a person is registered on a local authority list of childminders does not mean that the local authority is liable for negligent misstatement if that person proves unreliable or worse. The local authority would only be liable if a member of its own staff vouched for the childminder's reliability and assured a parent that the child would be safe in her care.

Also Note: Childminders are not required by law to have any particular childcare qualifications.

The Contract

You are a mature student. Most of your study is done by long-distance learning but you have to attend a week's full-time course at a university towards the end of your academic year. Your partner cannot take off the time to look after your two-year-old daughter. You want to find a childminder for the week and then use her services for three hours a day for a month thereafter while you prepare your thesis.

The advantage of childminding is its flexibility. You should be able to find a woman in your neighbourhood for your varying requirements.

Do remember: Childminding is negotiated on an individual basis, offering a flexible range of hours and arrangements – for example, a working mother may want a childminder to look after her toddler, as well as to pick up her child from primary school and care for him or her until she gets back from work in the evening. It is important, therefore, that you work out the terms and conditions of your specific needs very carefully before you enter into a contract.

See the draft contract on pp.63–4 which can be used as a basic document.

DRAFT CONTRACT
BETWEEN PARENTS AND REGISTERED CHILDMINDER

Details

Child's Name: _____

Date of Birth: _____

Home Address: _____
_____
_____ Tel No _____

Parents' name: _____

Place of work: _____
_____ Tel No _____

Childminder's Name: _____

Address: _____
_____

Terms

Start Date of Childminding: _____

Days: Monday Tuesday Wednesday Thursday Friday Saturday Sunday

Hours: From _____ am/pm   To _____ am/pm

Notice required to terminate contract (on both sides) _____

Meals to be provided: _____

Fees

£_____ per hour/day/week   weekly/monthly/in advance   Overtime: £_____ per hour

Parent responsible for payment:

Playgroup fees to be paid by parent

Charges for Absence

Holidays   _____ weeks
                     _____ weeks
Childminder's annual holiday
Parents' annual holiday   _____
Bank Holidays

Part 3 — Other carers

Sickness

Childminder's sickness
Child's sickness
Parent's sickness

Provisions (nappies, etc)

Parents to provide: _____

Childminder to provide: _____

Health and Safety

Emergency Contact: _____ Tel No _____

Child's Doctor: _____

Address: _____

_____ Tel No _____

Health Visitor _____

Immunisations/Vaccinations: _____

Infectious Illnesses: _____

Special Diet _____

Allergies/Health Problems _____

Permission to administer medication, eg Calpol _____

Discipline

'No-smacking' policy is/is not in force.

ACCIDENTS

Date	Time	Description of accident	Treatment given (if any)	Parent's Signature

Chapter 7 — Pre-school care

There are certain points which every contract must cover.

CHECKLIST of issues to be discussed and agreed:

- fee
- hours
- number of carers
- number of children being looked after
- provision of meals
- absence for sickness (involving either child or childminder)
- annual holidays and bank holidays
- safety procedures
- emergency arrangements
- deposit to reserve a place
- overtime hours
- reviewing the contract (i.e. if you need more or fewer hours, or the childminder wishes to increase fees)
- terminating the contract
- diet and any other special requirements
- method of payment
- who supplies what e.g. disposable nappies, or jars of baby food
- presence of pets – ascertaining, among other queries, whether the childminder has a dog or cat, or intends to acquire a pet or replace an existing one
- issues relating to discipline must be made perfectly clear (see immediately below).

In addition you must ensure that your childminder has the following in writing:

- your contact address
- your doctor's address
- any other medical information of immediate relevance, e.g. that the child is liable to asthma attacks.

An *accident report form* should be made available to the childminder to record any incident, including date and time of the event, the nature of the injury, and the treatment given. Every entry should be countersigned by the parent.

Do remember: arrangements about the persons who are authorized to collect your child have to be crystal clear.

Discipline

Parents will have strong views about whether to give to a childminder their authority to administer any form of physical punishment.

Under local authority guidelines, issued by the Department of Health, a childminder may be allowed to smack children

- where it is part of the contract between the parents and the childminder
- where it is a sanction of last resort.

Physical restraint is permissible only insofar as it is necessary to prevent a child harming himself, another child or an adult, or seriously damaging property.

Note of Warning: Shaking is never to be used. By law there are no circumstances which justify its use.

Certain local authorities still advocate a 'no smacking' policy. Check on the position in your area with the under-8s officer, the social services department or the local education authority.

Childminders and tax

Unlike nannies, childminders are treated as self-employed and have to pay their own tax.

B. PRIVATE NANNIES

Whereas childminders, as we have seen above, must be registered by a local authority and undergo police checks, there are no existing regulations which govern nannies or the agencies which recruit them. There are also no qualifications which nannies require by law although many do obtain suitable qualifications through appropriate training courses.

CHOOSING A NANNY

Despite the lack of legal regulation, efforts are being made to ensure that the needs of parents, children, and the nannies who work for them, should be more closely scrutinized. A compulsory register of nannies has also been suggested.

The Metropolitan Police issue a leaflet on *Choosing and Employing a Nanny* (Leaflet 8K/94), which outlines basic safety procedures and is available from your local police station.

You are strenuously advised

- to plan your questions in advance when interviewing a prospective nanny
- to check all references
- to check qualifications
- to enquire into a medical history
- to check a driving licence
- to check educational background.

The Professional Association of Nursery Nurses (PANN) has put together a nanny pack and has made calls for proper inspection, registration and police checks. Since 1995 it has become a separate section of the Professional Association of Teachers delegated to improve the standards and status of childcare workers (see DIRECTORY).

PANN has drawn up a Code of Practice and an information pack. The pack outlines a nanny's duties, as well as offering training and vetting qualifications. Only nannies with appropriate qualifications can become a member of the Association.

Do Note: nannies work in the education authorities, the NHS and the social services as well as in private homes.

The employment contract

By law, like any other employee, a nanny must receive a contract within eight weeks of starting employment, setting out basic terms and conditions. However, in addition it is better by far to discuss terms and conditions before the nanny commences employment.

These should include:

- hours
- overtime
- holiday
- sickness arrangements
- starting date
- probationary period
- notice period
- disciplinary procedures e.g. the circumstances in which an employer can summarily dismiss the nanny
- agreed circumstances and manner in which the nanny can discipline the child in her care.

Insurance

A nanny should be covered either by her employer's policy or by a policy issued by an organization such as PANN.

The policy should be taken out for injury to third parties and for loss and accidental damage to property.

Do remember: If your nanny is going to drive your car, please check with your brokers or insurers regarding cover under your car insurance policy. Make sure she has a clean driving licence.

Nannies and tax

As your nanny's employer, you have a legal obligation to the Inland Revenue to

- keep a proper payroll record
- pay regular income tax
- pay national insurance contributions on your nanny's behalf.

You will also have to pay the employer's national insurance contribution and provide a summary of all these deductions and payments.

Nanny-share

If a nanny works for two families so that she is employed by two different employers and looks after the children in the home of one of her employers, she does not act as a childminder. Arrangements regarding tax paid by more than one employer will have to be made.

Take heed: if a nanny works for more than two families, however, she must be registered under the Children Act as a childminder.

C. OTHER CHILDCARE ARRANGEMENTS – THE LEGAL ASPECTS

DAY NURSERIES

Day nurseries fall into two groups:

(a) *Under local authority auspices*
   Certain day nurseries are run by the local authorities on an all-day or sessional basis. The costs are means-tested to the parents and the nurseries are staffed in the main by nursery nurses. Pressure on places is very great and children are generally accepted on the basis of need, e.g. because their families are in difficulties (see also *Family centres*, below).

(b) *Private nurseries*
   Private nursery places are generally available all day usually from 8 in the morning to 6 in the evening. Parents can specify the hours that they will require.

   Day nurseries generally operate throughout the year and are not tied to school terms.

Registration of day nurseries

All nurseries must be registered and must display a registration certificate. The certificate will specify how many children can be taken care of, and their ages.

The staff/child ratio should be made clear (i.e. one member of staff for every three children aged 0–2; one staff member for four children aged 2–3; and one to eight for children aged 3–4).

In order to be registered, the nursery must meet certain requirements with regard to premises, persons employed, and record-keeping.

(a) Premises

The premises must have passed inspection by the police, fire officers, and the local authority under-8s officer.

The local authority will also issue guidelines on what constitutes adequate furniture and equipment and check toys for safety and quality. Regulations under the Children Act specify space standards per child.

(b) Persons

All staff will have been checked by the police, have filled in a health questionnaire and passed a social services computer check.

Certain minimum qualifications are specified. At least half the staff in a private nursery should be trained.

(c) Records

All nurseries must keep proper records of children in their care.

Parents must ensure that the records are up to date and accurate so that any change, e.g. in daytime telephone number, is recorded.

Do note: certificates should be updated annually.

PRE-SCHOOL PLAYGROUPS

Playgroup sessions can last just a few hours and can sometimes be booked at short notice.

The charges are per session and the playgroups are generally run by parent and voluntary groups.

All playgroups which run for more than two hours per day must register under the Children Act whether or not there is an element of profit involved.

Playgroups generally cater for children from two to five years. Staff ratios require one staff member for every four children aged between two and three; otherwise it is one to eight.

Staff

There must be a playgroup leader and half the staff should be qualified.

CRECHES

Creches are provided in community centres, leisure centres and shopping complexes. They are generally used by a transient group of parents and children for short periods.

Creches open for more than two hours per day must be registered.

FAMILY CENTRES

Family centres are intended to provide an integrated service for children and families in need. They may be run by voluntary groups or set up by the local authorities under the Social Services Department. In addition to being trained as nursery workers, staff may be qualified as social workers.

Chapter 7 — Pre-school care

BACK TO WORK SCHEMES FOR LONE PARENTS

Welfare-to-work policies are intended to help lone parents leave behind the 'benefit culture' and return to paid employment.

The benefits to be made available are outside the scope of this book and parents should seek advice from their nearest Benefits Agency or Jobcentre.

However, crucial to such plans is the provision of adequate childcare while mothers are at work. To this end, the government has proposed an expansion of 30,000 out-of-school clubs to be set up for nearly one million children over the next five years, as parents' problems of finding suitable persons to take care of their children do not cease once the children start school. For working mothers in full-time employment, arrangements have to be made for after-school hours and for school holidays.

Other schemes are to be put in place for assistance with the costs of childcare for working parents either by employers or the State, in what the government has described as its 'national childcare strategy'.

BABY-SITTERS

You have been looking for a baby-sitter. Your friend has recommended a 14-year-old school girl as level-headed and sensible. You have been told that no person under the age of 16 is allowed to baby-sit by law. You want to know whether that is correct?

The answer is 'no'. There is no specific age at which a person may be left alone in charge of a child.

The law specifies, however, that any person over the age of 16, who wilfully assaults, ill-treats or abandons a child left in his or her care, will be guilty of a criminal offence. This does not mean that a young person under the age of 16 may not look after a child. However, it is not advisable because a person under 16 cannot be held responsible in law for anything that happens to a child left in his or her care.

Note of warning: For that reason, the NSPCC advises that parents should ensure that only over-16s should baby-sit.

The Metropolitan Police, Youth Crime Prevention, issue a leaflet: *A Sreetwise Guide to Being Home Alone*. This very helpful leaflet contains safety procedures for parents employing a baby-sitter, as well as for children left in a house without adults and in charge of little ones. It is available from local police stations.

CHECKS ON YOUR CHILD'S WELFARE

In all cases where your child is being looked after by others, you must ensure that his or her health, well being, and physical safety are being properly cared for.

Note of warning: if you notice any changes in your child's behaviour, such as disturbed eating or sleeping, do not ignore these signs. Any bruises or any other injury must be satisfactorily accounted for.

If you do think that your child is at risk, you must contact your police force immediately. Specially trained officers are available to assist.

CHAPTER 8
THE EXTENDED FAMILY

As we mention in Chapter 4, a striking feature of the modern concept of parental responsibility is that it can be shared – not just between the child's parents but among other people with whom a child may come to share part of his or her life. This would indicate an acknowledgement in law that children of today often experience changes in their family relationships in the course of their childhood and dependency.

In this chapter we deal with the extended family, and cover

- Step-parenting
- Grandparenting
- Foster caring
- Bereavement and Guardianship
- Young people as carers.

Section A covers *living with relatives*; section B deals with *living with others*; and Section C deals with *family loss and illness*.

A. LIVING WITH RELATIVES

STEP-PARENTING

Stepfamilies are not a new phenomenon. Until this century, stepfamilies largely resulted from shortened life expectancy, in particular as a result of the numbers of women dying in childbirth. Today's numerous stepfamilies are generally the result of breakdown in marriages and partnerships although bereavement still plays a part in the statistics. According to the organisation StepFamily (see DIRECTORY), an estimated one in three people live in a stepfamily. It estimates that by the year 2000, children who will be living in stepfamilies will number about three million.

There are inevitable stresses and strains as children, parents, and step-parents have to adapt to changed relationships which can include step-siblings as well.

From the legal point of view, certain immediate problems arise for step-parents:

- the problem of co-existing with the natural parents (both present in the family and the absent parent) who will have their own views on matters such as change of name, discipline and maintaining contact.
- the problem of maintenance and inheritance.

What is a stepfamily?

A stepfamily is a household in which either the male or the female partner (or both partners) have a child or children from a previous relationship either living with them or regularly visiting them. Often the couple will have a child together too so that a further family dimension is created.

Basic duties

There are certain basic duties which a step-parent has in relation to a child in the household, whether or not the step-parent is married to the child's mother or father:

Chapter 8 — The extended family

(a) they may do what is reasonable in all the circumstances of the case to safeguard or promote the child's welfare (for example give the go-ahead for treatment in an emergency medical situation);

(b) they may not harm the child. Any person who looks after a child under the age of 16 is guilty of a criminal offence if he or she ill-treats or neglects that child.

(For the obligation to maintain a 'child of the family' see section below: *Stepfamilies and maintenance*, p.72).

Stepfamilies and adoption

About half the present numbers of adoptions are step-parent adoptions (see Chapter 3, section B). In order to adopt as a couple, the step-parent and the child's birth mother or father must be married to each other. Adoption is a final order which severs the legal links with the stepchild's birth parent.

You left your husband two years ago, together with your three-year-old son. You are now happily remarried and are expecting another child. You have lost contact with your first husband who has shown no interest in his son. You and your second husband would now like to adopt him formally.

You would have to make an application to court for an adoption order. Your ex-husband's consent will have to be obtained unless the court finds that his consent is being 'unreasonably withheld'. Your son may lose any contact with his birth family – for example, with a grandparent. His stepfather will now have to maintain him. Adoption entails the legal transfer of a child to another parent (see Chapter 3, section B, pp.22–5).

Stepfamilies and parental responsibility

Because adoption is such an irrevocable act in law, step-parents may seek to acquire parental responsibility instead. Parental responsibility entails having all the duties, powers, responsibilities and authority which a parent exercises in relation to his child.

In order to obtain parental responsibility, a step-parent would have to acquire a residence order which decides with whom the child is to live. A residence order would confer parental responsibility on a step-parent under certain limitations.

Step-parents must apply to court under section 8 of the Children Act. You can apply as of right

(a) if the child has been living with you for three years; or

(b) if you are married and the stepchild is being brought up as a 'child of the family', i.e. the child must have lived in the same household and have been treated by the step-parent as a child of his or her own family.

Otherwise you must get the court's permission to apply for a residence order under the Children Act. This is an order which decides on the person with whom the child is to live and it automatically carries parental responsibility with it.

In all these situations, a step-parent is advised to seek legal advice.

Limitations on parental responsibility

There are two legal limitations on the parental responsibility of a step-parent:

- he or she cannot appoint a guardian
- he or she cannot free a stepchild for adoption.

Janet, a divorcee with a young son called Max, met John who also had a child from a former marriage. They married and had a baby of their own. All three children live with them. John now wants to draw up a will appointing a guardian for the three children. At all times he has treated Max as a child of the family.

John can apply as of right for a parental responsibility order for Max but still will not be able to appoint a guardian for him in the event of his death (see also *Appointing a guardian*, p.79).

Stepfamilies and affinity

Marriage

According to the marriage laws, a step-parent cannot marry a stepchild unless both parties are over 21 and the child was never brought up as a 'child of the family'.

Stepfamilies and maintenance

Maintenance for children in the event of their parents' split-up is now regulated by the Child Support Agency. The CSA cannot order maintenance in a step-relationship unless the step-parent formally adopted the child.

Maintenance for stepchildren, therefore, is still dealt with by the courts. Thus where a child is brought up by married step-parents as a 'child of the family', and that marriage breaks up, a step-parent can be involved in maintenance arrangements under a divorce settlement.

The child, who must be under 16, has to have lived in the household as a fully accepted member of the stepfamily. The reasoning is that if a child has been treated as part of the household, it is 'as much his home as anyone else's that is breaking up'.

Stepfamilies, inheritance, and guardians

The question of who takes care of children in stepfamilies in the event of death raises two issues in the context of this chapter, as step-parents must ensure that

1. their children from a previous marriage will be adequately provided for;
2. a guardian is appointed in the event of their death.

(See also sections *Appointing a guardian*, p.79 and *Wills*, p.80.)

In all cases you should seek advice from a solicitor or from a legal advice centre in drawing up your will and appointing a guardian. Failure to do so can lead to awkward and unwanted consequences.

Maurice and Sally, who had two children under 12, were divorced. As part of a clean break settlement, Sally was given the matrimonial home where she lived with the children. She then remarried and her second husband moved into the house. Sally died tragically in a car accident. Her children are hoping to benefit under her will which she made when she was married to her first husband, Maurice.

All wills are automatically revoked [i.e. cancelled] by force of law on marriage or remarriage. Therefore Sally's will cannot take effect. Her estate devolves as though she had never made a will (i.e. as though she died 'intestate'). Therefore the rules of intestacy apply and her second husband will inherit her estate up to the sum of £125,000.

Her children will have to claim under the law which makes family provision for dependants.

Do note: in this context, if a stepchild can show that a step-parent was maintaining him at the time of the step-parent's death and that he was dependent on that maintenance, he could apply under the same family provision law.

For the position concerning name change in stepfamilies, see Chapter 4, section *Can you change your child's name?*, p.38.

Step-parenting and domestic violence

Under those provisions of the Family Law Act 1996, which came into force in October 1997, anyone can apply for a 'non-molestation order' provided he or she is 'associated' with the person who is responsible for the molesting. The category of an 'associated person' includes step-relatives. They must live in the same household whether or not the step-parents are married to each other. Under the Act a child or stepchild under 16 may apply with the court's permission for a non-molestation order.

'Molestation' is not defined but the court must have regard to all the circumstances including the need to secure the health, safety and well-being of the person applying for the order.

GRANDPARENTING

Grandparents are very often called in to help with looking after young children for parents who are working or indisposed.

An arrangement where a grandparent looks after a child for more than 28 days is not regarded as a private foster arrangement (see section on *Private fostering*, pp.76–7 below). Therefore none of the rules relating to private fostering apply.

However, a grandparent's actual legal rights are limited notwithstanding the closeness of the family ties.

What rights do grandparents have?

General rights

Anyone in charge of a child is entitled by law to do 'what is reasonable for the purposes of safeguarding or promoting the child's welfare'. This means that grandparents are empowered to take absolutely necessary decisions to safeguard the child.

You are looking after your grandson while his parents are on holiday. He falls and cuts his leg badly. You take him to the nearest casualty station where the doctor on duty advises a couple of stitches.

You are entitled to consent to essential medical treatment.

However in less urgent cases, although treatment may be required, you may find that the doctors will be less willing to accept a grandparent's consent. In one case the local education authority would not accept the grandmother's consent allowing her granddaughter go on a school trip, notwithstanding that the child had lived with her for years.

If grandparents wish to be granted an order under the Children Act 1989 (see section immediately below), in general they have first to apply to court for 'leave' [i.e. permission] before they can bring their case. In other words, grandparents would have first to persuade the court that they have a case worth hearing. They cannot generally bring their case as a 'right' in law.

Do note: Grandparents very often live on a pension so the cost of bringing an action in court can be prohibitive.

However, legal aid may be available to apply for orders under the Children Act if an applicant's capital and income fall below the legal limit. See also section below, *Attitude of the courts*, p.75.

Orders under the Children Act

Grandparents may be able to acquire certain orders under the Children Act. The orders available under the Act, in this context, are

- Parental responsibility
- Residence order
- Contact order
- Care order.

In certain circumstances, grandparents can also apply for

1. Adoption
2. Guardianship
3. Wardship (see section on p.75 below, and Chapter 9, section C, p.89).

(a) Grandparents and parental responsibility

As we have seen, having parental responsibility means being able to exercise all rights and duties in relation to a child. To have parental responsibility for a child you must

- be a married parent of the child
- be the unmarried father who has acquired parental responsibility
- have adopted the child or
- be the child's guardian
- have a residence order in your favour.

So grandparents looking after their grandchildren do not normally have parental responsibility unless they have a residence order (see immediately below).

(b) Residence order

A residence order is an order of court which decides upon the person with whom the child is to live. If grandparents receive a residence order in their favour, it automatically confers parental responsibility on them.

The parents will still retain parental responsibility.

(c) Contact order

A grandparent can apply for a contact order which requires that the person with whom the child lives should allow either visits or other forms of contact e.g. telephone calls.

> *Your son parted from his girlfriend in circumstances of great acrimony. Their child lives with the mother who has so far refused to allow you any contact with your granddaughter. You have always been close to her and wish to remain so. Even your birthday cards have been returned.*

You can apply to court for leave to bring an application for a contact order.

In a case where the mother opposed contact with the paternal grandparents, a court held that the grandparents' application had 'overwhelming merit' and that the child could actually be harmed if she lost contact with her grandparents. In another case, however, the Court of Appeal stated that the mother's implacable hostility to the grandchild having contact with her paternal grandmother had to be respected.

So each case depends on the facts and the view the court takes of them. (See DIRECTORY for names of organizations which can offer assistance, advice or support to grandparents who wish to maintain contact with their grandchildren.)

Chapter 8 — The extended family

Adoption by grandparents

A child must have lived with his or her grandparents for 13 weeks before they can make an adoption application.

At one stage it was felt that adoption by grandparents 'distorted' normal family relationships. However, the courts also recognize the importance to a child of a permanent arrangement rather than stop-gap measures. The courts will make the order most suited to a child's welfare in the circumstances of the case before them.

You apply for adoption of your granddaughter as both parents have become apparent strangers to their child. The court, instead, makes a residence order for her so that you acquire parental responsibility but not the adoption order which you wanted.

The court is entitled to make any order under the Children Act in a case before it.

Becoming a guardian to your grandchild

Guardians are appointed where

- the child has no parent with parental responsibility for him or
- a residence order was made for the child and the person under that order has since died.

Your unmarried daughter had a baby girl. Sadly your daughter has become terminally ill. The child's father has played no part in her life and does not have parental responsibility for her. You would like to take care of the child.

Your daughter can appoint you guardian of the child or, if it is too late for her to do so, you can apply to the court to appoint you as guardian.

Wardship

A grandparent could apply to court for wardship as an 'interested person'. Wardship is dealt with in Chapter 9, section C, p.89.

Grandparents and local authorities

The Children Act has encouraged – as far as possible – the view that a child is best left in the care of his or her genetic family, and specifies that it is the duty of a local authority to 'promote contact between the child and any relative' if a child is already in care.

When there is a proposal to take a child into care (see chapter 9, pp.85–6), because, for example, the parents are unable to care for their child, grandparents can apply to court for a care order.

They can also apply for a contact order if a grandchild has been placed in care.

Even if a care order is made in favour of the local authority, grandparents may still be able to look after the child. In fact a care order may be to their advantage as they will receive financial support if, for example, the child is disabled and has special needs.

Do remember: grandparents will still have to seek the court's permission to apply for a contact order or any of the other orders.

Attitude of the courts

Note of warning: Even if grandparents successfully obtain leave from the court, it by no means follows that the actual hearing will result in their favour. Indeed, in a recent judgment the court said that although there were 'cogent reasons why a natural parent should have contact, that approach did not apply towards any other member of the family: grandparent, aunt, uncle or anybody else'. It must always be the welfare of the child which is the paramount consideration.

B. LIVING WITH OTHERS

FOSTERING

Fostering is a temporary arrangement which can be

- entirely a private one (see immediately below) or
- under local authority jurisdiction (see pp.77–79).

Voluntary and involuntary foster care

(a) Voluntary arrangements

There are many reasons why a child may need short or long-term fostering. In private arrangements parents may be studying full-time away from home; they may need a respite period in caring for a disabled child; they may be unable to cope due to illness or bereavement. These arrangements are voluntary (see also p.77).

(b) Involuntary arrangements

Children are 'taken into care' by the local authority, on the other hand, where parenting is perceived to be seriously at fault and there is significant risk of harm to their children. However, for these children, too, fostering is the preferred local authority alternative to accommodating them in a children's home.

Private fostering

If you look after anyone's child for more than 28 days and you are neither

- a relative nor
- a guardian of the child,

  and

- the child is under 16,

  you are that child's foster carer.

  In the case of a disabled child, the age limit is 18.

Note: You do not have to be paid money for the task. You must notify your local authority Social Services Department not less than six weeks and not more than 13 weeks before the date when you will be taking care of the child.

The duty to inform the local authority lies on

- parents
- proposed foster carers and
- anyone else involved in proposed arrangements.

Note: In an emergency and you are unable to give six weeks' notice, you must give notice within 48 hours.

> Mrs Jones, a grandmother, looks after her grandson while he is at school as his parents work abroad. She falls and breaks her hip. You are a very close friend of Mrs Jones and are prepared to step in.

> You should give the local authority due and immediate notice that you will become the boy's private foster carer.

Chapter 8 — The extended family

The local authority must satisfy themselves that the welfare of the child who is being privately fostered within their area is being satisfactorily safeguarded. They are entitled to inspect your home and to speak to the boy there.

The local authority will also have to be satisfied that there is no one in the household who is disqualified from having a child in his or her care – e.g. because of a criminal conviction.

Failure to abide by the terms of the Act with regard to private fostering is in itself a criminal offence.

Local authority fostering

'Looking after' children by the local authority on a voluntary basis

There are many reasons why children are taken into care. Children can be looked after by a local authority on a voluntary basis where it is felt that it would promote the child's welfare.

For example, if a parent is ill or otherwise cannot provide the child with proper accommodation or care, a parent can approach the local authority to make application to court for a care order on the child's behalf.

The parents retain responsibility for the child and can remove the child at any time from the accommodation. The local authority is under a duty to

- ascertain the child's wishes
- ascertain the parents' wishes
- ascertain the wishes of any other relevant person.

The child's age and understanding, religion, racial origins and cultural and linguistic background must all be taken into account.

The most important aspect of looking after children in this way is the so-called 'family placement', i.e. placement in a foster family.

Your wife recently died. Your teenage daughter was very difficult during her mother's illness, and she has now become uncontrollable. You feel you can no longer cope and that she needs the kind of care which you just cannot give to her. You would like to consider the possibility of fostering.

You can apply to the local authority which will then investigate the entire family situation. Your daughter's views will also be taken into account. It is open to the court to provide for some other form of order, such as a supervision order which would entail a social worker or probation officer befriending and assisting a child and helping him or her over a present crisis (see Chapter 9, section *Supervision order*, p.85).

Assessment of foster carers

Assessment is usually a long-drawn-out process. Local authorities set their own criteria, for example, an age limit where they will not take on someone older than 65 or younger than 25 as foster carer. A social worker will then visit the proposed foster carer for an initial assessment. If there is a realistic approach on the part of the would-be foster carer to the task, they will be asked to attend a training group.

The next stage comprises an in-depth home study which covers all aspects of the home. It examines attitudes to religion, discipline and, very importantly, attitudes concerning contact with the birth parents.

Once the foster carers have been assessed as suitable by this in-depth home study, medical and police checks follow.

After that, their application goes to a panel of child care experts which would include not only social workers but paediatricians and others. If the panel makes the decision to approve the application, then foster carer and child will be matched.

In general, children of the same age would not be fostered together, and babies would not be placed with a working mother.

The process has been described as 'draining' for the potential carer, but very necessary in order to ensure a foster parent's suitability.

Remember: the child generally remains in contact with his or her natural parents and it is essential that a foster carer must be able to co-operate with them.

Review of child and foster care

The local authority is under a duty to keep the situation under review once child and carer have been 'matched'.

It must enter into a written agreement on matters such as

(a) the child's health
(b) contacts with parents
and, growing in importance,
(c) a financial allowance to cover costs.

Note: It is very important that the local authority supply a would-be foster carer with all relevant information. In a recent case, a social worker in the local authority failed to inform the family that a 15-year-old boy being placed for fostering in their home was a suspected sex abuser. When the foster carers' own children were allegedly abused by the boy, they were allowed to sue the local authority for damages on behalf of their children.

Duties of a foster carer

The foster carer must

1. care for the child
2. notify the local authority of any serious problem
3. allow a social worker to visit
4. notify the local authority of any change of address or any change of person living at the address.

You are a foster carer. You take in an 18 year-old student as lodger.

You must notify the local authority. The student will be vetted and there will be police checks on the student too.

In addition, a foster carer must

- allow the child to be removed on request
- not use corporal punishment.

The definition of a 'child of the family' in the Children Act excludes a child living with foster carers. This enforces the view of fostering as a temporary arrangement.

Foster carers and negligence

For issues relating to negligence by foster carers and subsequent allegations of harm by children in their care, see Chapter 11 on *Your child's safety*, p.107.

Conflicts inherent in the foster carer's role

Foster carers are expected to behave towards the children in their care as loving parents and to provide a family life to these children who are most in need. At the same time, the children are expected to be re-established with their natural parents in due course and are encouraged to keep in contact with them.

There are therefore inherent difficulties in the role of foster carer who has to be a 'parent' while knowing that their 'parent–child' relationship is, at best, a temporary one.

The 'Cinderella' service

Fostering is now the preferred option for children being looked after by local authorities. Nevertheless, it has been called the 'Cinderella' service. Although it plays such a crucial role in looking after very vulnerable children, there are simply insufficient funds, resources, training and support to meet the demands made on both local authorities and foster carers.

Recent surveys have shown that many children in need are not being fully assessed and that as a result they are placed in a foster home because the foster carer was willing to accept them instead of in a home which suited their specific needs.

The level of failed placements is causing concern. Children may move from home to home – sometimes as many as five or more times. This entails forcing them to adapt again and again to unfamiliar surroundings and schools as well as to new families.

In a recent report by Sir William Utting, a code of conduct was called for to provide proper vetting for the appointment of foster carers. He also called for the regulation of private fostering and demanded that unregistered foster care should be made a criminal offence.

C. FAMILY LOSS AND ILLNESS

PARENTING AND BEREAVEMENT

Parents with young families have to consider the painful questions of who would take care of their children in the event of their death, and how their children would be supported financially. In this context, we consider the appointment of a guardian and the need for parents to draw up a will so that their assets can be used to care for those minors left behind.

Appointing a guardian

A parent may appoint another individual to be the child's guardian in the event of his or her death. To appoint a guardian

1. you must have parental responsibility for your child
2. you should consult the person you wish to appoint.

The appointment must then be in writing, and has to be dated and signed.

The person you have appointed will then assume parental responsibility for your child provided the appointment comes into effect (see immediately below).

Do note: a person with parental responsibility under a residence order, such as a grandparent, cannot appoint a guardian.

When would the appointment come into effect?

The appointment of a guardian would come into effect

- on the death of the person making the appointment,
- provided that there is no other person with parental responsibility for the child.

Your daughter lived with your ex-wife. She has now died and has appointed her brother as guardian in her will. You have never liked him. What can you do?

You can apply to court to have a residence order in your favour as the natural parent.

A married man, even if he subsequently gets divorced from his wife, automatically has parental responsibility for their child and an appointment of guardian cannot take effect where there is someone else alive who has parental responsibility.

Can you refuse to act as guardian?

Even if you are appointed guardian in someone's will, you are not obliged to take up the appointment. The law gives you a formal right to refuse ['disclaim'] the appointment. However, disclaimers must be

1. in writing
2. made within a reasonable time of knowing that the appointment has come into effect.

Guardianship by order of court

If parents fail to appoint a guardian and the child is orphaned, then the court can appoint a guardian who will be given parental responsibility.

The other circumstance in which the court can appoint a guardian is if the surviving parent has no residence order and has taken no interest in the child.

Any relative or family friend can apply.

Guardian's allowance

A weekly tax-free benefits payment is available to someone who takes a child into the family where either

(a) both parents are dead or
(b) one parent is dead and the other cannot be traced.

Details are set out in Leaflet N1 14. To make a claim you must fill in form BG1 (see DIRECTORY).

Your sister never married but had a child while she was working abroad. She returned to England with her child as she had contracted a serious illness. She has since died and you have taken care of the child. The father is not known as your sister had steadfastly refused to discuss her relationship.

You are entitled to claim Guardian's Allowance. Do not delay your claim as it can only be backdated for 6 months.

If your claim were to be refused, you can appeal to an independent social security appeal tribunal.

Wills

If parents do make their wills, their assets will be used for the purposes for which they intend. This is particularly important in considering the needs of a young family, e.g. for education and physical care. Do seek legal advice in your family's interests.

Failure to make a will means that the intestacy rules apply and an estate up to the value of £125,000 devolves on the widow or widower. For estates above that figure, the surviving spouse is entitled to the first £125,000 plus the personal belongings and certain additional rights or interest in the matrimonial home.

Chapter 8 — The extended family

Definition of 'child' for the purposes of the intestacy rules

The definition of 'child' includes an illegitimate child and an adopted one but not a stepchild. However, a stepchild could claim under the law regulating family provision for dependants (see section on *Stepfamilies, inheritance, and guardians*, p.72 above in considering the effect of intestacy on a stepfamily).

Disability

Although legal aid is not generally available for making a will, it may be available for parents or guardians of children who are handicapped either mentally or physically. The legal aid limits will apply.

Certain organizations, such as Mencap, can offer advice on setting up a trust to ensure the future care for a child who is disabled.

Death of a child

Organizations exist to support parents who have to endure the loss of a child, including bereavement involving a miscarriage or still-born baby (see DIRECTORY).

In the strictly legal context, there are two matters to be drawn to parents' attention: their duty to bury the body and their possible right to compensation.

Burial or cremation

Parents are under a duty, by law, to bury or cremate their deceased child's body.

Compensation

Where parents can show that their child lost his or her life as a result of another person's fault, they can claim under the Fatal Accidents Act provided that their child was unmarried and under 18. The maximum compensation payable, so-called 'bereavement damages', is £7,500. It has been suggested that the level be increased to £10,000 (and index-linked for the future).

YOUNG CARERS

There are many children under the age of 18 who find themselves having to take care of a relative who is ill, either mentally or physically, or is disabled. Parenting roles are thus reversed with the concomitant loss of childhood for the young carer.

Seeking support

The local authority social services should be called upon to provide support and assistance so that the child does not have to bear the physical and mental stress alone.

Help can be sought under the following :

The Children Act, as young carers can be classified as 'children in need' (see Chapter 9, p.84);

Community Care legislation, under which the local authority must assess the ability of a 'carer', including a young person under 18, to provide for the person being cared for.

Local authorities, which may have 'Young Carer' officers and run support networks.

Voluntary sector organizations, which can be contacted for advice and assistance (see DIRECTORY).

Young carers and education

Although a crisis situation at home must affect a child's ability to cope with school, nonetheless it does not provide an excuse for missing school (see Chapter 13, *Ensuring a suitable education*).

It is important, therefore, that the situation be explained to the school authorities so that they provide understanding and assistance. Otherwise child and parent, who are in a situation not of their own making and who need sympathy and support, can instead find themselves at the receiving end of punishment and blame.

CHAPTER 9
WHEN PARENTING FAILS

In this chapter, we deal with situations in which a local authority intervenes in a child's life by order of court. Where compulsion is used the local authority takes over the parenting role and assumes parental responsibility. The local authority can only do so where the court is satisfied that parenting has demonstrably failed or is failing the child, whose welfare is therefore at risk.

Even in these circumstances, however, parents still retain parental responsibility although the actual day-to-day care of their child devolves on others.

It has to be stressed that the court can take whatever steps it thinks fit in the circumstances of each individual case. For example, in dealing with a private dispute over children between individual parents, the court may decide that it is in the child's best interests to make a care order in favour of a local authority.

As far as possible the law seeks to avoid situations which allow local authorities to take over responsibility from a child's parents and to transfer it to themselves. Its prime concern is to give children in need, as well as their families, the support that they require. Family ties between parents and children are to be nurtured provided that they are compatible with the child's safety and well being.

Section A deals with the laws relating to *local authority duties and powers*; section B covers *court-appointed guardians*; and section C deals with *making a child a ward of court*.

A. LOCAL AUTHORITY DUTIES AND POWERS

GENERAL DUTY

Every local authority has a general duty, imposed by law, to safeguard and promote the welfare of children within its area who are in need, and promote their upbringing with their families.

Duties of the local authority

The duties placed on the local authority by the Children Act 1989 are manifold. Among them are duties to

- take care of children 'in need' in its area
- protect children in danger
- provide accommodation in children's homes
- take children into care.
  In the past, the local authorities have been found to be both
- too officious in taking children away from their parents and putting them into care on mere suspicion of wrongdoing or abuse, and
- failing in their duty to children who have slipped through the net and have suffered terrible harm and even fatal injury as a result of local authority mismanagement.

Child Protection Registers

Local authorities work on an inter-agency basis to share decision-making and to pool information in dealing with children who may be in danger of suffering harm and in deciding whether to bring court proceedings for a care order. Child Protection Committees will include health professionals, social workers, members of the police, probation service etc. In the first instance a decision will be taken whether or not to place a child on the Child Protection Register. In the most recent figures, 32,370 children were on child protection registers in England. Of the 43,600 children who were the subject of initial child protection conferences, 67 per cent were placed on a register.

Children in need: court orders available

The orders in the Children Act are intended to cover a wide range of situations. They are intended to give a local authority sufficient flexibility to be able to make appropriate and measured responses to the problems it encounters.

Orders are directed to 'children in need'. This phrase is given a wide definition, i.e. a child is in need if he or she is 'unlikely to achieve or maintain . . . a reasonable standard of health or development'.

Do note: the definition is wide enough to cover more than a child's physical well-being; 'development' can relate to a child's emotional and psychological needs as well.

So far as is consistent with their duty, local authorities must work together with parents so that children are brought up at home if at all possible.

In assessing need the authorities must assess whether the need is intrinsic to the child or whether it is the parenting skills which are 'depleted or under-developed'.

Court's considerations

The welfare of the child is the court's paramount consideration.

The court must also pay heed to the checklist in deciding whether an order is justified (see Chapter 5, p.46). Finally in making any of the orders available to it, the court is obliged to decide whether

- an order would be in the child's best interest
- it is better to make an order than to make no order at all
- delay is prejudicial to a child's best interests.

Do remember: none of the orders listed below are available except under the authority of a court.

TYPES OF ORDER

The orders are

- child assessment order
- supervision order
- care order
- emergency protection order.

All these orders are dealt with below. For an *education supervision order*, where a child is habitually truant, see Chapter 13, p.160; for a *parenting order*, where a child may be likely to commit a crime, see Chapter 14, p.175.

First, however, we must examine some of the tasks imposed on a local authority under the Children Act:

- it has a general duty to take care of children 'in need'
- it is required by law to work with families of children in need
- it has a specific duty to investigate cases where a child suffers or is likely to suffer significant harm
- it must enter a child's name on the Child Protection Register if he or she is at risk.

Who has a specific duty to investigate?

Where a local authority has reasonable cause for suspecting that a child in its area is suffering or is likely to suffer significant harm, it must make enquiries necessary to decide whether to take any action to safeguard the child's welfare.

The National Society for the Prevention of Cruelty to Children is the only voluntary organization specifically named in the Children Act and given the statutory powers to take legal action to protect a child who is being abused or is at risk.

Assessment order

Where a local authority has reasonable grounds to suspect that a child is at real risk of suffering harm, it may find that those looking after the child do not co-operate when it tries to establish the true position.

An assessment order therefore is intended to cover a situation where there is some ground for suspicion that the child could come to harm and to enable the local authority or the NSPCC to have a medical or psychiatric examination made of that child.

The child need not be removed from home for an assessment. Removal can be permitted under the Act if the person who has care of the child fails to produce him or her for assessment. The court must be satisfied that

(a) there are reasonable grounds for suspecting that the child is suffering significant harm or is at risk of suffering significant harm;
(b) an assessment is needed of the state of the child's health or development or the way in which he or she is being treated in order to establish whether the child is suffering or is likely to suffer significant harm; and
(c) it is unlikely that such an assessment will be made in the absence of a court order.

The court must always decide on the basis that the child's welfare is paramount.

The court can issue an emergency protection order on the evidence before it. The order lasts seven days.

Supervision order

This order appoints a supervisor who has the duty to advise, assist and befriend the child. Such an order usually lasts a year. A supervisor can apply to extend the order but its maximum duration is three years.

Care order

Care orders apply to cases where a local authority takes a child into care and assumes parental responsibility for the child. Thus any residence order for the child is terminated. The child is taken from home and placed either in a local authority home or with local authority foster parents.

The local authority then assumes parental responsibility for the child under care.

A care order can only be made by court order. The court must be satisfied

- that the child is suffering or is likely to suffer significant harm (i.e. ill-treatment or impairment to health or development) and
- that harm is attributable to lack of reasonable parental care or
- that the child is beyond parental control.

Do note: the responsibility of the parents of a child in care continues as well so that a local authority cannot

- free a child for adoption or
- appoint a guardian.

Care orders may also be issued in other circumstances, for example in divorce proceedings or when a child is involved in criminal proceedings.

Care orders can last until a child is 18 but cannot be made for a child over 17.

Do note: In this context, the issue of parenting becomes crucial. The harm a child has suffered or is likely to suffer must be attributable to the lack of care which one would expect from a reasonable parent.

In a significant decision and by a majority of three to two, the House of Lords ruled that a child could not be taken into care under a care order unless a real possibility existed that the child would suffer significant harm. In order to convince the court that it should make the order there had to be more than just suspicion: there had to be facts.

This judgment has exacerbated the uncertainty about when a local authority should investigate allegations of harm and when to take care proceedings 'which has dogged child protection' (*New Law Journal*, 25 November 1994).

Children in danger – emergency protection order

A local authority, concerned about a child in a situation of danger or distress, can apply to court for an emergency protection order. The order only lasts eight days. Although it can be extended for another seven days, only one extension may be granted.

The court must be satisfied that

- significant harm has occurred or could happen
- there was no access to see the child in circumstances in which significant harm could occur.

The court can make an order for parental contact once the child has been removed from home, as well as make an assessment order for a medical or psychiatric examination of the child.

CHILDLINE, the national free helpline, exists for children in trouble. The number is 0800 1111. The number for children in care to ring is 0800 884 4444.

Who can apply to court for any of the above orders?

(a) Assessment, supervision, or care orders
Only a local authority or the NSPCC can apply to court for an assessment order, a care order, or a supervision order.

(b) Children in danger – emergency protection orders
Applications for emergency protection orders can be made by
- local authorities
- the NSPCC
- any other concerned applicant.
   (i) In making application to court for an emergency protection order, a local authority has to show that
      - it has been making enquiries on the child's behalf
      - its enquiries into the child's well-being are being frustrated and
      - access to the child is required as a matter of urgency.
   (ii) The NSPCC must show that
      - it has been making enquiries which have been frustrated
      - access to the child is required as a matter of urgency

Chapter 9 — When parenting fails

- it has reasonable cause to suspect that a child is suffering or is likely to suffer significant harm.
(iii) Any other applicant must show that
- he or she has reasonable cause to believe that the child is likely to suffer significant harm if not removed.

REPORTS BY CONCERNED FRIENDS OR NEIGHBOURS – CONFIDENTIALITY

Apart from applying for an emergency protection order, a concerned friend or neighbour can approach the court to make a child a ward of court (see *Wardship* below, p.89).

If you suspect that a child is being neglected, ill-treated or abused, you can report your suspicions to the local authority or the NSPCC. Confidentiality is ensured.

You suspect the couple in the next-door flat are abusing their child. You want to report the case to the NSPCC but do not want it known to the parents that you have taken this step. Can you insist that your name will not be divulged in any subsequent proceedings?

The answer is 'yes'.

CHALLENGING AN ORDER

Who can challenge an order?

While minor disputes can often be settled informally, serious problems can and do arise as a result of local authority intervention. Generally orders can be challenged by:

- the parents
- the child – provided he or she is of sufficient understanding and maturity
- any other person with parental responsibility with whom the child was living, e.g. a grandparent with a parental responsibility order.

A local authority may also wish to mount a challenge, e.g. if it has applied for a care order for a particular child but the court has refused to grant it.

Decisions on care orders and contact orders can be challenged in court.

However, there are other procedures available:

(a) Complaints procedure

Under the Children Act, every local authority must set up a complaints procedure. In addition to those listed above, a foster carer can make a complaint, as can any other person considered to have 'a sufficient interest in the child's welfare.'

Any person lodging a complaint must be given proper information on how the procedure works and be told the name of the officer handling complaints. An independent person, together with the local authority, must then consider the matter and put their decision in writing. If there is still no satisfaction, the complaint can be hear by a panel, provided a request for a panel hearing is made within 28 days.

(b) Secretary of State

The Secretary of State has the power to declare a local authority remiss in its duties. Generally speaking these powers are not used in individual cases.

(c) Judicial review

If a parent feels that a local authority has taken a decision without following the proper procedures, he or she can apply to the High Court for judicial review of the decision.

(d) Local government Ombudsman

A complaint can be made to a local government Ombudsman, provided that all formal complaints procedures within the authority itself have been tried.

(e) European Court of Human Rights

The European Convention on Human Rights is to be incorporated into UK law. It provides that everyone has the right to respect for his private and family life.

Cases have reached the European Court of Human Rights where a local authority has, for example, refused contact by parents with their child in care, or refused to give access to records.

Legal aid

Legal aid may be available for a parent who wishes to challenge an order provided that all the financial and other criteria for legal aid are met.

In need of care from 'carers' – protection for children

As we have seen, the Children Act tries to impose standards on those whose job it is to look after children. However, abuses do take place both within the family and outside it.

The problems are manifold: changing social patterns and attitudes; lack of public resources; conflict between the necessity for state protection of children and the undesirability of obtrusive interference in family life. Where requirements are made too onerous, can local authorities always enforce them? Difficulties in implementing the current legislation have become only too clear.

According to a recent report by Sir William Utting, nearly 35,000 children, being looked after by local authorities in England and Wales, were in foster homes. It was the preferred placement for two out of three children who had been taken into care. The report recommends that local authorities should follow existing guidelines and regulations on foster caring; that there should be inspections of the recruitment and support of foster carers; and that the government should introduce a code of practice.

The review also documents abuse of children who have been taken into care, covering a range of institutions. It 'presents a woeful tale of failure' at all levels of a whole system to provide a secure and decent childhood for some of the most vulnerable children. Elementary safeguards were not put in place on their behalf or not enforced.

In response to the report, the government has set up a ministerial task force to establish a programme of policy and management changes and to ensure that standards which are set will be met.

B. GUARDIANS BY COURT APPOINTMENT (*GUARDIANS AD LITEM*)

WHEN IS THE COURT APPOINTMENT OF A GUARDIAN NECESSARY?

The courts are obliged to appoint guardians to assist them in litigation involving children unless they are sure that there is no need for such an appointment and that the child's interests would be quite safeguarded without it.

The role of court-appointed guardians has been heightened by the need to take proceedings under the Children Act before a child can be taken into care.

They are also increasingly being used as litigation involving children becomes more complex. Such litigation includes local authority applications to court for emergency protection or care orders, supervision orders, proceedings involving contact with parents, and adoption.

The guardians are trained social workers and are appointed from a panel, which the local authority is obliged by law to set up. Their appointment is by the court. They are completely independent and are there to serve the child direct. The well-being and welfare of the child is thus their overriding consideration. They can instruct solicitors and obtain expert opinion.

C. WARDSHIP

WHAT IS WARDSHIP?

Wardship is a power of the court, used in very special circumstances, to transfer to the court all responsibility for a child's life. That child then becomes a 'ward of court'. The child must be a minor, i.e. under 18. No major step can be taken with regard to the child, once he or she has been made a ward of court, without permission of the court.

When is wardship used?

A wardship application is made to court when there is an urgent need to protect a child's interests. It has been used in life-threatening situations, e.g. when doctors wanted to turn off the life-support machine of a dying infant. It has also been used in deciding the question of sterilization of a mentally retarded girl.

However, wardship has been invoked in other circumstances, such as to ensure the proper supervision of property belonging to a child, or to prevent a child from being abducted from home.

Local authorities cannot apply to make a child a ward of court in order to take a child into care. Where a local authority does apply to court for wardship, it will have to obtain the court's leave (permission). Leave will only be granted if the local authority can show that

- the other orders generally available to it will not achieve the necessary results
- the child will suffer significant harm if not warded.

In general the courts have stated that wardship will not be granted where an issue can be settled by its powers under the Children Act.

Procedure

Although anyone can apply for wardship of a child, for example a non-relative such as a doctor or social worker, an applicant must have a proper interest in the child's welfare. Wardship takes effect immediately even before a judge hears the case. The hearing must then take place within three weeks.

PART 4
MINIMISING RISKS

CHAPTER 10
YOUR CHILD'S HEALTH

One of the most critical aspects of parenting is how best to safeguard your child's health and safety. Parents are involved in these issues from the very beginnings of their baby's life, e.g. in deciding on the safest way to put him or her to sleep in a cot. Because society as a whole is concerned to ensure that children should be cared for so that they can grow up to realize their full physical and mental potential, a range of services is provided to assist parents in giving their children a healthy start in life. Health professionals have the primary role in assisting parents in this task.

However, the law too is deeply involved in these matters. It recognizes the limited extent to which young children are able to take care of themselves and the need for laws that insist on safeguards for them.

On the other hand, the courts also realize that there are certain inevitable hazards in the very process of growing up and that children should enjoy a degree of freedom in their daily lives even though there may be some risk attached. The crucial question is how to balance safeguard and risk.

In endeavouring to answer this question, the law's involvement ranges from the purely practical (e.g. regulations requiring car seats for children), to consideration of issues of morality (such as the age at which young girls should receive contraceptive advice). Again it is a question of balance. How best can children's health be safeguarded? At what age can children be expected to take decisions on medical treatment? When should they be regarded in law as capable of looking after their own interests? Should the views of parents, lawyers, or doctors prevail over the child's own wishes and in what circumstances?

Thus we examine the legal view of the relationship between doctor, parent and child, as well as other more general issues concerning a child's health, e.g. entitlements under the NHS.

In this chapter we look at *Health issues*:

- Entitlements
- Consenting to or refusing medical treatment
- Hospitalization
- Mental health
- Medical negligence – pursuing a claim
- Private medicine.

Section A covers general health care; section B deals with the questions relating to consent and medical treatment; and section C deals with complaints about your child's treatment, and negligence-related claims.

In Chapter 11, we examine *Safety issues*:

- Parents, carers and negligence
- Safety in the home
- Safety on the road
- Safety at school
- Activities and sport
- Children causing accidents
- Occupier's liability.

A. GENERAL HEALTH CARE

ENTITLEMENTS

Numerous services are available to ensure that children receive regular medical checkups and any treatment they might need. In addition, other areas of their well-being are covered, such as education for children who have to miss school through ill-health.

For the registration of all new-born babies with a GP see Chapter 2, section *NHS Card*, p.16. The GP gives primary healthcare to parents and children throughout their lives and provides a link, if need be, to specialized treatment at hospitals and other clinics.

An initial physical examination of the baby soon after birth is carried out by a paediatrician, midwife or GP. The health visitor then takes over from the midwife, generally within two weeks of a child's birth.

(a) Health visitor

The health visitor maintains a record of the baby's health and development, carrying out health checks at 6 weeks, 8 months, 18 or 24 months, 39 months and at pre-school entry (about four and a half years).

Parents are entitled to keep the record which is later passed on to the school nurse. Thereafter children of school age are included in health care provided under the school health service, in addition to primary healthcare which is the responsibility of their GP.

(b) School health

The school nurse is employed by the local health authority, although the extent of her tasks and services varies from authority to authority, depending on whether or not a full school health service is provided in the area, as well as on budgetary restraints. A pre-school assessment of each child is carried out on enrolment at the school. This will include tests for hearing, sight, walking, speech and language. If these checks reveal a problem, a letter will be sent to the child's parents requesting them to see their GP.

The school nurse also plays an educational and counselling role with regard, for example, to healthy diet. Provision of immunizations is dealt with below.

The Department for Education and Employment (DfEE) together with the Department of Health issues schools with guidance on how best to support pupils with medical needs in schools.

Health benefits for children

Dental treatment

Free NHS dental treatment is available for all children until they reach the age of 18 years, irrespective of whether or not they are in full-time education.

NHS sight tests, and vouchers for glasses

All children under the age of 16 are entitled to free sight tests. Under-16-year-olds are also entitled to vouchers to help towards the cost of glasses for those who need them. Children in full-time education are entitled to these benefits until they reach the age of 19 years. Tests can be arranged with your local optician.

> *Your daughter, aged 16, has been diagnosed as having short sight. She would prefer to wear contact lenses.*

Vouchers are available to help towards the cost of contact lenses or glasses, but it would depend on the optician's clinical judgment whether these would be suitable for her.

Chapter 10 — Your child's health

Your son, aged 18, is a full-time student. He now needs glasses.
He is entitled to a free NHS sight test and vouchers towards the cost of glasses until the age of 19.

Do remember: children under 16 who have lost or damaged their glasses are entitled to a voucher towards the cost of their repair.

Free prescriptions

A child under the age of 16 is entitled to free prescriptions. The age range is extended to a child under 19 who is in full-time education.

Immunizations

The Health Education Authority and the Department of Health issue advice for parents on immunization for children: *A Guide to Childhood Immunizations*. The leaflet includes a timetable for immunization for children aged two months to 15 months (see TABLE below).

When is the immunization due?	Which immunizations	Type
At two months	Polio Hib (an infection which causes a number of serious illnesses) Diphtheria Tetanus Whooping cough	By mouth One injection
At three months	Polio Hib Diphtheria Tetanus Whooping cough	By mouth One injection
At four months	Polio Hib Diphtheria Tetanus Whooping cough	By mouth One injection
At 12 to 15 months	Measles Mumps Rubella	One injection
3 to 5 years (*usually before the child starts school*)	Measles Mumps Rubella	One injection
	Diphtheria Tetanus Polio	One injection By mouth
10 to 14 years (*sometimes shortly after birth*)	Tuberculosis (BCG)	Skin test plus one injection if needed

School leavers

13 to 18 years	Diphtheria	One injection
	Tetanus	
	Polio	By mouth

Immunizations at later stages of a child's life may be given routinely at school.

The leaflet also specifies how to obtain information on other immunizations required if, for example, parents are taking their child abroad.

Consent

Parents must consent to immunization.

Health authorities have standard forms which they make available to the parents of every newborn child in their area. Once parents sign, their formal consent to immunization is registered. A copy of this consent form is kept in the medical notes and a copy given to the health visitor. Thereafter, depending on the authority, consent may be required for each individual immunization.

Parents who are worried by the possible side effects of immunization are advised to discuss their anxieties with their health visitor, the practice nurse, or their GP before giving their consent.

It was in relation to whooping cough, in particular, that parents' fears regarding immunization were first aroused (see immediately below).

Do remember: As vaccinations involve the injection of foreign substances into a very small baby, adverse reactions can follow in a proportion of cases. Most of these symptoms are trivial and are readily accepted as a concomitant to the protection which the vaccine provides. Occasionally more alarming symptoms may occur. More rarely still serious conditions can result. However, statistics would confirm that children who are not vaccinated are more at risk than children who are.

Whooping cough

Vaccination for children against childhood diseases and others has been recommended by the Department of Health since at least 1955. Parents are actively encouraged by the health authorities to seek vaccination in all but a very few cases. Where there are contra-indications, guidelines have been issued to all health professionals to minimize risks. Vaccinations are not to be given where it is inadvisable to do so [the 'contraindications'].

In the middle of the 19th century whooping cough had been the highest cause of mortality among children under 15. In the early 1970s doubts arose about the safety and effectiveness of the whooping-cough vaccine and, to a lesser extent, the vaccine against measles. A number of children suffered damage following vaccination. Although a court case failed at the first hurdle to prove cause and effect, adverse publicity resulted in a marked decline in the number of parents who agreed to have their children vaccinated. In fact, the percentage of children being vaccinated against whooping cough halved. Notification rates of the disease increased.

The three-in-one immunization (Measles, Mumps, Rubella) has also led to on-going research into possible side-effects.

The *Guide to Childhood Immunizations* answers parents' most common questions about immunization and gives advice on treating possible side effects.

The Health Education Authority also issues an explanatory leaflet, *Protect your Child with the new Hib Immunization.*

Special needs – children under five

A child is said to have 'special educational needs' if he or she has learning difficulties and needs special help.

'Learning difficulties' mean that the child finds it much harder to learn than most children of the same age. This may be caused by a physical disability, for example a hearing defect; by a mental disability; or by a behavioural problem. The subject of special educational needs is dealt with in detail in Chapter 13, *Ensuring a suitable education,* Section B. It is referred to in this section in relation to very young children.

Your baby was born premature. You notice that she does not seem to have the same developmental range at two years as other children of the same age.

You must speak to your health visitor or your doctor as soon as possible. They will be able to put you in touch with specialist advice and may inform the local education authority. There are also a number of voluntary organizations which may assist you (see DIRECTORY).

Further once a child is two years old or more, the local education authority can make a statutory assessment of her educational needs unless they decide it is unnecessary. For the procedure regarding statutory assessments (see Chapter 13, section B.).

B. CONSENTING TO TREATMENT

WHO CAN CONSENT?

The parents

Parents with parental responsibility have not only the right but the duty to take decisions which affect a child's well-being.

Parents who were married to each other at the time of the child's birth acquire parental responsibility automatically (For the position of other parents see Chapter 4, Section A). This includes the right to consent to a child's medical or dental treatment. A 'child' for this purpose is someone under the age of 16.

However, the issue of consent is not a simple matter. In fact the law recognizes that an under-16-year-old child can make a decision on medical treatment provided he or she has sufficient understanding and maturity to do so. By law, after the age of 16, it is the child and not the parents who can consent.

Further, a parent who has parental responsibility may give consent to medical treatment in the absence of the other parent. If the parents disagree, doctors may proceed on the basis of the consent of one parent alone.

You are divorced from your husband and your ten-year old son lives with you under a residence order. Your son injured his ankle in the school gym and an orthopaedic surgeon has recommended surgery. You are willing to give your consent. Your husband is opposed to the operation as he believes that the injury is best treated by using complementary medicine.

In the circumstances, you may give valid consent without the agreement of your ex-husband. However, in a situation such as this, co-operation is always the best policy and you should encourage your ex-husband to consult the doctors together with you.

The child

Over-16-year-olds

According to the law, children over the age of 16 can give valid consent to any medical or dental treatment. Thus for the purposes of taking decisions on their health, children are fully-fledged adults at 16.

Do note: The age limit relates to consent to treatment; problems relating to refusal of treatment are dealt with on p.99 below.

Under-16-year-olds

However, in addition, a child under 16 can also give valid consent to treatment if he or she has the mental capacity to understand the nature and effects of the proposed treatment. Thus the law regards the child's developmental age as more significant in this context than his or her chronological age. There is no rigid age limit which determines whether or not a child can give consent to medical treatment.

Contraceptive advice

A landmark decision of the House of Lords arose from a challenge by Mrs Gillick, the mother of five daughters, to Department of Health guidelines on the giving of contraceptive advice to under-16-year-old girls without parental knowledge.

In the light of that decision, the Department of Health issued a circular which was sent to every GP. It laid down guidelines that stipulated the following:

1. in considering contraceptive treatment, doctors needed to take special care not to undermine parental responsibility and family stability;
2. young people should always be persuaded to tell their parents that they were seeking advice on contraception;
3. it would be most unusual for a doctor or other professional to provide advice to a person under 16 without parental knowledge or consent;
4. in those exceptional circumstances where it was not possible to inform the parents, because, for example, family relationships had broken down, a doctor could be justified in giving advice where he was satisfied that:

- the young person could understand the doctor's advice and the moral, social and emotional implications involved;
- the doctor could not inform the parents or persuade the young person to involve the parents
- the young person would be very likely to have sexual intercourse with or without contraceptive treatment;
- without treatment, the young person's physical or mental health would be likely to suffer and it was in their best interests to give contraceptive advice without parental consent. Decisions are for the doctor in his or her clinical judgment.

Other medical advice

You have been told that the above rules apply only to issues concerning contraception for under-16-year-olds.

Although the Gillick decision was concerned with contraceptive advice, the principles it laid down have extended to other cases where a child would want to consult a doctor without parental involvement. This view has been confirmed by guidance on consent issued by the BMA.

Chapter 10 — Your child's health

Questions of confidentiality

Doctors owe a duty of confidentiality to all their patients whether or not they are over 16.

With regard to children under 16, confidentiality can be breached where

1. the patient is immature and does not have sufficient understanding to appreciate what the advice or treatment may involve;
2. the patient cannot be persuaded to involve an appropriate person in the consultation; and
3. it would, in the doctor's belief, be essential to the child's best medical interests.

All three conditions have to be met before there can be disclosure without consent. Thus even if a doctor regards a young person as too immature to consent to treatment, the consultation should still be confidential unless there are very cogent reasons to the contrary.

Exceptional circumstances

Doctors are bound by patient confidentiality unless they feel that maintaining confidentiality would put a child in danger – e.g. if a child, being counselled on drug addiction, has received threats because he owes money to a dealer. Therefore doctors or other health professionals should make clear to their child patients the limits placed on their confidentiality, while assuring them that it would be safeguarded wherever possible (see also *Access to records*, p.103).

In all cases, therefore, in addition to making clinical decisions, doctors have to exercise their own judgment about whether or not to persuade the child of the need to involve the parents. In some cases, parental involvement might be very desirable – e.g. where the doctor knows that the parents would give the love and support their child needs. In other cases, the doctor may decide against disclosure because it might have a detrimental effect – e.g. where the parents are likely to show a marked lack of understanding or even to resort to harsh measures against the child.

Remember: in cases of emergency, doctors have to take all steps necessary to preserve life (see also section on *Emergencies* p.98).

To sum up: information given by a child who is capable of giving consent to a health professional in confidence, may not be made available unless

- the doctor can persuade the child that it is in his or her best interests to involve the parents
- there is a need to protect the child or others from harm or
- a court authorizes release of the doctor's records.

An example would be where a child consults a GP because of sex abuse but does not want to involve other family members. If the GP felt that the child was likely to come to serious harm, or if her siblings were also at serious risk of abuse, then confidentiality could be broken. The doctor then has to tell the patient that confidentiality cannot be maintained in the circumstances.

Responsibility of other carers

As we see throughout this book, children may be cared for by others, apart from their parents, during the course of their childhood. Continuity of health care is of vital importance.

Local authorities

One of the main principles of the Children Act is that local authorities and health authorities should work together to safeguard and promote the welfare of children in their area.

When children are taken into care, the local authority acquires parental responsibility for them, and it exercises this authority together with the parents. Therefore, while the local authority can give consent to medical treatment which is in the child's welfare, parents should still be involved wherever possible.

Under an Emergency Protection Order (see Chapter 9, p.86) a local authority may take reasonable action to meet its parental responsibility to safeguard and promote the welfare of a child.

Agencies should obtain comprehensive medical information on the child and provide information to those who currently have care of the child. Such information should be monitored and regularly updated.

Do note: Even if a child is in care, the general rules of consent prevail. This means that children over 16 can give their own consent to medical treatment. Children under that age may be able to give consent depending on their capacity to understand the nature of the treatment and it is for the doctor to judge their capacity and understanding.

A child in care has to be examined by a doctor within three months before being taken into care or within two weeks of placement.

Foster carers

A local authority can delegate consent to treatment to other carers in conjunction with the social workers and parents. It is obviously in the interests of all involved with the child to have clear instructions as to the kinds of treatment which can be authorized by the foster carer.

In addition, foster carers should be given a child's medical history and any other information which would assist them in safeguarding a child's health, e.g. any known allergies or special dietary requirements. Other problems should also be recorded and noted.

A four-year-old boy has been placed with you for foster care. He is supposed to have an examination by a doctor within two weeks of arrival. However, on the first night when you give him a bath, you notice some nasty bruising on his legs. You do not want to be blamed. You wonder what action to take.

Generally children placed for care should have a medical examination immediately before they enter their new home. In this case, you should make a note of the child's physical condition and inform the social workers immediately. Your note should then be counter-signed.

It is important to be extra vigilant to protect both yourself and the child. If need be, you can attend a casualty department of your hospital.

As a routine, children in foster care under two years of age should be examined every six months; other children at least once a year.

Relatives and friends

Anyone who has care of a child for whom they do not have parental responsibility must do what is reasonable in all circumstances for the purpose of safeguarding or promoting the child's welfare.

Your sister has gone abroad on a motoring holiday and left her 15-year-old daughter in your charge. Your niece falls and breaks a leg in a school hockey match and needs surgery to reset it. The doctor asks you to sign a consent form.

In this case, the girl herself could consent if she is not too upset. As far as your position as aunt is concerned, the Children Act would appear to give the right to consent to medical treatment to people who have temporary charge of a child. The situation might be different if you had to consent to elective treatment, i.e. treatment which a patient could choose to have or not, such as the removal of a tooth under anaesthetic. You would be advised in such circumstances to await the parents' return.

Emergencies

Where a child's life is in danger, e.g. where he or she has been in a serious accident, doctors can and must treat the child without waiting for consent. Indeed, they can carry out the treatment, provided the child's survival is at stake, 'notwithstanding the opposition of a parent or the impossibility of alerting the parent before the treatment is carried out'.

Refusing treatment

The law appears to have divided the question of medical treatment for parents and children into two components:

- issue of consent to treatment
- issue of refusal of treatment.

In fact, situations are not always that easily divisible. Where parents request, as has happened, that a life support machine for their child be switched off, consent and refusal become secondary to considerations of the quality of life. The law has then to take decisions that, in a profound sense, defy judgment.

Refusal of parents

In the most hopeless cases the courts have accepted the refusal of parents to consent to their children's treatment if the life the children were to endure would be full of pain and suffering (see Chapter 1, *Expecting a baby*, p.9, section *Prolonging life*). In one recent case, however, where the medical prognosis was good for an 18-month-old boy who required a liver transplant, the court nonetheless upheld the parents' refusal to allow the operation.

In other life-threatening situations, however, the courts have overridden the parents' refusal. Permission has been given for the go-ahead for blood transfusions to take place even though the parents had refused treatment for their children on religious grounds.

Legal decisions therefore are taken on a case-by-case basis and it is difficult to draw hard and fast rules where issues of life and death are at stake.

Refusal of children

Children who are mature and understanding enough can consent to treatment even though they are under 16 years of age (see above). However, the same principle does not necessarily apply to the refusal by children to have treatment – whether they are over or under 16. One such case involved a girl whose mental condition fluctuated but who refused medication.

In another case, the court decided that a child could not refuse to be assessed under the Children Act.

In particular, the courts have wrestled with the question of refusal of treatment with regard to eating disorders.

Eating disorders and compulsion

In August 1997, in response to many requests from clinicians for advice, the Mental Health Act Commission brought out a 'Guidance Note' regarding the treatment for eating disorders. It applies in particular to the treatment of persons with anorexia nervosa, which is defined as a 'disorder characterized by deliberate weight loss'. Anorexia chiefly afflicts adolescent girls but does occur among adolescent boys as well. The Note sets out criteria for diagnosis and states that anorexia nervosa may be considered a mental disorder within the Mental Health Act. If, in their clinical assessment of the patient, the doctors regard it as a mental disorder, it is for them then to decide whether they should resort to compulsory detention.

Do Note: Generally, compulsory detention should not be seen as necessary except in an extreme situation where someone's health is seriously threatened by a refusal to eat. Even then consent for treatment should be obtained if possible. Only if that proves impossible because the patient is not in a position to give a valid consent [in the words of the law, 'does not have the capacity to give consent'], does compulsory treatment become an option. Force-feeding in these circumstances can then constitute a medical treatment for mental disorder provided the doctors are sure that in treating the food refusal, they are treating the patient's mental disorder.

The Guidance Note stipulates that an authoritative interpretation of the law can be given only by the courts and that the Commission's view must not be treated as, or substituted for, professional legal advice.

A child can also be detained by order of the High Court without having to comply with the criteria laid down in the Mental Health Act. In a recent case a 16-year-old girl was detained at a special eating clinic and the judge authorized the 'use of reasonable force' to detain her there. The Mental Health Act could not be used in her case because the clinic was not a mental hospital.

The doctors

The role of the doctors is to preserve life. However, in certain instances and despite the pleas of parents, they have made a clinical judgment that treatment should not be carried out because they considered that it would not be in the child's best interests.

Decisions such as these have been taken when refusing treatment for a very premature baby (see Chapter 2, *The birth*, p.14) and when the doctors denied a liver transplant to a teenager who had taken the Ecstasy drug.

A recent fatal-accident enquiry called for a code of practice so that parents could be given reasons in writing when doctors have decided on medical grounds that they would not treat their children.

Wardship

The High Court has the power to make a child a ward of court and this power has been used where there has been controversy over the medical treatment of a child, e.g. whether or not to sterilize a mentally handicapped girl. For details concerning wardship, see Chapter 9, p.89.

HOSPITAL STAYS AND SICK CHILDREN

Hospitalization

In general, children should be cared for at home wherever possible. Children's community nursing teams work in the community and make home visits to provide support, treatment, and any equipment which is needed, such as a wheelchair.

If a child needs to go into hospital, the following facilities should be available:

- a children's ward for the reception of children (except in exceptional circumstances)
- a consultant paediatrician to supervise treatment
- a designated qualified children's nurse to care for the patient
- the opportunity for a parent to stay in hospital.

Admissions

Under-16-year-olds

Parents or guardians can arrange for the admission of their children under 16. However, health professionals should be clear that this does not give them a blanket consent to whatever treatment they wish to undertake on the child, and the parents' consent is therefore necessary for each aspect of treatment as it arises. 'Blanket' consent forms also cannot be used.

Do note: If a doctor decides that a child, even if under 16, has the capacity to make a decision for himself whether or not to be admitted to hospital, there is no general legal right to admit him to hospital or to keep him there against his will. (For compulsory detention of children, see also *Mental health and hospitalization,* below.)

16 years and over

Children aged 16–17 or over, who can express their own wishes, can admit or discharge themselves as patients to or from hospital irrespective of the parents' wishes. With regard to formal detention, see however, section on *Mental health and hospitalization,* below.

Education

Hospital stays

Under the Education Act 1993, every local authority must make arrangements for suitable education for those children who – by reason of illness – may not receive education unless proper arrangements are made for them.

Local authorities are now under a duty by law to provide such education.

It is self-evident that a child's education can be disrupted by even a short-term hospital stay – for example, a tonsils operation might happen to coincide in time with preparation for a major examination.

According to the National Association for the Education of Sick Children (see DIRECTORY) there is an urgent need to define and implement standards to meet the broad, general duty of local authorities under the 1993 Act.

Illness at home

Illness can also seriously jeopardize education where a child is forced to remain at home for a length of time, because, for example, he or she has a chronic illness such as diabetes or has to recover from injuries sustained in a road accident.

As a matter of good practice many local education authorities do not leave children at home without tuition for more than four weeks.

Your child was involved in a cycling accident and was hospitalized for two weeks. He has now been recovering at home for the past fortnight. You are concerned about his interrupted schooling.

Where a child has been in hospital for a period without tuition that period should be taken into account when considering the start of home tuition. In your case, therefore, four weeks have elapsed since your child had any tuition. Arrangements should be made for him to receive teaching at home until such time as he can return to school.

Mental Health and hospitalization

While many adolescents may suffer from problems which can cause them great distress, these have to be distinguished from mental illness requiring treatment. The Royal College of Psychiatrists issues a series of leaflets called *Help is at Hand,* which provide useful information. The address is 17 Belgrave Square, London SW1X 8PG. A stamped addressed envelope should be enclosed.

However in certain instances, treatment is required.

According to the Code of Conduct published by the Mental Health Act Commission, any 'restrictive intervention' in a young person's life which is necessary because of mental disorder must be as limited as possible. Segregation from family, friends and school must be kept to the absolute minimum.

C. COMPLAINTS ABOUT YOUR CHILD'S TREATMENT

COMPLAINING ABOUT NHS TREATMENT

All NHS organizations have a single complaints procedure.

Informal procedures

Complaints about your doctor, dentist, chemist or optician can be made informally or formally.

If you feel you have a problem, talk to your GP or other health professional first.

Local resolution of complaints

You called out your GP one night after your two-year-old son had been given a vaccination. You were afraid that he was having a serious negative reaction.

You were told over the telephone that the symptoms were not in themselves alarming and that you should come into the surgery in the morning. Although the symptoms gradually receded, you feel strongly that the doctor should have seen the child and made a home visit when you called him. You wish to take further action on behalf of other parents who might find themselves in the same position. You also feel that making a complaint using the practice's own complaints system would not be of great effect.

As a parent, you are entitled to complain on behalf of yourself or your child.

Complaints must be made within six months of the event. Generally the first line of call is to speak to the practice manager or someone else associated with the GP's surgery. In spite of your doubts, they may take the complaint seriously.

However, once you feel that you would rather speak to someone who is not involved in the practice, you can contact the complaints manager of your local health authority. If your complaint is put in writing, you should receive a written reply within four weeks.

Independent review

If you are not satisfied with the reply, you can ask for an independent review. Your case will then be considered by a member of the trust or health authority, known as the 'convener', and an independent lay person.

Only if they feel it justified will they proceed to an independent review conducted by a special panel. Three people sit on the panel, which will re-examine the case and then send you a copy of its written report.

You will be told of any action being taken as a result of the panel's recommendations.

MEDICAL NEGLIGENCE
Proving cause and effect

In cases where parents have cause to believe that their child has suffered injury as a result of medical negligence, they must seek informed advice. Accidents can and do take place in medical treatment for which no person is to blame. Even where an element of blame is involved, proving medical negligence can be difficult and often leads to protracted litigation.

Action for the Victims of Medical Accidents can advise on pursuing a claim or making a complaint and has a list of solicitors specializing in medical negligence actions (see DIRECTORY).

A specialist organization such as Mencap should be contacted where the complaint relates to a child with a disability.

Access to records

Under the Access to Health Records Act, a patient has a right to obtain copies of his or her medical records made after 1 November 1991.

Your seven year-old daughter has been treated in hospital. You are not happy with the treatment she received and wish to make a complaint. You would like to have access to her medical records.

A parent can apply under the Access to Records Act on behalf of his or her child. You must make your request in writing to the hospital. If your request is sufficiently clear, you should be given access to the records within three weeks provided the records themselves have been added to in the past 40 days. You may be charged a fee for postage and photocopying.

If the information is not forthcoming, you are entitled to issue a summons in the County Court.

Pursuing a claim – time limits

In general, a claim for medical negligence has to be brought within three years of the date of the treatment which resulted in the accident, or three years from when you first became aware that something went seriously wrong during treatment. However, the time limits with regard to children are different. They have three years in which to claim after their eighteenth birthday, i.e. they are entitled to sue until they are 21, although the alleged offence could have taken place long before the child reached the age of 18.

Suing on your child's behalf

If you wish to take legal action on your child's behalf before he or she reaches the age of 18 because, for example, you hope to obtain damages to assist you in caring for your child, you, the parent or guardian, can sue as the child's 'next friend'.

Legal costs

If you wish to sue on behalf of your child, but are concerned about legal costs, your solicitor or legal advisor will advise you about eligibility for legal aid.

(a) Legal aid – age limit

The age limit for legal aid for children is 16 and a parent or guardian can apply on behalf of their child.

(b) Legal aid – assessment

Do note: Children are assessed for legal aid in their own right. Questions of the amount of capital and income on which legal aid is assessed generally do not apply to children. Therefore most children will be eligible for full legal aid.

(c) Legal aid – 'merit' test

In all cases, any claim would have to pass the 'merit' test. This requires the legal aid board to agree that

(a) you have a good claim and
(b) the compensation you are likely to receive warrants the claim being pursued.

There is uncertainty as to the extent to which the 'no win, no fee' conditional fee system will eventually apply to medical negligence claims. In the short term, the present legal aid system continues.

Private medicine

The NHS complaints procedure does not apply to private medicine. If your child has been treated in a private hospital, you generally have entered into two separate contracts: one with the hospital and the other with the doctor.

If your complaint relates to the hospital you must put it in writing and the hospital should deal with it through its own complaints procedure. If you get no satisfaction, you can then complain to the local health authority which is responsible for registering and inspecting the premises, which should meet proper standards for facilities, staffing etc.

Complaints regarding the doctor's treatment should be addressed to the practitioner concerned. If you are not satisfied you should write to the health authority and, in a serious issue, make a complaint to the General Medical Council.

Do seek legal advice if you intend to pursue a claim.

CHAPTER 11
YOUR CHILD'S SAFETY

In this chapter we look at the hazards a child encounters in the most ordinary of circumstances – in the kitchen, going to bed, playing with toys, spending time outdoors, or at school. In this context, a health survey for England for 1996 showed a strong relationship between accident rates and age. The highest major-accident rate was for boys aged 14–15 (a 'major accident' being defined as one which involves subsequent medical attention).

Section A deals with *negligence and accidents involving children*; section B covers *schools*; section C examines *safety regulations*; section D deals with *road safety*; and section E looks at *occupiers' liability*.

A. NEGLIGENCE AND ACCIDENTS INVOLVING CHILDREN

ACCIDENTS INVOLVING CHILDREN

The law recognizes that children are vulnerable and unpredictable and that what is an obvious danger to an adult may be an allurement to a child.

Primarily it is the responsibility of parents, or of others who have charge of the child – even temporarily, such as a babysitter – to shield them from harm. Their safety involves both taking precautions at home (having safety gates on stairs and childproof containers for medicines) and taking particular care of children out of doors. Older children are expected to take some care for their own safety, e.g. when crossing the road.

We look below at situations where an accident happens to a child as a result of a failure to take proper care by the adults in charge, as well as at the circumstances in which a child causes an accident to another.

Taking care to avoid accidents to a child
Parenting and negligence

In dealing with the issue of negligence, the courts take a realistic view of the relationship between parent and child. The law acknowledges that accidents can and do happen to small children when a busy parent, perhaps looking after more than one small child, is distracted by having to answer the telephone or cook a meal.

The law is reluctant therefore to bring legal principles of negligence into ordinary domestic situations, which it comfortably describes as the 'rough-and-tumble of home life'.

(a) Psychological injury

The dangers are not always physical. Children have claimed that they have suffered psychological damage in their later lives as a result of bad parenting. In a recent case, the court said that parents are making decisions daily with regard to their children's future. It held, however, that 'it was wholly inappropriate that those decisions, even if they could later be shown to be wrong, should give rise to a liability for damages.'

(b) So when can parents be liable to their children for negligence?

Where a parent drives a car negligently and causes an accident and their child is injured as a result, the parent can be sued for negligence. The question of damages then becomes a matter for the insurers and not for the parents themselves.

Parents and criminal liability

Under the Children and Young Persons Act 1933, it is a criminal offence for any person over 16 years, who has responsibility for a child under 16, wilfully to assault, ill treat, neglect or abandon the child, in a manner likely to cause him unnecessary suffering or injury to health. The wilfulness distinguishes the criminal element from a negligent action which causes the child harm.

The Act covers any person who has parental responsibility or any person over 16 who has care of a child, e.g. a childminder (see Chapter 7 section A). Neglect includes failure to provide adequate food or medical attention.

For sex abuse against children by parents and others, see Chapter 15 on *Children as victims of crime*, p.181.

Other carers

Children may be looked after by persons other than their parents – in particular, those children who have been taken into the care of a local authority or have been placed in foster care.

Local authorities

In taking a child into care, or making any other arrangements regarding a child's future, a local authority acts under duties imposed by statute.

In two recent cases, attempts have made to bring actions against the local authorities for performing these duties negligently. The first case concerned five children, aged between five and twelve at the time of the proceedings, who alleged that they had suffered abuse and neglect by their parents. They alleged that, despite the fact that the local authority social services had received serious reports about parental neglect, the authorities had failed to conduct proper investigations or to protect them from further harm.

The court decided that the social services were always involved in particularly sensitive decisions. Social workers had to strike a balance between protecting the child from harm and disrupting the parent–child relationship. It would be difficult for those social workers and others who made these difficult and painful decisions if they were judged to have been wrong only with the benefit of hindsight.

In the second case, the plaintiff, now an adult of 24, had first been taken into care at just under a year and had then been moved from foster home to foster home no less than nine times in the course of his childhood. He alleged that as a result he had suffered serious psychological harm. He claimed damages against the local authority for his problems in adult life as a result of an alleged failure to take proper care of him after he had been placed in care. Again the court held that it was not in the public interest to make a finding of negligence against the social services.

The very fact that the local authority was in the 'position of a parent' brought home the 'public policy aspects of the situation', the court stated.

However, where a local authority placed a boy in a foster home when they suspected that the boy was a child abuser and failed to inform the foster family of that fact so that he allegedly

Chapter 11 — Your child's safety

abused their own young children, the family were allowed to sue the local authority (see Chapter 8, *The extended family*, p.78, *Review of child and foster care*).

Foster carers

For the purposes of the law of negligence, it would appear that foster carers are in the same position as natural parents. In general the courts have held that litigation of children against foster carers for negligence would not be in the public interest.

Childminders

The Children Act 1989 lays down guidelines for the registration by the local authority of all persons who look after children under eight for gain, for more than two hours per day (see Chapter 7 section A).

WHEN A CHILD CAUSES AN ACCIDENT

Parents' liability – the general rule

In general, parents are not liable for the damage that their children cause, although they may feel moral responsibility – for example, to pay for the replacement of a neighbour's window broken by their son's cricket ball.

In the rare case where the child has personally got assets, he or she can be sued for compensation. In one case a driver sued a 10-year-old boy for the cost of repairs to his car which was involved in an accident through the boy's own fault.

Note: an award of damages can be enforced when a child starts earning provided this takes place within six years of the date of the judgment.

Can parents be at fault?

It does happen, however, that parents can be personally negligent in not properly controlling their children. The fault is then theirs in failing to prevent an accident. In the case of a young child accompanied by an adult carer, it could be that the carer would be held wholly or partly responsible. For example, a driver who sees a little girl walking with her mother might reasonably expect the mother to prevent the child from running into the road. A parent who does not control children in a car, to the detriment of other road users, will also be held responsible.

> You have picked up two of your son's school friends for the school run and the three boys are being very rowdy in the back seat of your estate car. They unwind the car windows and start throwing conkers on to the road. Unfortunately, one hits the windscreen of an oncoming car so that the driver is distracted and has a minor accident.
>
> He complains that it was your duty to control the children in the car in the interests of other road users. Is he correct?
>
> The answer is 'yes'.
>
> A parent's liability for a child's actions is also related to the danger involved.
>
> You buy an adult's archery set for your 12-year-old son. While he is practising, he accidentally injures a neighbour's child who has come to watch him.
>
> In such circumstances, a parent may well be held liable for allowing their child to use a bow and arrow as a toy and then failing to supervise him adequately.

Part 4 — Minimising risks

Liability of other carers

When a child causes an accident while in the care of others, the same principles apply.

John, aged six, is being looked after by a childminder. While playing outdoors, he careers violently down the pavement on a skateboard and knocks over a passing pedestrian.

In this case, the childminder has failed in her duty of care. The age of the child coupled with the lack of proper supervision has led to a foreseeable accident.

In another case, a lorry driver was killed when he swerved to avoid a four-year-old who had wandered out on to the street from his local authority nursery school. The authority was held negligent in failing to supervise the child. The driver's widow was awarded damages against the LEA.

B. SAFETY AND SCHOOLS

SAFETY OF PREMISES, PUPILS AND EQUIPMENT

General duty

A local education authority is responsible for taking reasonable care for the safety of a child at a maintained school. The governing body of a fee-paying school owes the same duty of care to its pupils. In the case of opted-out schools, the board of governors is a formally constituted body. As such, it is required to have insurance cover against accidents on school premises. The duty of care requires the school to provide safe premises, just as the occupier of any other premises must.

Premises

Health and Safety Regulations, which cover the workplace and lay down a consistent set of standards for safety of premises, also extend to schools. The regulations apply to classrooms, grounds and parts of the buildings used by all staff and pupils such as stairs or corridors [the 'common parts']. These have to be maintained in good repair. For example, schools have to ensure that children moving from classroom to classroom in a short period of time should not slip or trip as a result of badly worn floors or carpeting in main corridors. Staircases need to be fenced and open stairwells protected by additional guarding.

The duties under the Regulations are manifold. They apply despite the fact that school buildings are often in a state of disrepair due to cuts in education funding.

Playgrounds and sports facilities are also required to be suitably designed and safely maintained. Safety at school must also be safeguarded by the provision of suitable materials and equipment (for example, round-ended rather than pointed scissors should be provided for younger children), and by a reasonable level of supervision. This does not mean constant supervision, although obviously more supervision is required the younger the child or the more dangerous the activity. It is not unreasonable for the duty to supervise to be delegated in appropriate circumstances to unqualified staff such as dinner ladies, or to prefects or monitors, provided that the supervision is adequate (see immediately below).

Negligent supervision

Children in class

Schools are responsible for the negligence of the staff in failing to protect pupils' safety. For older children, warnings about dangerous substances or practices may, in some circumstances, be a sufficient discharge of the teacher's responsibility to safeguard his pupils.

Where a teacher warned pupils in a chemistry lesson about the dangerous nature of a chemical, he was held not to be negligent when one of the pupils carelessly spilt some of the chemical on another pupil, causing burns. On the other hand, where a teacher had left an unmarked container of the dangerous substance in a position where pupils could get at it, he was held to have been negligent.

Children and break times

Teachers' duties do not extend to lunchtime supervision. Nor are staff expected to act as policemen or security guards when children play in the playground during breaks. Nevertheless there has to be an adequate system of supervision in place and it must be working properly.

On a rainy day, all the children are sent into the classrooms. One dinner lady is assigned to oversee the behaviour of the children in two classrooms. A child gets hurt because of the rowdy behaviour of a fellow pupil. The parents sue the local authority for negligence.

In a similar case, the court held that a teacher does not have to be on duty in each classroom. However, even if the kind of supervision was different from that required during lessons, it nonetheless had to be adequate. In this case, it was clearly inadequate.

Children and out-of-school hours

Schools often open their gates early in the morning for the convenience of parents and children. At what time should a school assume responsibility for children before school-time actually begins or after it ends?

There is no general rule. Liability if something went wrong would depend on the circumstances of the case, and the ordinary rules of negligence, as well as occupier's liability.

Your son Bernard, who is nine years old, was confronted by another boy, Neville, on his way to the school gate at the end of the school day. Neville had been waving his coat like a lasso and it had struck Bernard in the eye. You feel that the school ought to supervise the children from the school door to the school gate.

In a similar case the Court of Appeal held that there was no need for supervision in the short period in which pupils ran from the door to the exit gate. However, the need for supervision over the lunch period was obvious.

Parents should ensure a proper system is in place for the school to hand children over to those who come to collect them, and they must inform the authorities if there is any change to the usual routine, e.g. if an uncle, rather than the father, is picking up a young child.

School sports

Provided there is a reasonable level of supervision, a school may not be liable if a child is hurt during playground games, even if the injury is caused during organized sports activities.

A pupil was severely injured by a head-on tackle during a school rugby match. Some degree of instruction had been provided.

In this case, the school was found not negligent in failing to insure the pupil nor in failing to advise his parents to take out such insurance. The Central Council for Physical Recreation arranges bulk insurance through schools to cover this type of accident.

However, in another case a player, then aged 17, was seriously injured when his neck was broken in a collapsing scrum during a colts rugby football match. The court accepted that rugby football was a tough, highly physical game in which participants could expect minor injury. However, the Court of Appeal went on to rule that the referee had failed to take appropriate steps under the rules framed for the protection of players and therefore had failed to exercise the level of care required of him in the circumstances.

Parents, anxious for their children's safety, are entitled to withhold their consent to certain serious competitive games.

Outdoor activity centres, activity holidays, and school trips

Most outdoor activity holidays cause no problems. On the contrary, they are seen as enjoyable and valuable additions to the normal school learning programmes. While school trips can never be entirely risk-free, stringent procedures can help to ensure that risks are kept to the minimum.

Regulations have been tightened and new legislation was passed in 1995 following upon the death of four teenagers on a canoeing course in Dorset in 1993. The legislation applies to commercial centres which provide caving, climbing, trekking and watersports activities for under-18-year-olds.

Under these regulations, organizers of adventure activities for children have to be licensed and must comply with safety regulations which came into force in 1996. Inspectors from the Adventure Activities Licensing Authority visit the centres in order to assess standards.

Do note: the regulations apply to England, Scotland and Wales and their territorial waters. They do no apply elsewhere.

The regulations also apply only to activity centres which operate commercially. Therefore they do not apply to expeditions organized and run by the school itself.

Checklist

If your child is to go on a school trip, try to find out the following in advance:

1. the extent of the plans
2. the risk assessments
3. the experience and qualifications of supervisory staff
4. whether the school has undertaken exploratory visits to the centre
5. whether there is insurance in place (both for the costs if the operator goes out of business and for any illness or accident which might occur during the trip)
6. the content of the programme
7. the mode of travel
8. staffing details and staff-pupil ratio
9. telephone numbers in an emergency
10. the emergency procedure for contacting parents
11. the arrangements for medical treatment.

Parental consent

The guidelines require that parents should sign a parental consent form in advance for each pupil.

> *Your son and daughter, aged 14 and 16 respectively, are participating in an end-of-year orienteering course arranged by their school. You have received one consent form for both of them. Your daughter is a strong climber whereas your son suffers from fear of heights.*
>
> You should insist on two consent forms. There are also a number of issues that the consent form should cover which might apply to some children but not to others, e.g.

Chapter 11 — Your child's safety

- travel sickness or incontinence
- allergies
- medication (if any)
- special diet
- non-participation in certain activities, e.g. potholing
- swimming distance.

Note of warning: these lists are not exhaustive.

School trips abroad

The Department of Education is in the process of drawing up guidelines about safety on trips in Europe.

Again the need for tighter regulation was called for following on a tragic incident in which a 13-year-old girl was killed in a youth hostel in Brittany. However, children take part in school expeditions as far afield as Latin America and Asia where no proper accreditation exists for the organizers and there is no way of insuring that leaders are professionally qualified and that proper back-up is in place.

Staff claims against pupils

You are a teacher on playground duty. A pupil with a history of aggressive disruption throws a cricket ball with all his force at you and fractures a cheekbone. You want to know whom to sue.

You can claim damages from the education authority for failing to protect you from the risk of such an injury.

C. REGULATIONS AND SAFETY MEASURES

Safety regulations are in place to protect children against accidents – regulations, for example, covering the flammability of clothing and the safety of toys or nursery equipment. Where you feel that equipment or toys do not conform to safety levels, do inform the safety standards officer of your local authority who will take the matter up with the manufacturers and retailers. Standards officers have enforcement powers in addition to their investigative duties. You do not have to wait until an accident has occurred.

(Advice on safety can also be obtained from the Child Accident Prevention Trust and the Royal Society for the Prevention of Accidents, among other bodies, see DIRECTORY.)

TOYS

We like to think of children as contentedly playing with their toys. Unfortunately, about 30,000 children a year have accidents which involve toys. Most serious accidents are caused by choking on small parts of toys.

Ensuring the safety of toys

The UK has passed regulations to comply with a European Directive on toy safety. Under these regulations, toys must

- satisfy the essential safety requirements
- bear the CE marking
- be accompanied by warnings where necessary.

Under the regulations toys are defined as any product designed or clearly intended for use in play by children under 14 years of age.

These regulations make it a criminal offence to supply toys which would jeopardize safety or health when 'used as intended' or in a 'foreseeable way bearing in mind the normal behaviour of children'. This means that it is up to the manufacturers to try to envisage how children are likely to use the toys.

The regulations apply to anyone supplying toys in the course of any business. e.g. importers, shops, manufacturers.

You order a teddy bear, advertised on the back of a jar of children's food. The toy is supplied free of charge provided you enclose three further tokens. When you receive it, you see that it obviously poses a danger to small children as the bear's button eyes are insecurely attached to the fabric.

The regulations apply to all toys, whether free of charge or not, and to any business, not only a business dealing in toys. So a free toy given away in the course of a food manufacturer's business must still comply with safety regulations.

Day-to-day enforcement is the responsibility of the local authority trading standards department and you should complain to them. They can take enforcement action at any point in the supply chain and suspend the supply of products considered to be unsafe.

(a) The CE marking

The CE marking is not in itself a European safety mark or quality symbol intended for consumers. Its purpose is to indicate that the toys are intended for sale in the EU and that the manufacturer declares that the toys satisfy the safety requirements applicable to them. However, it does not require that toys are independently checked and tested. Therefore parents should also check for the marks below before making a purchase.

(b) Additional safety marks

British Safety Standards
All toys made in the UK must be manufactured to specific standards. Therefore on the box or label you will see BS5665. The standards stipulate, for example, that toys should have no sharp points or edges, or that dangerous dyes are not used.

The Lion Mark
This has been developed by the British Toy and Hobby Association and is backed by a Code of Practice. It is a symbol of quality and safety and can only be used by BTHA members.

(c) Age mark

A toy should carry a warning if it is not suitable for a child of less than three years old.

Do Note: Certain products are not regarded as toys. These include bicycles, Christmas decorations, toy steam engines, and sports and playground equipment.

Take care to check the toy before you buy it, as toys that are sub-standard are still sold. Also always heed warning notices e.g. that a toy is not suitable for a child under three.

FIREWORKS

According to consumer safety research conducted by the Department of Trade and Industry, accidents involving fireworks have risen by 90 per cent over the last five years.

Accidents are attributable to

- underage youngsters having greater access to fireworks
- the number of new outlets, including short-lease shops
- the willingness of some owners to sell to underage children

Chapter 11 — Your child's safety

- the decrease in parental control and supervision
- the greater availability of cheap 'pocket money' fireworks
- the growth in unregistered trade, with fireworks being sold from cars, vans, and private dwellings.

Selling fireworks – the legal way

Premises must be registered by the local authority trading standards department or the fire authority. Under measures introduced in October 1997

- fireworks should be classified by the BSI (BS 7114: Part 2 1988)
- generally sales should be for the three weeks up to 5 November
- fireworks should be sold in manufacturers' boxed sets
- many large fireworks have been banned.

It is an offence to sell fireworks to persons apparently under 18 years of age.

It is also an offence to keep fireworks on premises which have not been registered or licensed for that purpose.

Your 18-year-old son wishes to purchase some fireworks for a private party. He asks the shopkeeper if he can examine the fireworks so that he can choose them to his satisfaction. The shopkeeper tells him that he does not let customers handle fireworks while they are choosing.

The shopkeeper has an obligation to the general public and to his staff to take proper precautions in selling fireworks. This includes ensuring that customers do not handle fireworks while choosing them and that fireworks should be sold in manufacturers' boxed sets.

Do note: Special rules apply to organizers of fireworks displays.

NURSERY EQUIPMENT

There is an enormous range of nursery equipment available: prams and pushchairs, cots, playpens, safety gates, baby bouncers and walkers, high chairs, dummies and baby slings. Products are made in the UK as well as being imported from abroad.

Although not all nursery equipment carries a British Safety Standards mark, all products must nonetheless comply with consumer safety provisions under the Consumer Protection Acts. By law all manufacturers must make their goods safe, and consumers have the right to claim compensation for injury caused by defective products which result in death, ill health or other personal injury. Liability rests on

- manufacturers
- firms which market goods under their own label, or
- firms which import the goods into the EU.

Do remember: where a product carries a safety mark this means that the manufacturer declares that he has complied with an agreed safety standard after independent testing and inspection. For example, when you buy a cot to BS 1753, it will be deep enough to stop a baby climbing out and have a mechanism on the drop side which will be child-proof.

The Child Accident Prevention Trust (see DIRECTORY) issues a leaflet, *Keep Your Baby Safe*, which provides a guide to safe nursery equipment. It also includes safety tips and checklists, for use, for example, when bathing a baby or changing a nappy.

CLOTHING

Nightwear burns rapidly, so regulations are in place to ensure that babies' garments and children's nightwear and dressing-gowns meet set performance requirements for flammability.

Part 4 — Minimising risks

Babies' garments must carry a permanent label showing that they meet the required standards.

It is a criminal offence to supply any goods which contravene the regulations which apply to importers, wholesalers and retailers, as well as manufacturers.

You are expecting your first baby and wish to order baby garments from a mail order catalogue. You want to know whether the safety regulations will still apply to goods ordered through the post.

The regulations specifically include mail order traders. However, they do not apply to second-hand goods.

D. SAFETY OUT OF DOORS

ON THE ROAD

Note of warning: More children under 15 die as a result of a traffic accident than from any other cause.

Ensuring that young children are safe on the roads, therefore, involves the vigilance of parents (whether or not they are in a car), other motorists, planners, educationalists, and legislators. Children cannot be expected to have the skill of an adult in judging the speed and proximity of traffic. It is our job, therefore, to take care of them.

Child passengers in cars

When children are being driven in cars, they are required to wear seatbelts or appropriate child restraints by law (see Table). All child restraints should be labelled to indicate the appropriate weight and/or age of the child, and must carry either the BS Kitemark or the UN 'E' mark.

Each year over 5,500 children are killed or injured while travelling in the rear of cars and it is estimated that about two-thirds of such deaths or injuries could have been prevented by the proper use of child restraints.

Seat belts and children

	front seat	rear seat	whose responsibility
child under 3 years of age	Appropriate child restraint must be worn	Appropriate child restraint must be worn if available	Driver
child aged 3 to 11 and under 1.5 metres (about 5 feet) in height	Appropriate child restraint must be worn if available. If not, an adult seat belt must be worn.	Appropriate child restraint must be worn if available. If not, an adult seat belt must be worn if available.	Driver
child aged 12 to 13 or younger child 1.5 metres or more in height	Adult seat belt must be worn if available.	Adult seat belt must be worn if available.	Driver

An appropriate child restraint is a baby carrier, child seat, harness or booster seat appropriate to the child's weight.

Regulations govern the standards of child restraints. The latest version is ECE44.03 and the Department of Transport advise that only restraints conforming to these standards should be purchased.

Chapter 11 — Your child's safety 115

Note of warning: Where a car is fitted with an airbag for the front passenger seat, do not use a rear-facing child-restraint in the front seat.

You have to take your three year-old child to your local GP. You order a minicab but the manager of the firm tells you that they have no baby seats in any of their cars. You wonder what you can do.

It is safer for children of that age to wear an adult belt in the back seat rather than no restraint at all. See if you can use a booster cushion but on no account use a household cushion. Booster cushions are intended for children who are generally too large for a child seat. An adult seat belt can then be safely used.

Warning note: It is the responsibility, in law, of the driver to make sure that all children under the age of 14 comply with the safety-belt laws. Therefore if you do a school run for your neighbours, make sure that the children in your car and in your care are buckled up properly.

The Department of Transport advises that you should not let children sit behind the rear seats in an estate car or hatchback, and suggests that child safety locks, where fitted, are used when children are in the car. (See the Highway Code.)

Minibus and coach seatbelts

From February 1997, all minibuses and coaches first used from 1 October 1988, are required to have a seat belt for each child when a group of three or more children are on an organized trip. For the purposes of the legislation, a 'child' is 3 to 15 years of age inclusive.

It applies to all journeys which involve transporting children, and includes a journey to or from school even if driven by parents.

A minibus is defined as carrying more than 8 but not more than 16 seated passengers in addition to the driver.

Pedestrians

Parents should take on the basic responsibility of training their children in road safety from a very early age. Road safety programmes exist even for pre-school children.

Unfortunately statistics show that the risk of a road accident increases when children start school. Thus children should not be left to cross the road unsupervised until parents feel it is completely safe for them to do so.

Note of warning: Most accidents happen when children start secondary school, and happen close to home.

A booklet is issued by the Department of Transport: *Lesson for Life*, which sets out road safety practice for parents of 1- to 15-year-olds.

Cyclists

Parents should not allow young children to cycle on the roads unaccompanied by an adult. Again there are training courses for young cyclists run by local road-safety officers, the schools, and the police.

The Highway Code should also be studied (there is a special section for cyclists).

(a) Safety checks

Always check the following:
- cycle helmets (which should conform to a recognized safety standard), lights and reflectors
- brakes

- saddles
- tyres, and
- steering.

(b) Legal requirements

By law, all cyclists must use front and rear lights and a red rear reflector at night.

Mopeds

A moped is a vehicle not over 50 cc with a maximum design speed of not over 30 mph. A moped licence may be obtained for a child from the age of 16.

A safety helmet must be worn and this must have passed the BSI safety standards.

Motor cycles

A provisional licence is obtainable from the age of 17. Drivers with provisional licences must have approved 'L' plates in the front and rear and the cycle must not exceed 125 cc. A full licence entails passing a two-part test.

Learner car-drivers

Provisional licences are available for learner car-drivers from their 16th birthday. Learner drivers with a provisional licence can only drive with a driver who has been qualified for three years and is over 21.

Driving licences are issued to persons who are 17 or over and have passed the theory test and driving test.

General safety while travelling alone

The Metropolitan Police, in their *Streetwise Guide to Going Places*, give young people a series of tips for safety when travelling alone in trains and tubes, buses, coaches, taxis, and while travelling abroad. Among other advice, the leaflet advises a young person who feels that he or she is getting into difficulties or is lost, to approach a family group (rather than a single person) and to ask for help. Leaflets are available from your local police station.

Road accidents and contributory negligence

Damages for a child hurt in a road accident will be reduced by the extent to which its own carelessness contributed to any injury.

> *You are driving your car during rush-hour in a busy road at about 20 mph. An 11-year-old boy, without looking, runs into the centre of the road to retrieve a ball, and is struck by your car. The child suffers a broken arm. You feel that you were not altogether at fault for the accident.*

In a similar incident, the driver was held only 25 per cent to blame for the accident. The court felt that the child's blameworthiness, even taking account of his age, was considerably greater.

Where a four-year-old ran quickly into the road into the path of an oncoming car, the driver in that case was held not liable for her injuries. His attempt to avoid her was all that a prudent motorist could have done in the circumstances (see also *Parents' liability*, p.107).

CHILDREN AND OCCUPIER'S LIABILITY

Premises must be reasonably safe for children, and that means taking into account the fact that children are less able to take care of themselves than adults.

Your four-year-old is injured when she slips between the bars of an airvent in a walkway in a shopping centre. It is clear that such an accident could not have happened to an adult or an older child. Would the fact that an adult or older child would have been safe in the circumstances be a factor in assessing the safety of the premises as far as liability is concerned?

The answer is 'no'.

A two-year old girl, when visiting the zoo, put her hand through the bars of a cage where a chimpanzee grabbed it and bit off two fingers. The zoo was held at fault and responsible for the width of the cage bars.

A tree has been planted in a public park with attractive but poisonous berries. A child eats the berries and becomes ill.

The local authority which owns the park is liable as its officials should have realized the berries presented a dangerous attraction to children.

Children as 'trespassers'

The question of children who trespass on land and then get hurt is a vexed problem for the courts. There might be liability to children who trespass in certain circumstances:

(a) if there is a hidden danger on the land, or an allurement which tempts children to use it even without permission (e.g. a ramp suitable for skateboarders to practise stunts), and
(b) if the occupier knows that children trespass on the land and lets them do this,

he may be regarded as having given them 'permission' and will be liable if they are injured.

Playground equipment

There is no law which applies specifically to playgrounds but the general laws do apply, for example, that of occupier's liability.

A child is badly cut by pieces of glass concealed in a sandpit in a public playground.

The local authority which manages the playground can be held liable to pay her compensation.

Playground equipment for permanent outdoor installation, such as slides, swings, climbing frames etc., should meet safety standards (BSI 5696).

A properly run playground should also be regularly maintained and have impact-absorbing surfaces underneath the equipment, as most accidents result from falls.

A playground manager (such as the local authority) will be liable if a child is injured by

- unsafe or defective equipment
- unsuitable surfaces, or
- hidden dangers.

PART 5
PARENTAL CONTROL AND GUIDANCE

CHAPTER 12
KNOWING THE RULES

The questions at the heart of this chapter concern children's exposure to the world at large and the various pleasures, temptations, and dangers which they encounter in the process. Some of the topics fill parents with dread, such as drug-taking or alcohol abuse. We examine the various rules and regulations which govern these issues and try to establish when and how parents can turn to the law to assist them in giving guidance to their children or in controlling their behaviour.

In some cases, the rules would appear to be quite clear, e.g. under-age children are not permitted to purchase alcohol. However, when one looks closer, the questions of 'Who is under-age and for what?' become quite daunting. The rules are so manifold that they have to be presented in tabular form (see page 125). Similar uncertainties and inconsistencies bedevil some of the other legislation on gambling, drugs, and the rules concerning media entertainment.

In this context of 'rules and regulations', the number of self-regulatory bodies is also striking. For example, there is much public anxiety about the influence of video violence on susceptible children. In response the film industry – along with many others such as the drinks industry or the National Lottery – are concerned to show how much policing they themselves do in order to minimize harm. The Press Complaints Commission is another such body which has been much in the news of late. There are always 'rogue traders' in every industry, however.

In certain cases, there are no adequate legal rules at all – for example, there are as yet no satisfactory answers to the question of how to control pornographic material on the Internet. Today's information revolution may seem a surprising target to pinpoint as a cause for parental concern. However, while modern technology often leaves parents behind, it can bring to their children's attention images of sex and violence that even an adult would find shocking. Thus while parents are strenuously encouraged to 'get their children on-line' at an early age, dangers can lurk in cyberspace too!

Many of these issues are central to our current debates on social policy, education, ethics, and the extent to which the criminal law should – or indeed can – be used to curtail young people's behaviour.

The inescapable fact is that, in the end result, rules of law are only meaningful insofar as they command the respect of the majority, are enforceable and are enforced.

In this chapter, we deal with
- drugs and other substance abuse (sections A and B)
- under-age drinking (section C)
- unsuitable media entertainment (section D)
- under-age gambling (section E).

For the involvement of children in crime, either as perpetrators of crime or as its victims, see Chapters 14 and 15, which also deal with parental liability for juvenile delinquency.

A. DRUGS

All drugs affect our bodies or minds to some degree – indeed that is their purpose. Because of their effects – including unintended or so-called 'side' effects – all drugs can be potentially life-threatening. Even drugs which do not need a prescription, and which can be bought from a local supermarket, have possible lethal consequences. For that reason, the law controls the way in which drugs are made and supplied. It also controls their use.

It is the non-medical use of drugs which concerns parents, children, and law-enforcers. Indeed the issue of drug misuse or abuse among young people is rarely out of the headlines.

Reliable information on the subject, however, is not easy to establish. Surveys have to rely on children's subjective reporting of their own behaviour which – in this context – is illegal. However, the general picture does indicate a growing upward trend of drug-taking in young people.

According to a recent study on *Drug Use in England* issued by the Health Education Authority,

1. drug use would appear to be on the increase;
2. drugs are readily available – most users found the six most commonly used drugs very easy indeed to obtain;
3. a large proportion of young people have used drugs at some time in their lives (7 per cent in 11–14 year olds rising to 55 per cent in 16–19-year-olds). The figures were dominated by one drug, cannabis;
4. regular drug use was relatively uncommon;
5. most people who try drugs do not continue using them;
6. the initial uptake of drugs is mainly a teenage phenomenon and three-quarters of all those who had ever used drugs had tried them by the age of 18.

Thus drug-taking covers a spectrum of behaviour which can vary from transient curiosity to dependency and criminality. It can vary with a child's physical susceptibility, for example taking a single Ecstasy tablet can lead to the death of one party-goer but enhance the 'fun' for others. Drug-taking can vary too with mental susceptibility – for example, there can be a severe psychological reaction to a particular drug – even a long while after use.

Initial uptake during teenage years also applies to children who take up smoking and drinking – teenagers will have experimented by the time they are 18.

This confronts parents with an immediate problem: drug-taking for non-medical reasons is an illegal activity at any age. However, once children are over 16, they can smoke and over 18-year-olds can consume alcohol quite legally. Society has decided, therefore, to legitimize these activities while stigmatizing others. All these activities are nonetheless susceptible to abuse.

At present the question of whether to legalize [decriminalize] 'soft drugs' – in particular cannabis – is under debate. The Lord Chief Justice stated that while he would not express a personal view, the subject deserves detached, independent and objective consideration (*The Times*, 9 October 1997). However, the present Home Secretary is of the opinion that decriminalization would only serve as an encouragement, and is actively engaged in the war against drugs. An anti-drugs co-ordinator or 'drugs czar' has been appointed and the Prime Minister has described this appointment as a 'key post' in spearheading the anti-drugs campaign.

WHAT ABOUT THE LAW?

The two main laws on drugs are the Medicines Act and the Misuse of Drugs Act.

The Medicines Act 1968

This Act regulates the manufacture and supply of medicines.

There are three classes of licensed medicine under the Act:

(a) medicines that may be freely sold ('general sale list'; available in high street shops);
(b) pharmacy sale (available only from a pharmacist);
(c) prescription only (available only from a doctor).

Medicines are categorized according to health hazard and risk of misuse by the Health

Chapter 12 — Knowing the rules

Minister on the advice of various bodies, including the Committee on Safety of Medicines, and the Medicines Controls Agency.

The Misuse of Drugs Act 1971

This Act bans the non-medical use of certain drugs.

It specifies certain drugs as 'controlled' and categorizes them into different classes: Class A, B, and C (see Box below). The classes carry different penalties for illegal use – Class A being the highest.

The main drugs involved are

- opiates such as heroin
- stimulants such as cocaine, amphetamines and Ecstasy
- tranquillisers such as valium
- hallucinogens such as LSD
- cannabis.

Heroin, cocaine and cannabis are mainly imported into the UK; amphetamines and tranquillisers, as well as LSD and Ecstasy are manufactured drugs – produced either here or abroad.

Legal Status:

Class A	Class B	Class C
Cocaine	Amphetamines	Tranquillisers
Ecstasy	Cannabis	
Heroin	Barbiturates	Anabolic steroids
LSD		

The Misuse of Drugs Act makes it unlawful for an unauthorized person

- to possess a controlled drug
- to import or export a controlled drug
- to produce, supply, or offer to supply a controlled drug
- to grow a cannabis plant.

Possession

You go abroad for a holiday leaving your house in the charge of some recommended 'house-sitters'. You come back to find some illegal drugs hidden in a biscuit tin. You wonder what you should do.

If you have an illegal drug on your premises you are committing an offence and can be charged with possession. It is also an offence to allow someone to smoke cannabis in your home.

According to the Misuse of Drugs Act, you have a defence provided you can prove that you took possession of the drug to prevent someone else from committing an offence and that as soon as possible after taking possession, you took all reasonable steps either

- to destroy the drug or
- to deliver it into the custody of the police.

Premises

A person also commits an offence if he or she knowingly permits a drug on his or her premises

- to be produced
- to be given away or
- to be sold.

Note of warning: It is an offence to offer to 'supply' a drug albeit free of charge. There need be no element of profit involved for the offence to be committed.

For parents who do suspect that their children are involved in drug abuse, there are a number of agencies available to offer information and advice, as well as support and counselling services (see DIRECTORY). The National Drugs HelpLine, 0800 77 66 00, is open to anyone with a problem. The HelpLine also gives parents advice on how to talk to their children about drugs. The lines are available 24 hours per day, seven days per week and calls are confidential.

Information can be obtained from the Department of Health; and, under a project, Tackling Drugs Together, Boots has produced *A Parents' Guide to Drugs and Solvents* which is available free.

According to recent statistics, penalties for cannabis offences are not consistently enforced throughout the country. However, 56 per cent of possession cases in 1995 were dealt with by cautioning the offender. Where persons were involved in unlawful supply, however, 88 per cent of them were brought before the court, and custodial sentences [i.e. jail terms] were imposed in 44 per cent of cases.

Anabolic steroids

These drugs received a lot of negative publicity after prominent sports personalities failed 'dope' tests in competitions at the highest level. As children are encouraged to be successful in sports and young teenage boys are concerned about 'body-image' and muscularity, there was concern that they might be tempted into using steroids. In 1996, therefore, the law relating to the supply of steroids was tightened up. A number were added to the list of controlled drugs as 'Class C' drugs and are only available on prescription for medical use. It is not an offence to possess steroids in small quantities. However, possession with intent to supply them is an offence.

Drug education in schools

Certain aspects of drug education are part of the National Curriculum which schools are required to teach by law. Pupils should be taught the following:

- the role of drugs as medicines (5–7 year olds)
- the harmful effects of tobacco, alcohol and other drugs (7–11 year olds)
- the health risks resulting from abuse of alcohol, solvents and other drugs (11–14 year olds)
- the effects of solvents, tobacco, alcohol and other drugs on body functions (14–16 year olds).

In addition, individual schools themselves are then free to decide how and whether they want to extend provision for drug education beyond the requirements specified above – either within science classes or as part of a broader programme of personal/health education or current awareness programmes.

Parental involvement

Schools need the support and encouragement of parents in their efforts at drug-abuse prevention. PTAs can provide an opportunity for the school to explain its programme to parents, and parents' meetings – including the annual meeting – can be used as a forum to explain the school's approach to drug education.

> *You are concerned that your child is being 'taught' about drugs at school and that this will stimulate curiosity rather than act as a deterrent.*

> You can ask to see the school's teaching materials and to meet any outside professionals, who may play a part in the teaching, e.g. police officers or health professionals.

Chapter 12 — Knowing the rules

Public Entertainment Licences (Drugs Misuse) Act 1997

The Act gives councils the power to revoke the public entertainment licence of premises, such as clubs, where they have evidence that a serious drugs problem exists.

Your child is attending a club where you suspect drugs are openly sold in the car park of the premises.

The council's power under the Act to revoke an entertainment licence extends to 'any place nearby which is controlled by the licence holder'. You can complain to the licensing committee of your local authority.

Solvent abuse

Solvents are in fact everyday household fluids: text-correction fluids, dry-cleaning fluids, paint thinners, lighter fuel, aerosols – to name but a few. As it would be quite impossible to ban these items, possession of volatile substances (i.e. solvents) is not illegal.

However, sale to under-18-year-olds is controlled where a retailer suspects misuse (see immediately below).

In general it is children from ages 12 to 16 who try sniffing. It is supposed to give a quick 'buzz'. Sniffing can and does lead to fatalities – more than 100 children die from substance misuse each year.

Under-18s – Intoxicating Substances (Supply) Act 1985

It is an offence to sell solvents to a person under 18 (or a person acting on his behalf) if a shopkeeper knows or has reasonable cause to believe that they will be used for sniffing.

A retailer committing an offence faces a fine of up to £5,000 and six months in prison.

'Herbal highs'

There are public health concerns regarding several of the main active ingredients in 'herbal highs'. These products are sold through specialist retailers, at pop music festivals and through mail order. The drugs imitate the effects of widely known drugs such as cannabis but claim to be without health risk. In fact, they contain ingredients which clearly fall within the legal definition of a medicinal product and need a licence before they can be sold. By selling these products without a licence, the suppliers are therefore breaking the law.

According to the Department of Health, herbal high drugs are dangerous and can be killers.

B. SMOKING

Smoking is probably the largest cause of preventable death in the UK.

Public attitudes to smoking have undergone a remarkable change, resulting in no-smoking policies being implemented in workplaces, cigarette advertising being restricted, and the proposed banning of tobacco sponsorship of sporting events. Nonetheless the figures for young people show that about 450 children start smoking every day. There appears to have been a significant increase in the take-up of smoking among teenage girls.

CHILDREN AND YOUNG PERSONS (PROTECTION FROM TOBACCO) ACT 1991

This Act strengthened the law on illegal sales of tobacco products to children under the age of

16 (increasing penalties for doing so, and making illegal the sales of unpacketed tobacco).

Warning signs of age limits must be displayed in shops and on vending machines.

Shopkeepers are liable to a fine of up to £2,500 if they sell to under-age children. If you suspect that a shopkeeper is deliberately flouting the law on sales to children, you should report the matter to your local trading standards officer.

The law is to be further tightened so that the minimum age at which cigarettes can be legally purchased will be increased to 18.

Advertising

The Independent Television Commission, the Radio Authority, and the Advertising Standards Authority all have codes of practice which stipulate that advertisements for cigarettes should not be directed at those under 18 or contain anything which might appeal to them.

There is a voluntary code to prevent advertising of cigarettes near schools. However, the Department of Health announced that 19 out of 30 breaches of the voluntary agreement on advertising related to poster sites near schools. As a result an outright ban is likely to be introduced.

Anti-smoking education

The national curriculum requires that science lessons should teach children about the harm which smoking can do.

Many schools have a 'smoke-free' policy which prohibits smoking on the premises – not only for pupils but for staff and visitors as well.

C. UNDER-AGE DRINKING

The rules relating to young people and alcohol are set out below. From surveys and other information, it would appear that more and more young people are beginning to drink alcohol, and at an ever-earlier age. According to a Health Education survey, *Young People and Alcohol*, 13 per cent of 11- to 15-year-olds were found to drink regularly in 1988. By 1994 that figure had risen to 17 per cent. According to *The Times* of 8 August 1997, 55 per cent of 11- to 16-year-olds are 'regular' drinkers, rising to 71 per cent of 16-year-olds. Regular drinking is defined as 'usually having a drink at least once a week'.

These trends cause justifiable concern as alcohol abuse can lead to addiction, physical and psychological damage, and anti-social behaviour of all kinds. In addition, new sweet alcoholic drinks, known as alcopops, have been introduced into the market in the late 1990s, which some teenagers appear to find both trendy and nicer-tasting than traditional alcoholic drinks. Surveys show that alcopops were the easiest for under-age drinkers to buy although steps are being taken by retailers and the drinks industry to reduce accessibility.

PUBS AND OFF-LICENCES

Licensing laws control the sale of alcohol (the main piece of legislation is the Licensing Act 1964). By this statute, licences are to be granted to 'fit and proper' persons for sale of alcohol for consumption on and off premises. An opportunity is provided for anyone (including police and local residents) to object to the renewal of a licence on a wide variety of grounds.

What is intoxicating liquor?

Your daughter states that drinks with a low alcoholic content do not constitute 'intoxicating liquor'.

Chapter 12 — Knowing the rules

The definition of 'intoxicating liquor' includes, by law, any drink containing in excess of 0.5 per cent alcohol.

Rules relating to children and alcohol – a parent's guide

Under 5s may not be given alcohol except on medical orders.

It is not illegal for a *child over 5* to drink provided this does not take place on licensed premises.

The general rule is that *under 14s* are not allowed into a bar of licensed premises.

For children of *14 and over,* it is legal to go into the bar of a pub – but only for soft drinks and at the licensee's discretion.

At *16 or over*, a child can buy beer, cider or perry but only to drink with a meal in a sectioned-off area of the pub.

It is an offence in licensed premises, for a licence holder (or an employee) to sell alcohol to a person *under 18* or to knowingly allow such a person to drink on licensed premises (except as above).

Certain pubs have now been granted children's certificates (see below) which allow under-14-year-old children, accompanied by adults, into pubs subject to strict conditions and special licence.

Rules to curb under-age drinking in public places have also been introduced recently (this too is discussed below: see *New legislation – drinking in public*).

Licensees and retailers must – by law – refuse to sell alcohol to anyone who they think may be under 18. Licensees take pains to prevent under-age sales and may ask for proof of age. Nonetheless, sales to under 18-year-olds are on the increase.

TABLE

Age	Law	Act
Under 5	may not be given alcohol except on medical orders	Children and Young Persons Act 1933
5+	may consume alcohol at home	
Under 14	may not be present in the bar of licensed premises unless (i) accompanied by a person over 18; (ii) if it is before 9 pm; and (iii) a children's certificate relating to the bar is in force	Licensing Act 1964 Deregulation and Contracting Out Act 1994
14+	may be in the bar of licensed premises during permitted hours	
16+	may purchase beer, cider or perry with a meal in an eating area on licensed premises.	Licensing Act 1964
Under 18	may not purchase or be supplied with or consume alcohol in a bar	Licensing Act 1964
Under 18	may not purchase alcohol from an off-licence, supermarket or wholesaler	Licensing Act 1964
Under 18	may be employed in a bar of licensed premises under a job training scheme	Deregulation Order 1997

Children's certificates

Under the Deregulation and Contracting Out Act 1994, the Government has introduced a new system to certify bars which they consider provide a suitable environment for children who are accompanied by an adult.

Thus children may be present in a bar which has a certificate in force and operation, provided they are in the company of a person who is 18 or over. The regulations came into force in January 1995.

A children's certificate requires the following:

(a) a designated environment suitable for persons under 14 and
(b) meals available for sale in that area.

A 'suitable environment' takes in a host of factors such as the locality, existing clientele, facilities for children to play, etc.

The pub must provide a children's menu or children's portions and a full range of soft drinks.

Other conditions can be imposed such as opening hours, child safety standards etc.

New legislation – drinking in public

There are new police powers to confiscate alcohol from under-18s drinking in public and to ban adults from buying alcohol at the request of youngsters – the Confiscation of Alcohol (Young Persons) Act 1997. The legislation was brought in because of increasing concern that groups of drunken youngsters were making public places – e.g. shopping malls – unpleasant or even intolerable for the rest of us.

Under-18-year-olds

The 1997 Act allows police to destroy any alcohol in the possession of any person under 18 who is

- in a public place or
- in any other place which they have entered illegally.

The police must have reason to believe that the young person has been drinking or is about to drink.

Over-18-year-olds

You are over 18 and have bought 12 lagers quite legally at an off-licence. You pass one of the cans to your girlfriend while you are in the street outside a dancehall. She is 16. The police approach you and ask you to hand over all 12 cans.

Police can seize alcohol from any person who is 18 or over in a public place where the police believe alcohol will be passed to under-age drinkers.

Providing details to the police

The police can request the name and address of an under-aged drinker, and can request the name and address of any person from whom alcohol has been seized under these powers.

It is a criminal offence, punishable by fine, to refuse to provide a name and address to the police or to give them false details.

Drunk in charge of a child

Since an Act of 1962, a person found drunk in charge of a child under the age of 7 in a highway or other public place may be liable to a fine or a period of imprisonment.

Proof of age

Because the licensing laws are so age-dependent, proof of age is a critical issue: not only must licensees ban anyone who they think is under-age, they themselves commit a criminal offence if they sell liquor to an under-18-year-old – knowingly or not.

The drinks industry watchdog, the Portman Group, has published a guide for staff in licensed premises and off-licences entitled *Saying No to Under-Age Drinkers*.

It has also introduced a voluntary national proof-of-age scheme for those over 18. Proof-of-age cards are issued provided there is verification that applicants are indeed 18 or over. The card is tamper-proof and is available free from the Portman Group Issuing Authority, Admail 173, London W1E 2SJ. The Home Office has indicated that the scheme might become mandatory.

Alcopops

These are drinks with an alcoholic content of between 4 and 5.5 per cent which taste of lemonade or vanilla or such like in order to mask the flavour of alcohol. Marketing and packaging are said to be aimed at young people attracted to the rave scene – for example, cans and bottles carry labels which glow in the dark.

Alcopops attracted widespread media criticism and were accused of being designed to appeal to the under-18s who cannot legally buy them. Certain supermarket chains are now refusing to stock them. According to the most recent government study, alcopops were not luring youngsters to drink alcohol when they would otherwise have consumed only soft drinks (*The Daily Telegraph*, 31 October 1997).

The self-regulatory body of the drinks industry has introduced a Code of Practice for its members requiring that alcopops

- should not be targeted at under-18s
- should not use the imagery of under-18s culture
- should not use endorsements from under-18s' 'heroes'.

Words such as lemonade, orangeade or cola are to be 'used with the utmost care' so as to avoid confusion.

You are upset at the packaging of a brand of alcopops which you feel is deliberately aimed at the teenage scene.

Complaints about packaging or merchandizing can be made to The Complaints Officer, The Portman Group, 2d Wimpole Street, London W1M 711. You should enclose a product sample with your complaint.

Employment in bars for under-18-year-olds

In 1997, deregulation was brought in which would allow job-training schemes in pubs for persons under 18. It will apply to those who have left school at the compulsory school leaving age of 16. The schemes will be available subject to strict criteria.

D. MEDIA

One of the most striking features of the latter part of the twentieth century is our ever-developing capacity to transmit information. Apart from radio, TV and telephone, information now reaches us by E-mail, digital image, and CD-ROM. It crosses national boundaries, and transcends earthly confines. The technology involved even infuses our language with new words and concepts.

For parents and children, this information revolution poses a number of challenges.

First, there is the sheer excitement of being able to access vast quantities of information from our own home. No longer are children confined to looking up the books on their parents' shelves at home or even on the shelves of their local library.

Second, our patterns of recreation have changed. We can take our music with us when we go on holiday; we can play games on computer; we can surf the Internet; we can watch our favourite local TV programme or news service in practically any hotel room anywhere in the world.

But, as with most things, the benefits can present difficulties.

Parents do not necessarily know or understand what their children are doing and seeing. Methods of parental control – for example devices to blot out the undesirable depiction of violence on the screen – are at best imperfect.

The law has to grapple with three particular areas of complexity:

- difficulties of definition – where to draw the lines, for instance, in defining obscenity or pornography in the light of changing standards
- difficulties of keeping pace with technological development – for example, is 'downloading' the same as 'publishing'?
- difficulties in enforcement – global transmission of services, particularly on the Internet, presents a wholly new challenge in applying existing laws.
  In this section we deal with
- television and radio
- advertising
- videos
- video and computer games
- cinema
- magazines
- the Internet
- chatlines.

Protection from unwanted publicity for children is covered in Chapter 14, *In trouble with the law*.

TELEVISION AND RADIO

Children between the ages of four and nine watch an average of more than two hours of television a day. With the advent of cable and satellite television, viewing is increasing in most households.

Television brings undoubted pleasure and relaxation to most children. It has also widened their horizons. Debate has nonetheless centred on undesirable programme content for susceptible children.

How can parents prevent their children from viewing unsuitable material? Apart from the on/off switch which all parents use, much has been made of the 'V chip' to provide some of the answers.

The chip acts as a blocking device which allows parents to scramble programmes containing an unwarranted degree of sex, violence, or bad language. But even if there were to be a law which required that all new TV sets be fitted with a V-chip, there would still be many second-hand sets without one.

The responsibility which rests with the parents is therefore two-fold:

Chapter 12 — Knowing the rules

- they need to be alert in trying to oversee and influence their children's viewing, and
- they need to exert pressure so that broadcasters take parents' concerns into account.

The NSPCC has drawn up a booklet on screen violence: *What every parent should know*, which provides guidelines on the different stages of a child's development and the extent to which they can relate to screen images. It also contains suggestions on how parents can help their children to understand the images which they see.

Broadcasting standards

Parallel systems of guidelines and regulations govern the BBC, and commercial radio broadcasting and TV.

In addition the Broadcasting Standards Commission has a general monitoring function over all programmes (BBC and commercial). It considers issues regarding sex and violence, complaints of unjust or unfair treatment in programmes (TV and radio) and unwarranted infringement of privacy.

BBC

The BBC is established under Royal Charter, which was renewed in 1996. Under the Charter and its licence from the Home Secretary, programme standards should not include anything which offends against good taste and decency or would be offensive to public feeling. The criteria are similar to those applied by commercial stations in their Programme Code for family viewing (see immediately below). Further, in order to 'show concern for the young' programmes should be scheduled at appropriate times. This refers to a 'watershed' of 9 p.m. which is also dealt with in greater detail below.

Complaints about the BBC can be addressed to the BBC or the Broadcasting Standards Commission (see DIRECTORY).

Independent Television Commission (ITC)

This is a public body which licenses and regulates commercial TV services (covering ITV, Channel 4, Channel 5, Teletext and a range of cable and satellite services).

Do Note: The BBC and ITC do not 'censor' programmes. They have no powers to preview scheduled programmes in order to decide whether or not to transmit them. However, films may be vetted; for example, bad language can be excised so that films can be shown earlier in the evening to boost audiences.

ITC programme guide and code – 'family viewing'

In general, the content of programmes should not offend 'good taste and decency'.

In particular the ITC has drawn up a programme code which covers
- language
- sex/nudity
- scheduling
- violence
- behaviour easily imitated by children
- the need to issue warnings about possible upset to viewers.

The 'watershed'

The ITC Programme Guide requires that early evening broadcasts conform to the requirements of the Family Viewing Policy. This policy states that nothing should be broadcast before 9 p.m. which is unsuitable for viewing by children aged 15 and under. Even after the 9 p.m. watershed, the Code warns against bad language and profanity with regard to any religion.

After 9 p.m. – with transmissions continuing until 5.30 a.m. – requirements become progressively less strict on the assumption that fewer and fewer young persons may be watching late at night and in the small hours of the morning.

It is expected that parents, too, should be responsible for deciding what their children watch after 9 p.m.

Do remember:

(a) not all programmes before the watershed are suitable viewing for children – for example, an older child may understand that a film is mere fiction but could be very upset by images of real violence on the early evening news;

(b) the 'watershed' presupposes that there is only one TV set in the house and that children are packed off to bed at 9 p.m. However, two out of three teenagers now have their own TV sets in their bedrooms so that the exercise of parental control over their children's viewing at night becomes increasingly difficult.

Films on TV

As regards material considered by the British Board of Film Classification (see below, *The classification process*, p.132), the code states that

'R18' [restricted 18] material should never be shown on TV but is to be confined to viewing in licensed sex shops only;

- '18 rated' material should not start before 10 p.m.
- '15 rated' material should not start before 9 p.m. and
- '12 rated' material should not start before 8 p.m.

Advertisements

In their hours of TV-watching, children are also being exposed to advertisements and mass consumerism. Hence the need to ensure that adverts, too, conform to certain rules when it comes to their effect on children.

In all, there are three systems of guidelines and regulations to protect the interests of children as well as adult consumers.

- The ITC covers TV adverts
- The Radio Authority covers radio commercials
- The Advertising Standards Authority covers non-broadcast advertisements including print, posters and cinema advertising.

These bodies are all self-regulatory. Therefore it is in the interests of parents to keep a careful eye on adverts aimed at their children to ensure that guidelines are not only drawn up but are also being observed.

The guidelines

- Guidelines include the following:
- children should not be shown in hazardous places or talking to strangers;
- advertisements should not exploit their credulity, immaturity or inexperience;
- children should not be misled about size/quality/performance of product or services and should not be made to feel disloyal or inferior for not buying;
- advertisements should not exhort children to ask parents or others to buy;
- they should not invite children to make direct purchase by mail or phone;
- they should not encourage children to be a nuisance to parents or others;
- children should not be encouraged to eat frequently throughout the day;

- restrictions on drinks, cigarettes, medicines and slimming regimes which are not to be directed at under-18s; and
- restriction on how prices are expressed, i.e. advertisements should not use words like 'only' or 'just'.

Guidelines are reviewed to take account of changes in current opinion and advances in technology, science and medicine.

Clearance for adverts

TV and radio advertisements are pre-vetted according to these guidelines. Adverts found to be in breach can be withdrawn or re-scheduled.

Every year thousands of commercials are checked before transmission.

Complaints about adverts

The regulatory bodies monitor and log all complaints. Those that show a consistent negative response may be withdrawn. In serious cases of breach of the code penalties can be imposed and the licence can even be revoked.

> *Your child has been nagging you to buy a computer game advertised regularly on TV. When you make enquiries, you are shocked to discover that the retail price is £55. You feel that the advert is taking advantage of children's gullibility and their capacity to cajole their parents into making ill-considered and expensive purchases.*

According to the guidelines, adverts for 'expensive' toys and games must include an indication of their retail price. A product is considered expensive if it is over £20.

You should make a note of the date, time of day, TV channel and details of the product, and write to The Advertising and Sponsorship Division, The Independent Television Commission, 33 Foley St, London W1P 7LB. (For addresses about complaints concerning radio adverts and printed ads, see DIRECTORY).

VIDEOS

Videos pose particular enforcement problems. Age categories can be specified on the box but viewing takes place at home where there is 'no gatekeeper at the box office to turn younger children away'. Only the parents can act as gatekeepers!

The effect on children of video 'nasties' is also the subject of intense public concern. Home-viewing also allows for images of film being seen out of context, i.e. the freeze/slow motion/speed buttons mean that a video can be seen in a way not anticipated at all by the director.

Because of these problems, classification standards for home videos are stricter than for films shown in cinemas.

By law, since 1994, special regard has to be paid to 'any harm that may be caused to a potential viewer [which includes a child or young person] , or through their behaviour to society'. So the legal stipulation is two-fold: harm which can be done to an underage viewer, in particular, because of the violence of the images; and harm that these images may lead a child to do to someone else.

Harm is thus the main criterion in determining classification content and is categorized by the manner in which a video work deals with criminal behaviour, illegal drugs, violent/horrific behaviour or human sexual activity.

Part 5 — Parental control and guidance

Who is a potential viewer?

The term 'potential viewers' includes those below the minimum age specified in the certificate. In other words, it includes underage viewers who are likely to watch adult material – whatever the category. If a significant proportion of underage viewers is likely to view, then the work must be classified in a form suitable for these potential viewers and contain more cuts.

It is a criminal offence to supply any title given an age-restricted classification to someone below that age.

The classification process

1. Films and other programmes have to be classified by the British Board of Film Classification (BBFC) before being released.
2. As well as films and programmes on video (including tapes and discs), computer/video games and software products can also be covered as can a wide range of other future devices.
3. Examiners are employed on a full-time basis and include teachers, social workers, academics and others. Members of the ethnic communities vet foreign-language videos. Because of the concern to protect children, many examiners are parents.
4. Certain video works are exempt from the classification requirements – for example, educational or sports videos.

Consumer advice

In 1997, in order to provide clear and accurate information to parents, a system of Consumer Advice was introduced. It is a standard format that appears on the sleeve of all videos and indicates any potentially disturbing material and the frequency and intensity of the key issues of language, sex/nudity, and violence.

In addition there is the more familiar Category System: see immediately below.

'U'	UNIVERSAL	Suitable for all
'Uc'	UNIVERSAL	Particularly suitable for young children
'PG'	PARENTAL GUIDANCE	General viewing, but some scenes may be unsuitable for young children
'12'		Suitable only for persons of 12 years and over
'15'		Suitable only for persons of 15 years and over
'18'		Suitable only for persons of 18 years and over
'RESTRICTED 18'	RESTRICTED	To be supplied only in licensed sex shops to persons of not less than 18 years

Video Standards Council (VSC)

The Video Standards Council was established in 1989 to develop and oversee a Code of Practice and Rules designed to promote standards within the video, computer and video games industry. The VSC has a complaints board procedure to investigate alleged breaches of the rules (see DIRECTORY). It also offers advice and guidance to the public.

> *You took out a 'U' rated video for your eight-year-old niece as a treat. You were upset to discover that the trailers to the feature film contained some very undesirable material for such a young child to view. You wonder what the legal position is.*

Where a video contains a feature film together with trailers of other films the entire video must be labelled with the category of the most restrictive classification. Thus if the feature film has a 'U' classification and the trailer has an '18' rating, then the whole video must be labelled as '18'.

Offences

Offences connected with videos include the following:

- possessing an uncertificated video
- supplying or offering to supply a video to a person below the age specified in classification;
- supplying or offering to supply a 'Restricted 18' video anywhere other than a licensed sex shop.
Conviction carries fines and terms of imprisonment.

You are upset to discover that your 14-year-old son has been watching 'R18' videos at a nearby house.

Material such as this is restricted to licensed sex shops. You must therefore make a complaint to your local trading standards officer. Wide powers of search, seizure and arrest are entrusted to local trading standard officers (numbers will be in your local telephone directory).

Video and computer games

In general video games are exempt from the need for classification applied to video films, provided the product is

- designed as a game in the first place
- educational in content; or
- concerned with sport, religion or music.

However as technology develops, 'virtual reality' will begin to blur the lines between 'real life' and the fantasy situations we usually associate with games. In future, therefore, there are likely to be stricter criteria applied.

CINEMAS

Under the Cinemas Act 1985, cinemas must be licensed by local authorities (London boroughs, and district councils elsewhere). By statute local authorities must prohibit the admission of children to films classified as unsuitable for them.

The British Board of Film Classification (BBFC)

The BBFC is not a statutory body (in relation to film) and its powers are only those of advice. While a film may not be exhibited to the public without BBFC certification, a local authority can override its advice on whether a film should be shown to the public with regard to the particular category which the BBFC has assigned to it. For example, a recent film was given an 'R18' category by the BBFC. A single local authority decided to allow it to be shown in its area as suitable for general viewing to all those over 18, and not to be confined to licensed sex shops.

It does not follow that a video will receive the same classification as a film.

Teenage magazines

Coverage of sex-related issues in teenage magazines has attracted considerable adverse publicity. To ensure that teen magazines provide accurate and responsible information about sex, the industry has produced its own guidelines on how such material should be treated. The guidelines cover such matters as encouragement for young readers to seek support from their parents; discouragement of under-age sex; and the need for responsibility about contraception and safer sex generally.

The Teenage Magazine Arbitration Panel [TMAP] has drawn up these guidelines as a result of discussions between publishers, retailers and editors.

They apply to magazines where young women aged under 15 years make up 25 per cent or more of the readership. A complaints mechanism has also been set up.

If you are unhappy with an article in a teenage magazine, you must write to the editor and if you are not completely satisfied with the editor's response, you can write to the Teenage Magazine Arbitration Panel (see DIRECTORY). All complaints are carefully considered. If the magazine is in breach of the guidelines, TMAP will write to the editor and inform him or her of the breach. A list of breaches will be reported in their annual report: see TMAP's *How to make a complaint.*

THE INTERNET

Access to the Internet offers a brave new world to parents and children. Its importance will only grow in the future. The Internet enables people to keep in touch – world-wide – with others who share hobbies and interests; information can be exchanged, and vast quantities of data can be accessed.

The problem

Users access the Internet through Internet Service Providers who have no responsibility for the material which is put on the Internet through them. According to surveys about 15 per cent of traffic is to 'adult' sites.

Existing obscenity laws can deal with the producers of material. However the Internet presents new challenges for enforcement. Legislators all over the world have, as yet, been unable to control a medium which disseminates child pornography world-wide. It also enables child abusers to get in touch with children who are using the Net. Parents who let their children surf the Internet without supervision have been likened to parents who allow their children to wander alone out of doors.

Protective software can prevent access to specified pictures and words or to certain Usenet groups but it is thought that most computer-competent children would be able to get round the system. Tightening up of protective software is developing apace.

Making the Net a safer place

The Protection of Children Act 1978 (amended in 1994) makes it an offence to own computer-generated images of child pornography.

In 1996 the Department of Trade and Industry announced an agreement with UK Internet Service Providers to reduce potentially harmful material on the Net. The Internet Watch Foundation (IWF) has been established to implement the proposals. The Platform for Internet Content Section of the IWF is developing a ratings system for sites, with the aim of shielding children from sexually explicit and violent material on the Internet.

If you find something on the Net which is offensive, particularly material involving children, you must contact IWF. It can act to try to get it removed from the Net and will inform the police where appropriate. The phone number is 01223 236077; the IWF web site is at www.internetwatch.org.uk.

CHATLINES

The telecommunications industry was first liberalized about a decade ago with the main purpose of providing telephone information and entertainment services. However, 'adult' and chatline services very soon evoked strong public criticism.

In response to public anxiety, the industry set up its own regulatory mechanism, the Independent Committee for the Supervision of Standards of Telephone Information Services (ICSTIS), which became its watchdog. It regulates the content of premium rate services – which are charged on a different basis from ordinary calls – through codes of practice.

With regard to the Live Conversation Service ['one-to-one'], the Code of Practice calls on operators 'to do everything practicable' to prevent persons under 18 taking part. If they suspect that the person is underage, the caller should be cut off.

You have seen adverts at the back of your newspaper for 'adult' chatlines. You are concerned that your teenage children may be tempted to call them.

BT insists that adult services operating on its network have its own dialling codes. Customers wishing to dial these numbers have to have a special PIN code and a separate account which is only available to over-18-year-olds. In other words, a customer has to be an adult and has to 'opt-in'.

The Code of Practice for service providers includes provisions concerning decency, honesty, promotion and pricing. There are special rules applying to children's services.

These regulate content, as well as cost – stipulating that the service is only to be used with the agreement of the person who pays the telephone bill.

You discover that your child has been using the phone to access a quiz competition. She has run up large bills quite unwittingly because the competition form gave her a premium rate number to dial to discover if she had won a prize. It appears that the calls were kept deliberately long by the service provider because unnecessary information was spelt out. Also you feel that the competition itself was designed to mislead a gullible child.

Call-barring enables customers to block certain services – do look in your telephone directory which will tell you how to proceed.

However, if you feel that the industry's Code of Practice has been breached, e.g. because of misleading information on the competition form and the length of the call, you can make a complaint on a free complaints line: 0800 500 212. You can also write to ICSTIS FreePost WC5468 London WC1V 7BR. Do provide as much detail about the service in question as possible and send an example of the misleading material. Anonymity is respected. Scratch card competitions by chatline for children are to be outlawed.

E. GAMBLING

Gambling is not a new phenomenon. However, certain manifestations are new – such as the National Lottery. Restrictions on gambling have generally been relaxed over the years, and with the advent of the National Lottery, gambling as a national leisure activity has achieved respectability.

The prize-draw on TV is the second most popular programme for 10–15 year olds and the lottery logo is recognized more than any other corporate symbol including Pepsi and McDonalds (*Daily Mail*, 18 September 1997).

As far as young people are concerned, the law has endeavoured to control the attraction of gambling by setting age limits on playing and betting. The rules are complicated and their logic sometimes bemuses. For example, fruit machines with a £10 payout are restricted to 18-year-olds and over. Children over the age of 16, however, can buy Lottery tickets and scratch cards where the jackpot can run into millions of pounds.

There is evidence to suggest that problems of gambling addiction can develop among young people. On the whole, these problems are confined to two areas: fruit machines and scratch cards. However there is evidence to show that scratch cards are fast replacing fruit machines as the most addictive form of gambling for children because of their accessibility and excitement which make them very attractive to young people.

Organizations have criticized Camelot, which runs the National Lottery, for introducing the 'heartstopper sequence' (i.e. giving players the feeling they have just missed the prize).

A national charity, GamCare, which targets young gamblers among others, has set up a national hotline for anyone concerned about their own or someone else's gambling; the number is: 0845 6000 133. Counsellors offer safe and confidential counselling, crisis support information and, if need be, a referral service. A major educational initiative in secondary schools will highlight the dangers of gambling.

LICENSING LAWS

Generally speaking betting can only take place on premises that are licensed for the purpose. Bookmakers, to operate within the law, are required to hold a permit.

Permits and licences are granted and renewed by local betting licensing committees. Grounds for refusing to grant or renew a permit or licence include the appropriate authority's belief that such a person is not a 'fit and proper person' to hold a licence or permit.

Under-18s

The rules are as follows:

- No person under 18 may take part in gaming on licensed premises.
- It is an offence to take bets with any person who is known to be, or appears to be and is in fact, under 18, or to employ such a person to place a bet in a licensed betting office, or to receive or negotiate any bet through him.
- No person who is apparently under 18 may be admitted to or be allowed to remain on licensed premises.
- Notice relating to the non-admission of under 18s must be displayed.

Gaming by machines is regulated by law.

Basically there are three types of slot machine.

1. *Jackpots with a £300 payout:* these are restricted to licensed clubs and casinos which operate a strict 18-plus age limit.
2. *Fruit machines with a cash payout of £10:* the maximum stake is 30p. This information should be displayed on the machine.

   By law, these are restricted to the 18-plus age-group. These machines are found in the following places:

   (a) an amusement arcade which must contain a designated area for such £10 payout machines;
   (b) an amusement arcade which provides these machines exclusively;
   (c) pubs which are considered a 'supervised environment' where age restrictions already apply. However, 14–18 year olds can frequent pubs (see above, *Rules relating to children and alcohol*, section C). Machines should display signs stating an 18-and-over age restriction.

Chapter 12 — Knowing the rules 137

3. Fruit machines with a limit of £8 cash payout or tokens for the value of £8. There is no legal minimum age for playing these machines. They can be found in cafés or fish and chip shops for example.

You send you daughter aged 15 to your local fish and chip shop to buy chips. She returns to say that while she was waiting her turn, she played with a fruit machine which has just been installed in the shop. She tells you that it has a cash payout of £10. You wonder what you should do.

You must telephone the local trading standards officer of your local authority and he will check out the machine. If it is indeed one with a cash payout of £10, it is an illegal machine and he will take action accordingly.

Do note: All machines are required by law to return a minimum of 71% of stake money.

The British Amusement Catering Trades Association (BACTA) runs a voluntary code of conduct for amusement arcades which many arcades adhere to.

Arcades

Inland arcades – the age limit is restricted to over-16-year-olds. If the arcade only has machines with a £10 payout only over-18s are allowed on the premises.

Seaside arcades – School age children are not allowed on the premises during school hours unless they can show that they are on holiday.

National Lottery

It is illegal to take part in the National Lottery until you are 16 (including 'instants' and on-line games) and operators stand to lose their franchise if they allow sales to be made.

Members of the public are asked to report retailers who sell to under-16s.

You see a young child, apparently no older than 12, purchasing a lottery ticket at a local newsagents. You wonder who to contact.

Camelot, which runs the National Lottery, has a Telephone Helpline available (0541 56 16 16) to report incidents concerning underage sales (also see DIRECTORY).

PART 6
EDUCATION

CHAPTER 13
ENSURING A
SUITABLE EDUCATION

The legal requirement for free state education to be available to all school-age children was fully established in the Education Act of 1944, at a time of radical national reconstruction. The 1944 Act set up a Ministry of Education (later Department) under a Secretary of State for Education and laid down the pattern of education for the next four decades. In the main, the Act firmly placed responsibility for the provision of educational services on the local authorities. It also placed a legal obligation on all parents to ensure that their children were suitably educated according to their needs.

Although some changes were introduced in the years between 1944 and 1980, particularly in relation to comprehensive schooling, the duties placed on local authorities remained on more or less the same terms.

Since the beginning of the 1980s, however, the question of how best to educate our children has reached the top of the national and political agenda. During this relatively short period, from 1980 onwards, education in this country has undergone major changes. Still more radical changes are on the agenda, incorporated into the far-reaching School Standards and Framework Bill. Some of its features are discussed at the end of this chapter.

Thus far, crucial legislation on education has

- reduced the role of local authorities
- extended parental choice
- enhanced the parental role in running of schools
- introduced assisted places
- allowed schools to opt out of local authority control
- increased the role of school governors
- introduced different methods of funding
- set up the national curriculum and league tables
- insisted on raising teaching standards and methods to deal with failing schools
- established appeal bodies
- extended special needs facilities, e.g. by setting up appeal tribunals.

Apart from its intended results, this mass of legislation has also brought in its wake two somewhat unlooked-for but interrelated consequences. First, promises to parents about choice in education and range of educational opportunity for their children cannot always be met. Second, parents and pupils (as well as former pupils) are becoming increasingly litigious; claims have reached the courts concerning poor exam results, undetected learning difficulties, and inability to help victims of bullying.

Some nine million children attend school, of whom about 93 per cent receive free education in state schools. Thus in numerical terms, the number of children attending fee-paying schools is small. Nonetheless the private sector in our education system remains of much significance and fuels the continuing and intense debate over how the nation's schools can and should deliver the best for our children.

In this chapter, we examine the legal aspects of the following:
- the duty to educate

- choosing a school
- parent-teacher meetings
- parent governors
- special education needs
- national curriculum
- discipline
- preventing trauma
- proposals for change

Within the chapter, section A deals with the parent's role; section B covers special needs; section C outlines what is taught in schools; while section D deals with problems which a parent may encounter, including issues relating to discipline, truancy, and school security.

A. THE PARENT'S ROLE

DUTY TO EDUCATE

Ensuring that your child's educational needs are met is an integral element of parenting. Our aim must be to enable all children to acquire learning and social skills, and to equip them to cope with the demands that will be made of them as adults to the best of their abilities.

Parents therefore have the primary legal responsibility of seeing that their children, who are of compulsory school age, receive efficient full-time education suitable to

- their age, ability and aptitude, and
- any special educational needs they may have,

either by regular attendance at school or otherwise.

Who is a 'parent'?

Under the Education Acts, the duty to educate applies to all parents with parental responsibility for their child. It thus applies to married parents, to unmarried mothers, and to fathers who are not married to the mothers but who have a parental responsibility agreement or order.

Do note: In this context the definition of a 'parent' extends to any person who is not the child's parent but who has parental responsibility for the child, e.g. a local authority which has taken a child into care. It also applies to someone involved in the full-time care of the child on a settled basis, e.g. a step-parent or a foster carer.

As there are many divided families, schools sometimes have inadequate information about their pupils' parental background.

Conflicts can also arise where the natural parents are separated or divorced, as each has parental responsibility, and the concomitant duty to educate their children, and it is important in such cases for the mother and father to attempt to agree on the education which is most suitable for any child or children.

The School Standards and Framework Bill intends allowing the governing body or LEA to determine who is to be treated as the parent of a registered pupil at the school for the purposes of regulations dealing with voting rights at annual parents' meetings.

What is the compulsory school age?

A child is of compulsory school age when he or she attains the age of five (however, see also *Primary schools*, p.142 for the admission of the 'rising-fives'). School-age children are not entitled to leave school until the last Friday in June in the school year in which they reach the age of 16.

These requirements apply whether the child is being educated at a school or otherwise at home, and no child may be in full-time work while of compulsory school age.

Registering your child

You must register your child once he or she has reached school-going age. If you fail to do so, a school attendance order [SAO] can be served on you by the LEA. It will insist that the child be registered at a particular school unless you can show that the child is receiving education otherwise than at school – for example, by suitable home-based education (see section below).

Failure to comply with the order can result in a prosecution of the parent.

The subject is further discussed under *Truancy*, see p.159.

Categories of school

It is the duty of every local education authority to ensure sufficient primary and secondary schools for all pupils in the area, with education suitable to their different ages, abilities and aptitudes.

The system of funding and managing schools is complex. In broad terms, mainstream schools fall into three legal categories:

1. *county* (maintained by the local education authority [LEA])
2. *voluntary* (maintained by the LEA but with a distinctive, usually religious, character). As there are differences of self-government, autonomy, and maintenance requirements, voluntary schools comprise (a) voluntary controlled, (b) voluntary aided, and (c) special agreement categories
3. *grant-maintained* (funded by central government and outside the control of the LEA).

Local authority maintained special schools and the 21 grant-maintained special schools for special educational needs form separate legal categories.

Do note: the present government has already issued proposals regarding changes to the classification of schools (see *Proposals for change*, pp.161–2). The proposals envisage three new legal categories of school: *Community, Foundation*, and *Aided*. These will subsume all the above existing categories of mainstream school.

Nursery education

Initially, you may wish to send your child who is between the ages of two and under-five to a nursery school. These are separate schools.

Nursery school vouchers were first made available in 1996. In order to attract the additional funding to their schools, some primary schools increased the size of reception classes to attract the 'rising-fives'. The nursery voucher scheme is now being phased out.

Home-based education

Education is compulsory, schoolgoing is not.

> *You decide you no longer want to send your child aged 10, who is a gifted chess player, to school. You are a former headteacher and a chess player of note and feel that, in the circumstances, your child would be better educated at home. Are you entitled to withdraw him from school?*

The Education Act 1944 states that it is the duty of parents of school-age children to ensure that they receive efficient full-time education 'either by regular attendance at school or otherwise'. So in fact, while the parents' duty to ensure that their children are being educated is enforceable by law, this education can be 'at school or otherwise'.

Further, the education which every child receives has by law to be efficient, full time, and suitable to his or her needs, age, ability and aptitude.

If you decide to take your child out of school, you would first have to persuade the LEA that you are able to fulfil those criteria with home-based education. There are organizations which give advice and support to parents who wish to educate their children at home (see DIRECTORY.) You would be well advised to seek this advice before removing your boy from school.

Take heed: Once registered in a school, a pupil's attendance there is compulsory until such time that the LEA agrees to his withdrawal.

Primary schools

Although as we see, there is provision to educate your child at home, the norm is to send your child to a school which will meet the legal educational requirements.

Primary schools are for children aged from four to eleven years. Generally they are divided into two:

- infant schools for children up to the age of seven; and
- junior schools for children from seven to 11.

Do note: not all local authorities follow the same pattern.

Although the law stipulates that the compulsory school age commences at five, many local authorities admit children to reception classes in the academic year in which their fifth birthday falls – either at the start of the autumn term if their birthdays fall between 1 September and end of February, or at the start of the spring term if their birthdays are between 1 March and 31 August.

Parental preferences

In general a pupil is to be educated in accordance with the wishes of the parent. Local authorities are under a duty to enable parents to express a preference for the school which will provide their children's education. Parents should also be given an opportunity to give reasons for their preference.

For each school year the LEA must publish particulars of arrangements for admission to the schools which it maintains, as well as of admission appeal procedures.

If you consider that your child has or may have a learning difficulty, special provisions may apply. This is dealt with in section B.

Walking distance

A school must be within walking distance, *viz.* two miles for a child under eight and three miles for over-eight-year-olds. If there is no suitable school within these distances, local authorities are obliged to make free transport available.

If the distances differ from the statutory mileage, e.g. if the distance from school is 2.8 miles for a nine-year-old, the LEA has a discretion whether or not to provide transport.

> *You are a member of the Church of England and you wish to send your daughter to a C of E secondary school. The school is six miles from your home. The LEA has refused to pay for transport on the grounds that there is a suitable school for her within walking distance. You want to know what the legal position is.*

Parental choice is a factor that the LEA must take into account when deciding whether or not to make transport arrangements for a child to attend a particular school, and it should pay heed to the parents' wishes for a school which provides religious education in the denomination to which the parents adhere. However, after taking all factors into consideration – such as religious preference – an LEA is nonetheless entitled to make arrangements for your daughter to become a registered pupil at a school nearer your home or to refuse to pay for transport.

Admission refusals

All schools must admit pupils up to at least the number published in their prospectus.

You understand that all LEAs have an 'open enrolment arrangement'. Yet your five-year-old has been refused a place at the school for which you have expressed a preference.

Your child may have been refused admission to a primary school because the admission numbers would be exceeded, as the government wishes to restrict class sizes to 30 children for years 1 and 2. It is also possible for a religious-based school to refuse admissions on the basis that the admission of children who are not within their faith would constitute a significant change in the character of the school. Admissions may also be refused on the grounds that an increase in pupils would require a significant alteration to the school premises.

However, either the LEA or the school concerned must give you details of the procedure for an appeal you might wish to make against that refusal.

Admissions procedures and the appeals structure are subject to change according to a new government Bill, the Schools Standards and Framework Bill, published in December 1997 (see *Proposals for change*, pp.161–2).

CHOOSING A SECONDARY SCHOOL

Before you decide which secondary school to apply for you should collect as much information as possible.

You might wish to consider the following:

(a) The type of school you want for your child, such as:
- comprehensive or selective;
- single sex or mixed;
- county (maintained by the LEA);
- voluntary – also maintained by the LEA but with a distinctive, usually religious character;
- City Technology College [CTC] – schools established (mainly in urban areas) through a partnership between the government and business, with a special emphasis on technology and science;
- grant-maintained [GM] or self-governing state schools. These schools are managed by their governors and directly funded by the Department for Education and Employment.

(b) What values the school promotes; what it expects from its pupils in terms of behaviour and work.
(c) How your child would travel to a particular school, how long the journey would take and how much it would cost.
(d) Any links a secondary school may have with your child's primary school.
(e) How the school could provide for any special educational needs your child may have.
(f) The school's academic record.
(g) Any extra-curricular activities which are available at the school, e.g. societies and sports clubs.

Get first-hand information where possible by contacting the school and making arrangements to visit and talk to the headteacher, staff and pupils. Discuss possibilities with the staff of your child's primary school and attend any open evenings at schools. It is important to look at all the published information that is available. Each year your LEA will publish admission arrangements for all its schools. These leaflets, usually available from your child's primary school, also contain information on home-to-school transport and grants for clothing.

The governing bodies of all state-funded schools must publish a prospectus each year. This will tell you the school's aims and values, organization of teaching, public examination results, National Curriculum Assessment results, attendance figures, admissions policy, the number of applicants in previous years, the number admitted, and the school uniform policy. You should also look at the school performance tables published each year by the Department for Education and Employment. These are usually published in November and copies are sent to all primary schools to be given to parents of pupils who are due to start secondary education the following September.

Making an application

When you decide to make an application, remember that you can apply to more than one school and to schools outside your own LEA area. It is not legal for admissions authorities to discriminate against children because of the LEA in which they live.

Ensure that you send your applications to the correct admissions authority. Applications for grant-maintained schools are usually sent to the school's governing body and applications for LEA-maintained schools are usually sent to the LEA. If you are in doubt about the procedures, ask the admissions authority for advice.

Allocation of school places

All maintained schools must admit pupils up to at least the number published in their prospectus. If there are more applicants for a school than there are places available, the admissions criteria, as published in the school's prospectus, must be used to decide which children to admit. Admissions criteria must be objective and reasonable so that you can judge the chance of your child being offered a place. Admissions criteria may give priority to children who, for example:

- have brothers, sisters or other relations who attend or have attended the school
- live nearest to the school, or have the shortest travelling time to the school
- live within a clearly defined catchment area; or
- attend a named feeder school.

In general, admissions authorities cannot offer places for 'non-selective' schools on the basis of academic ability or aptitude, although some schools may offer up to 10 per cent of their places on the basis of ability or aptitude in certain subjects, such as music, art, sport and technology.

Admissions criteria should not

(a) discriminate against applicants on the basis of their race or (unless they are single sex schools) by sex;
(b) refuse to offer education to pupils with special educational needs;
(c) refuse to admit children who have been labelled potentially disruptive or difficult, such as those who have been excluded from other schools;
(d) charge entrance fees for admission;
(e) allocate places randomly (by lot, for example);
(f) give priority on a 'first-come, first-served' basis; or
(g) take account of religious beliefs (unless they are church schools).

Refusal of a school place

Most children are offered a place at the school of their parent's first choice unless the number

Chapter 13 — Ensuring a suitable education

of applicants is in excess of the school's capacity. If your child is refused admission, the refusal letter must tell you about your right to appeal. You can appeal regardless of the age of your child or the number of schools to which you applied.

The committees are composed of local councillors, teachers and parents. Nobody directly affected by your appeal is allowed to sit on the committee.

Appeal committees are required to be fair, and to consider each case individually, according to the school's admission criteria. If your child meets none of those criteria, your chances of success at an appeal will be low.

Should you feel that your appeal was not handled properly by the appeals committee, you can refer the case to the Ombudsman. Your LEA will be able to help you to contact your Ombudsman.

You may also complain to the Secretary of State at the Admissions Team address shown in the DIRECTORY. Any letter to the Secretary of State should explain the basis of your complaint and include copies of any relevant papers and letters you have received from the admissions authority and appeals committee. However, the Secretary of State can tell the admissions authority to offer your child a place only if he is convinced that either

- the authority acted unreasonably in refusing your child a place; or
- it failed to carry out a statutory duty, such as by turning children away although the school was not full.

Note of caution: The Secretary of State can consider your complaint only if you have already appealed.

Admissions policies and appeals procedure are likely to be changed under government proposals for education reform (see *Proposals for change*, pp. 161–2 below).

ANNUAL PARENTS' MEETINGS

County, voluntary, and maintained special schools are required to hold a parents' meeting once in every school year. That meeting is to be open to

- all parents of registered pupils at the school;
- the head teacher; and
- such other persons who may be invited by the governing body.

The purpose of the meeting is to discuss

- the governors' report, and
- how the governing body and the head teacher have discharged their duties.

Parents of all registered pupils should receive copies of any report not less than two weeks before the annual meeting.

No person who is not a parent of a registered pupil at the school may vote on any question put to an annual parents' meeting.

Governing bodies of county, voluntary or maintained special schools are required to consider any resolution which is passed at an annual parents' meeting and refer the resolution, depending on its terms, to either the head teacher or to the LEA.

A maintained special school in a hospital, or a school in which 50 per cent are boarders, need not hold an annual parents' meeting in a year when the governing body considers that it would be impractical to do so.

ELECTION FOR GRANT-MAINTAINED STATUS OF SCHOOLS

One of the significant features of the legislation introduced in the 1980s was its emphasis on centralization – indeed, the whittling down of local authority predominance in educational services inevitably brought with it a degree of centralization. In order to compensate, more autonomy was given direct to the schools themselves. Grant-maintained status was one of the results. Grant-maintained ('opted out') schools are taken outside local authority control but manage their own affairs on a budget direct from the State.

County and voluntary schools are generally eligible for grant-maintained status. Under present law, the school's governing body is required, at least once in every school year, to consider whether to hold a ballot of parents on grant-maintained status.

Request from parents

A ballot on opting out can only be held if it has been requested by parents of at least 20 per cent of the registered pupils at the school.

The governors must allow you to inspect at the school (at all reasonable times and free of charge) a list containing the name and address of parents of pupils registered at the school – other than where parents have made a written request for the information to be withheld. A fee, not exceeding the cost of supply, may be made if you want a copy of that list.

Do note: The grant-maintained status of schools will be absorbed into one of the three categories of school proposed by the present Secretary of State for Education.

It is expected that most GM schools will become foundation schools. Parental ballot and the governing body's discretion in choosing a school category are still at the consultative stage (see *Proposals for change*, pp.161–2 below).

PARENT GOVERNORS

Every school has a governing body which must include parents elected by other parents of children at the school; teachers; and usually the head. The governing body has very important tasks in ensuring the quality of education; in selection of the head teacher; and in improving the school's performance etc.

The number of parent governors is determined by the size of the school. However, if the number of parents standing for election is less than the number of current vacancies for parent governors, the required number of parent governors can be appointed by the other members of the governing body.

In opted-out schools, the board of governors is a formally constituted body.

For future proposals regarding parent representation and the need to ensure that there is at least one elected parent governor with relevant voting rights on the Education Committees of the local authorities, *Proposals for change*, pp.161–2.

B. SPECIAL NEEDS

CHILDREN WITH LEARNING DIFFICULTIES

The issue of learning difficulties can be very painful for the parents and children involved. However, it is not particularly out of the ordinary for a child to require special provision in education – about one in six children needs help at some stage in his or her schooling. While most children get over their difficulties quite soon and have their needs met in ordinary schools, about one in fifty children may have problems which need longer-term provision.

Parental disputes with local authorities about the education or special provision their children ought to receive can add to an already stressful situation. The 1993 Education Act, therefore, wished to underline that as far as possible parents should work together with the

Chapter 13 — Ensuring a suitable education

local education authorities, the health sector, and other caring and voluntary bodies. There are also a number of support groups which parents can contact (see DIRECTORY).

The law requires that children with learning difficulties should be educated – insofar as is possible – in ordinary schools. They are also entitled to a broad education which should incorporate as much of the National Curriculum (see section C) as possible.

Defining special educational needs

A child has special educational needs if he or she has learning difficulties and needs special help.

A child has learning difficulties if he or she finds it much harder to learn than most children of the same age, or has a disability which makes it difficult to use normal educational facilities. For example a child may have difficulties due to

- a physical or mental disability;
- a problem with sight, hearing or speech;
- emotional or behavioural problems;
- a medical or health problem;
- difficulties with reading, writing, speaking or maths.

Your child will not be taken as having a learning difficulty solely because the language in which he or she is taught differs from the language (or form of language) which is spoken at home.

If your child is under five but over two you can ask your LEA to make a statutory assessment of special needs: see Chapter 10, *Your child's health*, p.95.

Where you consider that there is a learning difficulty you should talk to the child's teacher or the head teacher. Every school is required to publish information about its policies for children with special educational needs and it should deal with your child's needs step by step or in stages. The school must give you a copy of its special needs policy on request.

Code of Practice

In order to ensure that the aims of the 1993 Act are carried out, the statute set up a Code of Practice and an appeals system.

The Code is available free of charge and lays down guidelines for investigating and then assessing special educational needs (SEN). It is used in schools, by LEAs, and by other services.

The law states that schools must have regard to the Code of Practice, i.e. they should always take into account what the Code advises, but it does not lay down what has to be done in every case. This is often left to the discretion of the teacher and the school involved.

The Act requires schools to draw up a policy for dealing with SEN children and the Code specifies that the policy should tell you the following:

- the name of the teacher who deals with SEN
- the school's arrangements for deciding on which children need special provision and how they will be providing that provision
- the way in which parents will be closely involved
- the way in which the school deals with parents' complaints.

The Code lays down three stages for meeting the needs of children.

Stage 1

If there are learning difficulties, these should be recorded by the teacher.

The school should approach you about the problems and will ask you to assist them in providing information on

- the child's behaviour at home
- possible reasons for the problems
- any health or development problems during the pre-school period.

It is hoped that by focusing on the problems (in conjunction with the child, parent and teacher at this very early stage) the difficulties might be overcome altogether. If this is not the case, then the second stage will be reached.

Stage 2

This involves the SEN teacher, who will speak to you and the child's other teachers. Together, an individual education plan will be drawn up which will

(a) set targets
(b) set a date for review to see whether the targets are being met
(c) perhaps ask for permission to talk to your doctor.

You may be asked to help the child at home too.

Again, the hope is that the work put in at stage 2 will mean that the difficulties are overcome. Failing that, stage 3 is reached.

Stage 3

The school generally has to approach specialist assistance from outside the school. A new individual education plan will be drawn up in conjunction with the outside specialist and the other teachers involved. Progress will be carefully monitored. You should be able to attend the review meetings.

If these remedial methods are not working to the extent that had been hoped for, then the head teacher must decide whether to ask the LEA to make a statutory assessment.

Note: some schools may have two, three or four stages in order to deal with learning difficulties at the pre-assessment stage. In all cases, however, they must pay regard to the Code of Practice, and involve the parents at all stages.

Statutory assessment and Statement

You will be consulted by your child's school or by your child's medical adviser before any request is made to the LEA for a statutory assessment. Equally, you yourself may apply to the LEA for a statutory assessment if you think your child is falling seriously behind other children of the same age and that his or her school cannot provide all the help that is needed.

You have received a letter from the LEA telling you of their intention to make a statutory assessment of your child who has learning difficulties. You would like to put your views to the LEA and to attend any medical or psychological examination.

Where an assessment is to be undertaken, you should let the LEA know your views, either in a letter or in person. If your child is required to go to any interview, medical or other test during the statutory assessment, you also have a right to attend. However, the professionals may request to see your child alone if they think your presence may affect your child's behaviour.

Who can ask for an assessment?

(a) the parent
(b) the doctor
(c) the teacher.

Chapter 13 — Ensuring a suitable education

What is an assessment?

This is a detailed examination to establish the child's special educational needs and the help which is to be provided.

Procedure for an assessment

If the LEA goes ahead with the assessment

(a) you must be informed;
(b) you will be asked to provide information and to submit your views;
(c) you are entitled to visit other schools in your area which may be able to provide additional help;
(d) you can attend interviews and tests with your child (unless the professionals think your presence unhelpful);
(e) your child may be consulted;
(f) you can appoint a Named Person to assist and advise you in giving your opinion.

Note: A 'Named Person' is normally independent of the LEA – for example, someone from a voluntary organization. He or she may be appointed at the beginning of the assessment process to attend meetings with the parents and to assist them with advice and information.

The LEA can then decide whether or not to make a Statement. This should be done within 12 weeks after deciding to make an assessment.

Statement of special educational needs

A Statement is made when the LEA reaches the conclusion that not all the special help your child needs can be provided within the school's normal resources.

Resources must take into account:

- money
- staff time and
- special equipment.

You will receive details of schools in the area, both mainstream and special schools. You will also receive information of 'non-maintained' special schools and independent schools which are approved for children with special needs.

Content and purpose of Statement

After your LEA have collected all the advice and comments about your child's special educational needs, they will normally tell you within 12 weeks whether or not they have decided to make a Statement. Any such Statement is to be set out in six parts:

Part 1: name, address and other details of parents and child
Part 2: details of learning difficulties and disabilities identified by the assessment
Part 3: a description of

- the special help the LEA consider that your child needs;
- the long-term objectives to be achieved by that special help;
- the arrangements for setting short-term targets and reviewing progress

Part 4: details of the school to which the child should go, or arrangements for education to be made other than at a school
Parts 5 and *6:* the non-educational needs a child may have, e.g. transport to school; and how that help will be supplied.

Should the LEA decide not to assess your child you have a right to appeal to the Special

Educational Needs Tribunal. A booklet entitled *Special Educational Needs Tribunal – How to appeal* can be obtained from schools, public libraries, or the LEA.

Disagreeing with special needs Statement

If you disagree with the Statement, you may ask the named officer at the LEA for an explanation and, if you are still unhappy, you may appeal to the Special Educational Needs Tribunal against the description of your child's learning difficulties, the help to be given for your child, or the type of school named. You may also appeal to the Special Educational Needs Tribunal if either

- the LEA refuses to reassess your child; or
- the LEA decides that there is no necessity to continue to maintain your child's Statement.

Note of warning: the appeal procedure should not delay any special educational help your child needs. Therefore you must apply to the Tribunal no later than two months after the LEA make their decision. Time limits are extended only in exceptional cases.

You may be able to make a complaint to the Local Government Ombudsman (see DIRECTORY) if your complaint is about something which the Tribunal cannot deal with, e.g. the LEA's failure to

- keep within time limits;
- provide the necessary help, as set out in the Statement.

For the position of special educational needs pupils and the National Curriculum, see section *Special needs*, p.152.

Special needs children over 16

Education for young people with special educational needs does not stop at 16. Depending on your child's interests and abilities, he or she can stay on at ordinary or special school, or can move to a college of further education. If your child has a Statement of special educational needs, further education will be considered when a transition plan is drawn up at 14.

Some students with learning difficulties or disabilities attend ordinary courses at colleges with the help of special equipment or support. If you have any questions about the choices open to your child after 16, the careers service can provide help and advice

Gifted children – assisted places

Unlike special needs children, children with advanced or special talents are not generally catered for in relation to their educational needs. If you consider that your child is gifted, you should select a school which may be most sympathetic and helpful in relation to your child. A placement in an independent school is an expensive option.

In such a case you may apply for a place under the assisted places scheme under which the government pays fees and other costs on a sliding scale according to parental income to enable bright children to go to independent schools. However, the Government intends to phase this scheme out.

Sick children

If your child is unable to attend school because of illness or injury, the LEA must make suitable arrangements for education in a hospital school, hospital teaching unit or service, or by tuition at home. Children should not be left at home without tuition for more than four weeks. For absences of less than four weeks, 'home schools' are normally expected to provide work to be done at home if the child's condition allows. As a parent, you may be able to give

Chapter 13 — Ensuring a suitable education

valuable help by providing additional liaison with your child's home school – both at the beginning and end of a stay in hospital – or with the home tuition service if the home tutor is not the same person as the hospital tutor.

Wherever possible you and your child should be kept informed about the education available for your child while in hospital. Some hospitals provide booklets giving useful information about educational services they have available.

Disagreeing with changes in provision of help

Your daughter has suffered a debilitating illness since the age of seven. She has since had difficulty in attending school, or deriving benefit from it when she did attend. She has been receiving five hours per week of home tuition. As a result of local authority budgetary restraints, those hours have been reduced to only three hours per week. You feel she is losing out as a result. You wonder what your legal position is as there has been no reduction in your daughter's needs.

In a similar case, the Court of Appeal held that the LEA was entitled to take into account its resources when setting a policy and allocating provision for special educational needs.

C. WHAT IS TAUGHT IN SCHOOLS

THE NATIONAL CURRICULUM

The National Curriculum was introduced in 1988 by the Education Reform Act. It heralded a dramatic shift away from the education system as it had been established for decades. Apart from the A- and O-level (later GCSE) syllabuses, which were set by the various examination boards, the local authorities had been responsible for syllabus content which, as a result, was marked by diversity.

The particular impetus behind the introduction of the National Curriculum was that school standards were perceived to be slipping. It was increasingly argued that children were not being sufficiently instructed in the basic elements of the 'three Rs'.

Moreover the introduction of a National Curriculum was an essential first step in the monitoring of the performance of schools, as well as of individual pupil assessment. It made possible the publication of league tables of successful schools, while bringing to public attention those schools which were seen to be 'failing' the standards set.

Since its introduction some concepts have been revised and teachers' views taken into account. Consultation on aspects of the National Curriculum remains an on-going matter in the light of experience, social change, and the demands of parents, children and their teachers – as well as those of the politicians.

The subjects and the stages

The school's prospectus must explain the National Curriculum, its organization for different age groups, and how it is taught.

Pupils aged between 5 and 16 in state schools are taught the following subjects: English, mathematics, science, design and technology, information technology, history, geography, music, art and, for pupils between 11 to 16, a modern foreign language. The Curriculum is divided into four key stages which depend on a pupil's age. These are stage 1 – age 5 to 7, stage 2 – age 7 to 11, stage 3 – age 11 to 14, and stage 4 – age 14 to 16.

The Curriculum sets standards of achievement in each subject for each pupil aged 5 to 14. For most subjects these standards range from levels 1 to 8.

Those levels are not used for music, art and PE. Instead there is a single description of the standard that most people are expected to obtain by the end of a key stage for each of these areas.

Testing

Teachers are required to monitor their pupils' progress and to assess their progress at the ages of 7, 11 and 14. There are national tests for 7-, 11- and 14-year-olds in English and mathematics. Pupils aged 11 and 14 are also tested in science. The tests give an independent measure of how pupils and schools are doing compared with the national standards in those subjects. Most 16-year-olds take GCSEs or similar qualifications such as the GNVQ.

At least once a year parents are to be provided with a written report on their child's progress in all subjects and their results in national tests or public examinations taken during the year.

You are not entitled to withdraw your child from any part of the National Curriculum, but it may be that a child with special educational needs will be withdrawn from an unsuitable section because of those special needs (see section immediately below).

The Secretary of State may direct that for a specified period the National Curriculum shall not apply or it may be modified in specified ways for the purpose of enabling development work or experiments to be carried out by a particular maintained school. Such a direction may also be given to a county, controlled or maintained special school on an application by one of the following:

(a) by the governing body with the agreement of the LEA,
(b) by the LEA with the agreement of the governing body, or
(c) by the appropriate curriculum authority (the School Curriculum and Assessment Authority in England or the Curriculum and Assessment Authority in Wales) with the agreement of both the LEA and the governing body. See DIRECTORY.

Special needs

The provisions of the National Curriculum may also be excluded or modified for pupils with Statements of special educational needs. The head teacher of a maintained school may make similar temporary exceptions for individual pupils. If this happens in relation to your child the head has to advise you of

(a) the fact that such action has been taken, its effects and the reasons for the decision;
(b) the provision that is being made for your child's education during the period of the direction, and
(c) either a description of the manner in which it is proposed to secure full implementation of the National Curriculum after the end of the period, or an indication that he or she has (or probably has) special educational needs for which special educational provision should be made.

Where you are unhappy with such a direction by your child's head teacher you may apply to the school's governing body which may confirm or alter the proposed action. You will be notified in writing of the governing body's decision.

Religious education

Schools are to maintain agreed syllabuses of religious education which must reflect the fact that the religious traditions in Great Britain are in the main Christian whilst taking into account the teaching and practices of the other principal religions represented here.

Under the European Human Rights Convention, the State must respect the right of parents to ensure that the education provided to their children is 'in conformity with their own religious and philosophical convictions'. At present, the Human Rights Bill is being introduced into Parliament. It reserves the right for the UK government to accept this principle only so far as it is compatible with the 'provision of efficient instruction' and does not lead to unreasonable public expenditure.

Religious worship

Schools are to make arrangements for collective worship on each school day on the school premises. On special occasions, the act of collective worship may take place elsewhere than on school premises. Collective worship in county schools is to be wholly or mainly of a broadly Christian nature.

However, variations may be made taking account of particular circumstances relating to pupils' family backgrounds in determining the character of the worship which is appropriate, based on the composition of the entire school or of any class of pupils at the school, as well as pupils' ages and aptitudes. In any event, individual parents have the right to withdraw their children from participating in RE or worship (see immediately below).

Religious education and collective worship – special arrangements

If your child is at a maintained school you, as a parent, may request that he or she be wholly or partly excused from religious education, or from attendance at religious worship, or from both. Also, if the LEA or governing body responsible are satisfied of the following:

a) that you wish your child to receive religious education of a kind which is not provided at the school,
b) that you child cannot reasonably be sent to another maintained school where religious education of the type you desire is provided, and
c) that arrangements have been made for the child to receive religious education during school hours elsewhere,

the pupil may be withdrawn from the school during such periods as are reasonably necessary for the purpose of receiving religious education in accordance with those arrangements.

Do note: no withdrawal will be permitted unless those arrangements will not interfere with attendance of the pupil at school except at the beginning or end of a school session.

Pupils cannot opt out of RE classes.

Your teenage son has asked his form teacher whether he can be excused RE on the ground that he does not believe in the existence of God. The teacher has refused.

Only parents can request the withdrawal of their children from RE classes. Perhaps you could suggest to the RE teacher that your son's views be aired in a debate within the context of his class.

If you are a parent of a boarder at a maintained school you may request that your child be permitted to receive education in accordance with the tenets of a particular religion or religious denomination outside school hours, or be allowed to attend worship on Sundays or other days exclusively set apart for religious observance by the religion to which you belong. The governing body must make arrangements for giving your child reasonable opportunities for doing so. It may be that facilities for such education can be made available on the school premises but such arrangements should not involve the governing body having to meet any expenditure.

Sex education

The LEA, governing school body and the head teacher are to take such steps as are reasonably practical to ensure that sex education is given in a way which will encourage the pupils to have regard to moral considerations and the value of family life.

The governing body is to keep up to date a written statement of their policy on sex education, and copies of that policy are to be made available to the parents of pupils at the school. If you wish to receive a copy of that statement, it must be provided to you free of charge.

You have the right to request that your child be wholly or partly excused from receiving sex education at the school. Your child is to be excused accordingly, except so far as such education is part of the National Curriculum.

In order to tackle the problem of unwanted and teenage pregnancies, the Department of Health is to set up task groups which are intended to bring together health, education and social services, and the voluntary sector (see also section on *Teenage mothers*, p.158).

Careers information and guidance

All registered pupils at

(a) county and voluntary schools;
(b) grant-maintained schools;
(c) maintained or grant-maintained special schools (other than those established in hospitals);
(d) city technology colleges and city colleges for the technology of the arts; and
(e) pupil referral units

are to be provided with a programme of careers education.

This is given in the period beginning at the same time as the school year in which the majority of pupils in a class attain the age of 14 and ending with the expiry of the school year in which the majority of pupils in a class attain the age of 16. In this context 'career' includes any training, employment or occupation, as well as any course of education. Pupils must be provided with access to guidance materials and to a wide range of up-to-date reference materials.

Political education

A key element in educating children is to prepare them for an active role in society once they become adults. To this end, they are to be encouraged to have a proper understanding of the nation's democratic processes and a clear appreciation of their rights and duties as future citizens. The LEAs, head teachers and governors are therefore encouraged to tackle political issues.

Political indoctrination

However, biased teaching which does not support the principles of a free and open society, and other forms of political indoctrination, are outlawed.

In relation to maintained schools, the LEA, governing body and head teacher are to forbid both the pursuit of partisan political activities by 'junior pupils' [i.e. under-12-year-olds] and the promotion of partisan political views in the teaching of any subject in the school. If the activities referred to take place outside the school premises, the participation of junior pupils is to be forbidden where arrangements to take part are made by a school staff member or anyone acting on behalf of the school or of a staff member.

D. DEALING WITH PROBLEMS

The responsibilities of parents and carers of school-age children extend beyond ensuring that the children attend school. They have a vital role in encouraging good behaviour, and should also ensure that their children arrive at school on time, that they take their school work seriously, see that homework is completed on time, and actively encourage and reward progress.

Parents must also be alert to problems which their children may be experiencing, both in and out of school, including behavioural difficulties, truancy, and bullying.

Questions relating to negligence for which the school may be responsible are dealt with in Chapter 11, *Your child's safety*, section B.

DISCIPLINE

Parents need to co-operate with the school in matters of discipline and to reinforce the school's efforts at home. Behavioural problems which affect the school generally may be reviewed at the governor's annual meeting with parents, and discussed at the meeting between inspectors and parents before a school inspection.

Some schools use home–school agreements to specify parental responsibilities and the expectations of pupils, parents and the school. Such agreements are voluntary and do not have any legal effect.

The School Standards and Framework Bill stipulates that all maintained schools and CTCs must adopt home–school agreements. Parents will be called upon to sign a 'parental declaration' stating that they have noted the school's aims and values – as set out in the agreement – and that they accept their parental responsibilities in ensuring their children's education.

Sanctions

Where a child is considered to have misbehaved at school, the school may impose various sanctions, such as

- interruption of break or lunchtime privileges;
- detention;
- withholding of privileges, such as participation in school trips or sports events where these are not an essential part of the curriculum;
- completion of assigned work or additional work; or
- carrying out a useful task in the school.

Other measures, in addition to a straightforward reprimand, may include

- moving the pupil's position in class, or isolation from his or her peer group;
- enlisting the support of senior staff; and
- contacting the parent.

Special rules apply in relation to truancy (see p.159) and in specified cases a pupil may be excluded from school – see p.156.

Corporal punishment

With the exception of privately funded pupils in independent schools in England, all pupils are protected from being subjected to corporal, i.e. physical, punishment from any staff member of a school. This includes children at private schools on the assisted places scheme.

In practice, very few independent schools now administer corporal punishment, but if they continue to do so, that punishment must not be inhuman or degrading. In determining whether punishment is inhuman or degrading, regard should be had to all the circumstances of the case, including the reason for giving it; how soon after the event it is given; the nature;

the manner and circumstances in which it is given; the persons involved; and the mental and physical effects on the pupil concerned.

If your child in the state sector is subjected to physical punishment by a member of staff, you may wish to take action.

1. Approach the head teacher or another senior teacher with your complaint.
2. Ask for an apology and an assurance that it will not happen again.
3. Enquire whether disciplinary action will be taken against the staff member involved.

You can also make a formal written complaint to the school governors or to the LEA.

The police will only be involved where there has been a serious assault. Although it might be possible to take civil legal action and sue the staff member and the LEA, always seek legal advice before contemplating such a move.

Do note: a teacher can use restraining measures in the following circumstances:

- in order to prevent the child from committing an offence, or
- if there is an immediate danger of personal injury to any person (including your child), or
- if there is an immediate danger to property.

Restraint can also be used to maintain good order and discipline whether during a teaching session or otherwise, e.g. during playtime.

Detention

Where a child has misbehaved, a school may impose sanctions in the form of withdrawal of break or lunchtime privileges or by way of detention. Detention after the end of any school session is not unlawful even without the parent's consent if

(a) the school's policy on detention is generally known within the school;
(b) the detention is imposed by the head teacher or by a teacher authorized by the head teacher;
(c) the detention is reasonable in all the circumstances; and
(d) parents have been given at least 24 hours' notice in writing.

In determining whether a detention is reasonable the following matters are relevant:

- whether the detention is a proportionate punishment in the circumstances of the case; and
- any other circumstances which are known to the teacher, including
  1. the pupil's age;
  2. any special educational needs;
  3. any religious requirements; and
  4. special arrangements that would have to be made for the child to travel home, and whether the parent can reasonably make suitable alternative arrangements.

The detention rules apply to pupils under 18 attending

- a school maintained by a LEA;
- a grant-maintained or grant-maintained special school; or
- a city technology college or city college for the technology of the arts.

Exclusions

A school's head teacher has the power to exclude a pupil from school (whether by suspension, expulsion or otherwise). The head may not exclude a pupil for one or more fixed periods which result in the pupil being excluded for more than 45 school days in any one school year. Nor may the head exclude a pupil for an indefinite period.

However a power exists to exclude a pupil from a school permanently.

Chapter 13 — Ensuring a suitable education

The parent of a child under 18 must be informed of the following without delay:

(a) the period of exclusion, including permanent exclusion
(b) the reasons for the exclusion; and
(c) that the parent can make representations about the exclusion to the governing body and the LEA.

Where the head decides to exclude a pupil, and this would result in his or her exclusion from the school for a total of more than five school days in any one term, or if the pupil would lose an opportunity to take any public examination, the head must also inform the governing body and the LEA of the period of, and the reason for, the exclusion.

Where a head decides that any exclusion for a fixed period should be made permanent the parents of a pupil under 18 must be informed of the decision and the reasons for it, and told of their rights to make representations about the decision to the governing body and the LEA. A pupil over 18 has similar rights.

Reinstatement of pupils excluded from county, voluntary or maintained special schools

Where the LEA has been informed of the permanent exclusion of a pupil it may, after consulting the governing body, consider whether the pupil should be reinstated immediately, reinstated by a particular date or not reinstated. If reinstatement is decided on, the head teacher will be directed accordingly. You as parent, or the pupil if aged over 18, will be informed of the authority's decision.

Similar provisions apply where a pupil has been excluded for a fixed period in excess of five school days in one term, or would lose the opportunity to take a public examination.

Reinstatement of pupils of aided and special schools

In these cases, it is the governing body which considers whether a pupil who has been permanently excluded should be reinstated immediately, reinstated by a particular date or not reinstated. You and the LEA will be informed without delay where reinstatement is not recommended.

Appeals against exclusion or non-reinstatement of pupils

A parent – or a pupil over 18 – must be given written notice of rights to appeal against an exclusion or a refusal of readmission of a pupil to a school and of the time limit imposed upon the making of any such appeal – generally within 15 school days after the decision.

An appeal is to be made in writing setting out the grounds on which it is made.

In general any such appeal is to be considered by the appeal committee within 15 school days of the day on which the appeal is lodged. The appellant pupil or parent is to be given an opportunity of appearing and making oral representations, and can be accompanied by a friend or be represented. LEAs and governing bodies may also make written and/or oral representations and may be represented.

Generally, appeals are held in private. However two or more appeals may be considered together if the appeal committee considers that expedient because the issues raised are the same or connected.

PUPIL REFERRAL UNITS

Where a pupil has been absent from school for a while, whether because of an exclusion, habitual non-attendance, pregnancy, or being a young mother, but an immediate return to mainstream education is not practicable, it is important that the child's education is continued and that the child be able to return to mainstream education as soon as possible. To this end, LEAs may set up pupil referral units (PRUs). The curriculum of any such unit is to be balanced and broadly based and should promote the spiritual, moral, cultural, mental and physical development of pupils. However PRUs are not obliged to provide the full National Curriculum because of their varied and different circumstances.

However, education at a PRU cannot be regarded as an acceptable long-term alternative to a placement in a mainstream school. Parents therefore cannot opt for their child to attend a PRU instead of school.

PRUs usually have more intensive staffing than mainstream schools and their staff should be equipped to deal with disruptive behaviour. However, there may be cases where a pupil poses a threat to his or her own safety or well-being, or that of others. Accordingly a pupil may be excluded from a PRU on disciplinary grounds. The LEA may require reinstatement of the pupil or may confirm the exclusion. A parent may make representations to the LEA against any such exclusion.

Where a child's behaviour is such that it cannot be contained in a PRU and permanent exclusion is necessary, it is possible that the child has special educational needs of a kind which require the LEA to prepare a written Statement of their proposed action (see above, *Statement of special educational needs*, pp.149-50).

Teenage mothers

England has one of the highest rates of teenage conceptions in the developed world, and under-16 conception rates (13–15 year olds) are 18 per cent higher than they were in 1980. The government is initiating a national programme – which will include health, education, social services, and the voluntary sector – to give young people the support that they need. Teenage pregnancy is seen as leading to a cycle of deprivation.

From the point of view of their education, mothers under 16 are taught at a PRU, through homebased tuition or, where possible, in mainstream schooling (see also section on *Sex education*, p.154).

PREVENTING TRAUMA

The saying 'your school days are the happiest days of your life' is well known, but is far from true for all pupils at all times. Your child may have worries about his or her performance in a particular subject or subjects, be afraid of bullying within school premises or on his or her journeys to and from home, or even have worries in relation to the security maintained at the school.

You can look out for tell-tale signs of any such worries, such as the development of mysterious symptoms of illness on days when particular classes are scheduled, general reluctance to attend school, the incidence of nightmares or even a suspicion that your child is truanting. If you have any suspicions about trouble at school, it is important to persuade your child to talk about his worries or fears and to try to resolve the problem in consultation with the school.

Poor progress in class

If your child admits to you that there is a problem with a particular course or courses and that he or she has difficulty in attaining the same levels as their peers, it is suggested that you talk to the relevant teacher and elicit his or her views on the seriousness of any problem. The teacher may agree to keep a particular eye on your child and try to help to tackle the subject(s) more effectively. If possible, you too could provide the child with additional help and information at home. In some cases it may be necessary for your child to have temporary private tuition to resolve the matter.

If the teacher has not previously identified any problem it is unlikely that you will be required to apply for an assessment of special needs as detailed on pp.148–50.

Bullying

If your child is being bullied by other pupils, either on school grounds or after school, it is important to inform the school immediately and work with its authorities to resolve the problem. Information and advice on bullying is available from a number of organizations which specifically target this problem (see DIRECTORY).

A parent has recently complained to the headmaster that your son has been bullying children in the playground. The headmaster has asked to see you.

In some circumstances, it may be found that your child is one of the bullies, rather than being bullied. In any such case, you should co-operate with school authorities in an attempt to discover the motivation behind the bullying and to stop it before the matter becomes serious enough for the law to become involved.

Should your child complain that it is a teacher who is bullying or harassing him or her, you should take the matter up with the head teacher, so that the allegations may be investigated and resolved in a satisfactory way. You should endeavour to discuss the matter with as much objectivity as possible – children have been known to exaggerate their grievances against those who are in a position of authority.

Truancy

New guidance for schools and LEAs has been made available by the Department for Education and Employment to reduce levels of unauthorized absence from schools. Regular attendance is seen as of key importance in raising school standards, as well as in tackling petty crime. The intention of the guidance is to nip irregular attendance in the bud before it becomes a habit that is hard to break.

It proposes a joint initiative bringing together schools, education welfare officers, the police and other community interests in setting up a Truancy Watch.

Pilot schemes are in place which, for example, use electronic pagers to let parents know instantly that their child is not in school. 'Pupil passes' coupled with Truancy Watch schemes are intended to deal with a situation in which a child is present at roll call and then leaves school premises.

Justified absence?

Some absence from school may be justified if your child

(a) is sick
(b) has a religious holiday or
(c) has some cause for not attending, for example, ill-health.

In this last case, the cause for the absence must involve the child and not the parent. In other words, you cannot withhold your child from school if you are sick and you want your child to help at home.

You would also be entitled to keep your child at home if he or she is not within walking distance of school and the LEA has failed to make adequate arrangements for transport (see *Walking distance*, p.142).

In the case of a 'young carer' where there are on-going problems at home, you are strenuously advised to contact the school and explain the situation so that your child can get the support he or she needs (see also Chapter 8, *The extended family*, section on *Young carers*, p.81).

Holidays

You want to take your two children out of school in term time to attend their grandparents' golden wedding anniversary party. Their grandparents live abroad.

Pupils may be absent with permission during term time for the purposes of going on an annual holiday with their parents for a maximum of two weeks.

Do note: the government has indicated that unscheduled holidays of this kind will no longer be allowed. Indeed parents who take their children out of school for holidays could face prosecution under new government guidelines.

Parental role

Apart from the above, it is your responsibility, as parents, to ensure that your child attends school, so it is in your best interest to make full enquiries if you discover or suspect that he or she is truanting.

Schools keep an attendance record which could confirm any suspicions you may have in this regard. Should you find there have been instances of truancy, you must talk to your child to establish his or her reasons and try to resolve any underlying problems. Discussion with the school may also prove beneficial.

Problems relating to poor scholastic performance or to bullying may lie behind the truancy and these should be tackled early on (as outlined above).

Education supervision orders

A local authority can apply to court under the Children Act 1989 for an education supervision order [ESO] if a child is not attending school regularly. Under the order a social worker or education welfare officer is appointed to 'assist and befriend' the child and to help the parents meet their responsibilities in ensuring that their child is being properly educated. The order lasts for one year but can be extended.

Note of warning: if parents fail to comply with these directions, criminal sanctions can be imposed. On summary conviction they could be liable to a fine, currently £1,000 per absent child. Similar penalties can be imposed for parental failure to comply with a School Attendance Order (see *Registering your child*, p.141) or failure to secure a child's regular school attendance.

While there is no power to imprison a parent under any of these provisions, failure to pay a fine may incur imprisonment.

In December 1997 the government issued draft guidance to heads, teachers, governors and welfare officers indicating that LEAs 'should adopt a vigorous stance in prosecuting parents of non-attenders'. In certain cases 'block prosecutions' could be mounted 'in order to demonstrate to parents how seriously the LEA regards truancy and unjustified absence' which is condoned by the parents.

Parenting orders

Under proposed legislation, 'parenting orders' may be imposed on parents who are prosecuted for failing to ensure that their children attend school. This would involve the parents in attending courses themselves.

SCHOOL SECURITY

Some horrendous attacks have taken place on pupils and staff either in or just outside school premises. Thus security in schools has become a cause for national concern.

In recent years, schools have been pursuing attempts to increase school security, but in some cases, the measures may not be sufficient to allay fears for you or your child. The provision of such security is both difficult and expensive, as, for example, schools have often been built over a large area with several entrances.

If you have any particular worries or suggestions on e.g. limiting access to the school, take them up with the head teacher or the governing body, or raise them at the parent governors' meeting.

PROPOSALS FOR CHANGE

In July 1997 the Government published a White Paper entitled *Excellence in Schools*, setting out a wide-ranging programme for raising standards which aims to keep parents better informed on their children's education and more involved in schools; and to reduce levels of truancy and exclusions. A significant number of these proposals have been given effect in the School Standards and Framework Bill which is at present before Parliament.

(a) *Parent representation*. It is proposed that parents will be given direct input into LEA education policies by ensuring that there is at least one elected parent governor representative with relevant voting rights on the Education Committee and two or three representatives on larger LEAs. Such parent representatives would be elected by all current parent governors of maintained schools in the LEA and would themselves have to be serving parent governors. It is proposed that parent representatives' terms of office should be aligned with those of elected members and that they should be able to serve out their full term even if during their term they ceased to have a child at school.

(b) *Categories of schools*. The proposals would allocate each existing school to a new category which best reflects its existing characteristics and enables a school to choose which status will best suit its character and aspirations. It is suggested that the initial categories could be as follows:

- *Community* category: county schools
- *Foundation* category: voluntary and grant-maintained schools
- *Aided* category: voluntary aided schools, special agreement schools
- *Community Special School* category: LEA special schools and GM special schools.

Where the governing body wishes to choose a different category, or a significant number of parents are unhappy with the proposed new status, a ballot of parents is to provide the mechanism for testing whether parents agree with that choice. The governing body's choice is to prevail in any case where

- fewer than 50 per cent of parents vote in the ballot; or
- parents' preferences are divided between the three categories of school.

(c) *Admissions procedure*. A reform of admissions policy is proposed under which parents should have clear information about admission arrangements. LEAs will be required to publish information relating to all Community, Aided and Foundation schools, covering basic admission policies and oversubscription criteria, the procedures parents must follow, and the timetable.

The new admission framework is intended to prevent schools from adopting admission criteria which includes the selection of some pupils by general academic ability, although schools specializing in a particular subject may continue to give priority to children with a particular aptitude.

It is also proposed that where parents are refused a place for their child, they should be able to appeal to a committee which would be entirely independent of the school and the LEA, and give consistency in their membership regardless of the category of school.

It is further proposed that the jurisdiction of the Local Government Ombudsman should cover all admission authorities, not just LEAs as at present.

(d) *Home–school agreements*. All schools are to be required to have home–school agreements. Such documents will include a parental declaration that parents acknowledge their responsibilities in connection with their children's schooling and accept the school's statement of aims and values. Parents may be required to undertake to read with their children at home for at least 20 minutes a day to help children attain targets for full literacy at age 11 by the year 2002.

Places are not to be refused on the grounds that parents do not sign such a home–school document which is not to be legally binding in any event.

(e) *Class sizes*. It is proposed that by the academic year 2001–2 no class of reception, year 1 or year 2 pupils should have more than 30 pupils. Legislation relating to admissions is to be amended accordingly.

(f) *Pupil exclusions*. The government wishes to standardize provisions regarding pupil exclusions and invites views on the subject. It suggests a model for all schools, giving responsibility for the initial consideration of parental representations, with the possibility of reinstatement, to governing bodies. Responsibility for arranging any independent appeal would then rest with the LEA.

(g) *Education action zones*. In order to deal with socially disadvantaged areas, 25 education action zones are to be established which will be run by private companies or consortiums of schools, as well as by community groups. Extra funds will be allocated to these zones which will also receive priority in other government schemes, such as homework clubs.

(h) *Failing schools*. Government will have power to close failing schools and incompetent teachers will become subject to faster dismissal procedures.

In addition the government has announced the setting up of a national network of 8,000 homework clubs which will offer the chance for extra tuition and access to computers, as well as the opportunity for supervised study, in particular as a support for children from less-advantaged homes. The homework clubs and other out-of- school-hours learning activities are also intended to complement the current programme to provide after-school childcare.

Overall the proposed changes are intended to bring about both a radical improvement in school standards and a far greater degree of parental involvement in their children's school progress.

PART 7
CRIME

CHAPTER 14
IN TROUBLE WITH THE LAW

The duration of childhood for legal reference purposes is uncertain. Various ages are referred to in various Acts of Parliament and in court decisions relating to 'children'. The ages of 10, 14, 16 and 18 are all relevant and some Acts of Parliament refer to people between 16 and 18 as 'young persons'. However for the purposes of both civil and criminal law one finally ceases to be a child at the age of 18 and in this chapter the word 'children' is used to describe all persons who are under 18. Special courts have been set up to deal with crimes committed by children and some special rules of evidence in relation to them are in the course of being developed with the help of electronic gadgetry.

The law relating to crimes committed by children represents a difficult compromise between opposites and is currently in flux. On the one hand children are viewed as innocent victims who, if they commit harmful acts, do not understand what they are doing and whose evidence must be treated with the greatest suspicion as they cannot distinguish between truth and fantasy. On the other hand, they are regarded by some as small monsters against whom society must be protected. The 'monsters' are relatively few in number but they are responsible for a disproportionately large share of juvenile crime. Home Office statistics published in 1994 showed that 1% of males born in 1973 who were convicted of six or more offences before the age of 17 accounted for 60% of all convictions for that age group.

Though there has apparently been some diminution in child crime in recent years it remains a serious problem. A senior police officer recently said that the young are committing more than 13 crimes a minute, that is 799 crimes an hour, or 19,178 crimes a day, at a cost to victims and the Government of between £5 billion and £10 billion a year. Many of the crimes would appear to be drug-related although there can be no firm statistics to show the correlation. Only 3% of offences committed by young persons lead to arrest or action in the courts and only 19% of the offences are recorded by the police. Gangs of young people can also terrorize neighbourhoods simply through rowdiness and petty acts of vandalism.

The stated intention of the present government is to endeavour to shift some of the burden of control from the State on to the family. As at the moment of writing, a Crime and Disorder Bill is before Parliament intended to introduce new court orders to deal with anti-social behaviour and disorder caused by young offenders.

Local authorities and the police are to work together to formulate and implement a strategy to reduce crime in their area and to set up youth offending teams. In addition, parents of children who are in trouble with the law are to be made the subject of 'parenting orders' requiring them to attend counselling or guidance sessions.

In this chapter we examine the following:
- Police procedures
- Youth justice
- Penalties
- Offensive weapons
- Parental liability
- Proposals for change.

Do note: If your child is in trouble with the police, you are strenuously advised to seek legal advice at the earliest opportunity. Ways of accessing a solicitor are dealt with below.

Section A details the procedures to be followed when your child becomes involved with the law; section B takes that involvement a stage further and examines the youth justice system; section C outlines the penalties which can be imposed on children; and section D deals with the law in relation to children and offensive weapons. Section E outlines parental liability for their children's wrongdoing and also indicates how the law in this regard is likely to be extended.

In the next chapter we deal with children who are the victims of crime.

A. WHEN THE POLICE BECOME INVOLVED

A 'GUILTY INTENTION'

To be found guilty of a crime you generally have to do a wrongful act and also to understand that what you are doing is wrong, that is, to have a guilty intention.

Under the age of 10 children are not able to commit crimes because the law regards them absolutely as being unable to form the necessary criminal intention.

Between the ages of 10 and 14 the law presumes that they are unable to form the necessary intention unless it can be shown affirmatively that the child knows that his actions are 'seriously wrong'. The House of Lords stated that this principle of law may give rise to anomalies and even absurdities. At present there is legislation before Parliament, the Crime and Disorder Bill, which abolishes the need to show that children between the ages of 10 and 14 know that their actions are wrong. It also contains provisions to deal with children under 10 who cannot be charged (discussed at the end of this chapter).

Once 14 is reached, the young person is treated as an adult, though of course age will be relevant in the court's coming to a decision as to whether the necessary criminal intention was present. However, youth courts in which children and young persons up to the age of 18 are dealt with are special juvenile courts and the crimes are normally dealt with by youth and community sections of the local police service. Custodial sentences are served in special detention centres.

POLICE PROCEDURES

Stop and search

Your daughter, who has been to a teenage disco, is one of a crowd of girls milling around the street outside at about midnight. Two members of the police, one male and one female, approach the group and single her out for questioning. They ask for her name and address and proceed with a number of other questions. She is then told that she will be searched. You wonder if the police followed the correct procedures.

Children should give their name and address. If the police continue to ask questions and wish to conduct a search, they must have reasonable grounds for suspecting that an 'arrestable offence' has either been committed or is likely to be committed. Thus your daughter is entitled to be told the reason for the questioning and the search. She is also entitled to be told the names of the police officers and the station from which they operate.

The police can also search her if they have reasonable grounds for suspecting that she is carrying illegal drugs. Only her outer clothing and bag can be searched within view of other people.

They are also entitled to search a person, or a car, if they suspect on reasonable grounds an arrestable offence, which would involve having

- stolen goods
- an offensive weapon (the laws relating to offensive weapons and young persons are discussed below in detail, see section D)
- means to commit a crime e.g. someone else's credit card.

Note: An 'arrestable offence' is one such as theft, assault, carrying an offensive weapon, or possessing or supplying illegal drugs.

Extension of powers of search

Under the Criminal Justice and Public Order Act 1994, if a serious and violent incident is feared, a senior police officer can give orders to stop any person or vehicle to search for offensive weapons. They do not have to have reasonable grounds for suspecting that the person whom they stop has actually broken the law.

The Prevention of Terrorism Act also widens powers to stop and search. Its use would be dependent on location and perceived need. For example, stop and search powers were extended in Central London by the Commissioner of Metropolitan Police acting together with the Home Secretary during the last IRA bombing campaign. As a result, a number of other offences were detected, e.g. drug-related crimes.

Raves

The police also have powers to remove persons attending or intending to go to an unlicensed rave.

They can be stopped within five miles of the site. While the provisions apply to any age group, young persons are generally most likely to be affected by them.

Under-age drinking

Police have powers to stop and search under-18-year-olds suspected of being in possession of alcohol. This is discussed in greater detail in Chapter 12, *Knowing the rules*, section C.

IN THE POLICE STATION

A child or young person who is capable of committing a crime, i.e. is over 10, and is thought by the police to have committed one, may be brought to a police station. However, the policeman concerned may, either immediately or after the child has been taken to a police station, decide that the matter is trivial and that there should be no proceedings of any kind. If the child is taken to the police station, the officer who arrested the child will stand before the station sergeant and will explain to the sergeant in the presence of the child why he or she has been brought in.

The 'appropriate adult'

The procedure followed is laid down in codes of practice issued by the Home Secretary under the Police and Criminal Evidence Act 1984. This requires the police immediately to seek the presence of an 'appropriate adult'. Statements made by the child before the appropriate adult arrives can in no circumstances be used in evidence. The appropriate adult will normally be the child's parent but if parents are not available, the social service will supply someone to act in that role. Notices must be served setting out the rights of arrested persons, and the reasons for the child's detention must be explained. The notices given show that the appropriate person or the child if necessary can speak to an independent solicitor free of charge. The solicitor cannot be the 'appropriate adult'. The appropriate adult must be present when the child is

- interviewed (except in urgent cases)
- cautioned

Chapter 14 — In trouble with the law

- asked to sign any documentation
- asked to give consent regarding any identification procedure
- charged.

The appropriate adult is required to be present to ensure that the interview is being conducted fairly.

However, he or she may not be in a position to know whether to advise the child to answer questions and may not be able to assess whether indeed an interview is being conducted fairly.

Do take heed: This highlights the need for insisting that an interview must take place in the presence of a solicitor.

Seeking legal advice

Your son has been brought into the police station because a neighbour telephoned the police to say he was acting suspiciously near an expensive car parked in the street in which you live. You are called in to be present as the 'appropriate adult'. You are served with all the proper notifications. The police begin to question the boy and you can see that he is getting tearful.

You telephone your solicitor but his secretary tells you that it will be some time before he will be free to attend to you.

You should ensure that your son waits for the attendance of your solicitor before continuing with the interview. In fact, once you have asked the police for legal help, they should not question him further. You can always ask for a duty or local solicitor to be present if your own solicitor is unavailable.

Parents should take advantage of the availability of a solicitor when the child is brought into the station. Each station has a panel of duty solicitors who will attend at the station at any hour of the day or night. The solicitor will advise on whether or not the child should admit the offence with which he is charged if either a formal warning or a formal caution is proposed. Duty solicitors are not employed by the police and everyone is entitled to free legal advice at a police station whether arrested or being questioned by the police.

In addition the police have a list of local solicitors. You can also ask the police to contact your own solicitor for you.

Do remember: There are three ways of accessing a solicitor in these circumstances:

(a) via the duty solicitor scheme
(b) via the police list of local solicitors
(c) by using your own solicitor.

Right to silence

There is no longer an absolute right to silence. In other words, if the police question a suspect and he or she has a defence, the police should be told of it. If the explanation is not divulged until the trial, the judge is entitled to comment on the fact that the suspect remained silent during police questioning. This can throw doubt on the explanation which may then not be believed.

Further enquiries

If the crime of which the child or young person is suspected is a serious one it is likely that the child will be bailed while a decision is made on whether or not he or she should be charged. One of the forms served on the parent or guardian of the child (as the appropriate adult) states that enquiries could include a visit to his house by a police officer in plain clothes from the Youth and Community Section to discuss the child's general background, and points out that it is important that both the parent and child are present at the interview.

The parent is asked to inform the custody officer before leaving the station of days or times when he or she will not be available. The Youth and Community Section will give further information if contacted.

Formal warning

When a child is brought to the station a custody record setting out the various steps taken must be kept and may be inspected by the appropriate adult and the child's solicitor. The matter may be dealt with immediately. The police may decide to take no action at all or to issue a formal warning. This is the modern equivalent of the once favoured 'clip round the ear'. The child in the presence of the parent or guardian is required to admit the offence for which he has been brought to the station. A record of the admission is kept at the station. However, it is not a criminal record or citable in court. It would be consulted by the police themselves if the child committed a further offence and the police then had to decide whether he should be prosecuted.

Page 1 of a formal warning form is reproduced below.

```
Metropolitan Police Service                              Form 8700
Formal Warning Form

Ref. No _____ Date _____
Officer _____ Stn./Branch _____
Person's details
Surname _____
Forename(s) _____ ID Code ___
Address _____
_____ Post Code _____
Date/place of birth _____
Occupation _____
ID confirmed  [Y]  [N]   How? _____
Offences/brief circumstances (show date/time/place)
_____
_____
_____

Offender (confirming admission and acknowledging warning)
I have admitted the offence(s) detailed above. I understand that a record will
be kept which will not be used in court. Should I offend again this record may
be considered when deciding whether I should be prosecuted.

Signature _____
Signature (parent/guardian) _____
Officer warning _____
Date/time/place of warning _____
```

Formal caution

In more serious cases, the matter may be dealt with by way of formal caution. Again, the child is required to admit the offence but is told that after consideration of all the circumstances it has been decided that on this occasion will not be necessary to proceed with the matter by court action. A record of the caution is kept in the station for five years and may be taken into

Chapter 14 — In trouble with the law

consideration when deciding whether to prosecute should the child re-offend. Though it is not a criminal record, it may be cited in court if the child is convicted of a future offence. This is a commonly used procedure. Indeed it is often used for children and young persons who have offended on several occasions.

The police may ultimately decide that none of these procedures is appropriate and that the possibility of charging must be investigated.

Conditions may be attached to bail given to the child while the decision as to whether or not to charge is being made. They include a curfew or a condition to keep away from a particular address (see also *Bail,* p.172).

A copy of the 'Record of Formal Caution' is on page 170.

The Crime and Disorder Bill published in December 1997 proposes significant changes and developments in the warning/caution system. The basic suggestion is that it should only be used twice and that on the occasion of the next or any subsequent offence the matter should go to court. This may overburden the already heavily burdened court system.

Formal warning or caution – the implications

Do remember: As a general rule, the formal warning is likely to provide a salutary lesson to a first offender and as the admission cannot be used in court it can do little harm. If on offer it should generally be accepted.

The formal caution is a different matter. The child is being required to admit an offence, and the caution, though it is not a conviction, is kept at the station for five years and may be cited in court if the child is subsequently convicted of an offence. If that is an unlikely occurrence it may well be considered that it is worthwhile accepting the caution as if it is not accepted it may lead to a full court hearing. It thus can give rise to difficult dilemmas.

> *Your child is accused of stealing a record from the local record store. The store detective saw him walk out without paying. He had enough money on him to pay and says that he just forgot. He has never been in trouble with the police before.*

If the case were to go to trial, the defence might not be believed so he risks a conviction and a penalty. If he agrees that the matter should be dealt with by a caution there will be no penalty. If he never offends again no record of the caution will be kept at this station after five years. Nevertheless if your son really did forget to pay, which it is easy enough to do, he is admitting to a crime that he did not commit.

Parents and children will have to make their own judgment and decide whether the matter should be dealt with as one of risk assessment, or to stand on their principles as a matter of morality where the parent thinks it highly unlikely that the child will be in trouble with the police again.

Note of Warning: Given the technicality of the criminal law and the seriousness of admitting to an offence by a child, parents and others in charge of children are strenuously advised to obtain legal advice before the child makes any statements and before irrevocable decisions are taken.

Do note also: The Criminal Justice Bill is to introduce a system of reprimands and warnings which is intended to limit the current procedures.

Laying a charge

Once a child is charged, a solicitor must be found and he will advise. The service is usually funded by the Legal Aid Board (see DIRECTORY) and the solicitor will act in the child's defence.

METROPOLITAN POLICE SERVICE
RECORD OF FORMAL CAUTION

COPY FOR PERSON CAUTIONED

Station Code
Custody/other Ref.

OFFENDER'S DETAILS
Surname... Former/Maiden Name..................................
Forename(s)..
Address...

Date of Birth................................... Sex..................................
School Attended (if juvenile)..................................

DETAILS OF OFFENCE(S)   See attached ☐ (✓ if offence details shown on separate sheet attached)
Date......./......./....... Place..................................
Offence(s)..................................

Method used (brief details)..................................
Officer in case (Name).................................. Rank.............. No..............

DETAILS OF THE CAUTIONING PROCESS
I am satisfied that for each above offence there is sufficient evidence to prosecute and that the offender has admitted it.
Admission(s) recorded vide (show reference, e.g., tape master seal(s), written record (MG15), note book, etc.)..................................

Signed.................................. Date......./......./....... Time..............
Name.................................. Rank.............. No..............
(Officer proposing to administer the caution)

I acknowledge that I have admitted the offence(s) detailed above.

Signature of person to be cautioned.................................. Date......./......./.......
Signature witnessed by.................................. Date......./......./.......
(Parent/guardian if person is a juvenile or appropriate adult as applicable for adult)

Information to offender (To be read out/explained by officer administering caution)
"After considering all the circumstances and because you have admitted the offence(s), I now propose to Formally Caution you for the offence(s). This does not involve court proceedings and it is not a criminal conviction. You must however understand that Police will keep a record of the caution and this may be taken into consideration when deciding whether to prosecute you if you re-offend in the future. A caution is not a criminal record but a court may be told about it if within three years you are convicted of a further offence. You should clearly understand that you cannot be cautioned unless you give your agreement knowing what a caution means. If you are *unsure, please say so." (* explain further if person unsure)

Acknowledgement of Caution
I agree to be cautioned for the offence(s) I have admitted and I accept an official caution knowing that it may be taken into consideration if I re-offend and that it may be mentioned in court if within three years I am convicted of a further offence.

Signature of person cautioned.................................. Date......./......./.......
Signature witnessed by.................................. Date......./......./.......
(Parent/guardian if person is a juvenile or appropriate adult as applicable for adult and in full knowledge of consequences)

Caution Administered
On (date)......./......./....... at (time).............. at (location)..................................
Signed (Officer administering the caution).................................. Rank..............
Authorised by (if different) Name.................................. Rank.............. No..............

M.P. 1436/97

Form 8701

Legal Aid

Children are generally assessed for legal aid in their own right. As few children are likely to have means of their own, they are generally eligible to receive financial assistance from legal-aid money to have the services of a lawyer.

The Legal Aid Board produces a leaflet, *Criminal legal aid at the police station and in court* (April 1997) available from its Press and Publications Section, 85 Gray's Inn Road, London WC1X 8AA.

B. YOUTH JUSTICE

THE COURT SYSTEM

Once a decision to prosecute has been made, most trials of people under 18 are conducted in youth courts, which are a special kind of Magistrates Court with less formal rules than those which apply in the adult Magistrates Court. The magistrates who sit in Youth Courts are chosen from a special panel and must be made up of not more than three magistrates amongst whom there must normally be at least one man and one woman. As in adults' courts they rely for legal guidance on justices' clerks who are full time paid professionals. However, magistrates who are unpaid members of the public may be replaced by a single stipendiary magistrate, a professional, who sits alone. In a few very serious types of case such as murder and indecent assault on a woman, the young person may be tried in a Crown Court.

Protection from publicity

Section 29 of the Children and Young Persons Act 1933 provides protection from publicity for young persons [up to the age of 17] who are involved in youth proceedings. Under the Act,

(a) no newspaper report of the proceedings shall reveal the name, address or school or include any other particulars calculated to lead to the identification of any child or young person in the proceedings. The prohibition applies to a child who appears in any capacity, whether as defendant, as a witness, or on behalf of the prosecution.
(b) A newspaper cannot publish a picture of any child or young person concerned in proceedings unless publication has been permitted by the Court.

The public is not allowed to attend sittings of youth courts. While the press may attend and report the proceedings, they must not identify those being tried unless the court allows identification, which it will normally not do.

The proceedings in Crown Courts which try more serious cases usually apply the same set of rules governing identification of children in their proceedings.

Other constraints on publicity

According to the Code of Practice of the Press Complaints Commission, which was further tightened in December 1997:

- Journalists should not normally interview or photograph children under the age of 16 on subjects involving the child's welfare or that of any other child without consent of an adult.
- Children should not be approached or photographed while at school without the consent of the school authorities.
- There must be no payment to minors for material involving the welfare of children nor payment to parents for material about their children unless demonstrably in the child's interests.
- Children of famous people are to be protected.

Sex cases

Among other matters, the Code of Practice, with regard to sex cases, specifies:
- Even where the law does not prohibit it, the press should not identify children under 16 who are involved in sex cases whether as witnesses, victims, or defendants.
- The word 'incest' should be avoided where it could lead to identification of the child.

Bail

Bail will normally be granted to the accused child or young person unless the child
- has nowhere to stay
- is likely to abscond or
- is regarded as a serious danger to the public.

In such cases, there will normally be a remand to local authority accommodation – generally a community home but sometimes a private lodging or the house of a relative depending on the circumstances. A child or young person can be remanded to secure accommodation or, in the last resort, for boys aged 15 and 16, they could be held in prison on remand.

It is intended that this practice should cease once enough places become available in secure accommodation.

C. PENALTIES

The range of penalties available to the courts is outlined below. The Crime and Disorder Bill also envisages further orders, *viz.* a reparation order or an action plan order, upon conviction. These proposals are further discussed at the end of the chapter.

COURSES OF ACTION AVAILABLE TO THE COURTS

In the event of a guilty finding, the court may
- discharge the child
- order a financial penalty
- order a community sentence or
- order a custodial sentence.

Discharges

The position is the same as in the case of an adult.

(a) absolute discharge

The court may give an absolute discharge which means that the matter is at an end.

(b) conditional discharge

A conditional discharge means that the child may be punished for the offence if he is found guilty of another offence at a later date.

Financial penalties

The court may do one of the following:
- award a fine
- make a compensation order
- order the payment of the costs of the prosecution.

Chapter 14 — In trouble with the law

Where the offender is 16 or 17, the court has the power to order the parent or guardian to pay but is not obliged to do so. When the child is under 16 the courts are under a duty to order the parent or guardian to pay. Youth courts may also make an order to pay compensation to the victim of the crime, up to a maximum of £5,000.

Binding over

(a) Under-16-year-olds: the court's duty

Where children and young people under 16 are convicted of an offence, the courts have a duty to bind over their parents to take proper care and exercise proper control over them if the court believes this will help to prevent them from committing further offences.

(b) 16- and 17-year-olds: the court's power

In the case of 16- and 17-year-olds, the courts have power to bind over their parents should they wish to do so. Binding over means that parents may be ordered to pay a sum of money specified by the court (up to £1,000) if they fail to look after their children properly. If they refuse unreasonably to be bound over, they can be fined up to £1,000.

Community sentences

Community sentences have been introduced to give the courts greater flexibility in dealing with youth crime.

1. Young offenders may be ordered to spend part of their leisure time at attendance centres for periods of time which vary with the age of the child up to a maximum of 36 hours in the case of a 16- and 17-year-old. Attendance centres are local centres usually run by the police.
2. The court has power to make supervision orders placing the child or young person under the supervision of a social worker or probation officer for up to three years. There are conditions that may be attached to supervision orders, for instance requiring the offender to live in a particular place or take part in various forms of activities, and they may impose a curfew.
3. When the offender is over 16 the court may impose a probation order, which is considered as a sentence in its own right. Requirements can be imposed such as attendance at a day centre or participation in intensive probation programmes.
4. The court may impose community service orders for offenders aged 16 and 17 for offences punishable with imprisonment. These require young offenders to do work for the benefit of the local community for between 40 and 240 hours.
5. The courts may also make orders which combine probation and community service orders for 16- and 17-year-olds.
6. The Criminal Justice Act 1991 makes provision for electronic tagging during curfew periods for 16- and 17-year-olds.

Do note: These orders can be made either singly or in combination.

In all cases the court must have regard to the child's welfare.

Custodial sentences

The court is required to restrict the use of custodial sentences for young offenders and cannot pass a custodial sentence unless it is of the opinion that

- the offence is so serious that only such a sentence can be justified for the offence, or
- the offence is a violent or sexual one so that only such a sentence would be adequate to protect the public from serious harm from the offender.

When making a custodial sentence a court has to give its reasons for doing so.

In general the minimum age for a custodial sentence is 15.

Sentences which are available for young people aged 15 and above are normally served in special young-offender institutions. However, 12- to 14-year-olds who commit a high number of offences may be sent to a new form of institution known as a secure training centre, although this plan has yet to be put into operation.

In a recent case, a girl aged 16, who had been convicted of robbery, was sent to an adult prison for an initial assessment. The High Court ruled that unlawful. While there were no young offender institutions specifically for young girls, they were to be held only in juvenile female-offender units located within women's jails.

The rules governing young offenders' institutions, with regard to education and pastoral care, are more stringent than those for adult jails.

Sentences for murder

Any child aged 10 to 17 who has committed murder will be detained 'at Her Majesty's Pleasure' in a secure unit. In the case of the two boys convicted of the murder of the toddler, James Bulger, the then Home Secretary increased the minimum period that they would be held before their possible release could be considered. The House of Lords ruled that his action was not lawful.

D. OFFENSIVE WEAPONS, CHILDREN AND THE LAW

There have been striking changes in the legislation governing the purchase and possession of firearms and offensive weapons in the past 12 months. The changes were brought about in response to a series of horrific attacks in and around schools over the past 18 months. In particular, the Firearms Acts of 1997 creates a general prohibition on small firearms so as to prohibit handguns including small-calibre pistols. There are, however, certain exemptions, e.g. for members of pistol clubs.

AGE LIMITS

The legal stipulations as applied to under-18-year-olds are set out below. The government has indicated that there could be further legislation to increase the age limits for children who currently are allowed to hold shotguns and air weapons.

Stabbing incidents involving young persons have also led to a tightening-up on all the rules relating to the possession, sale and marketing of knives. These rules are also outlined below.

Firearms/Shotguns

Under 14

- It is an offence for a child under the age of 14 to have in his possession a firearm or ammunition;
- it is an offence for a person under 14 to have an air weapon.

Under 15

- It is an offence for a person under the age of 15 to have an assembled shotgun except when accompanied by a person over 21.

Under 17

- It is an offence for a person under the age of 17 to have an air weapon unless covered with a 'gun cover'

Chapter 14 — In trouble with the law

- it is an offence for a person under the age of 17 to purchase or hire any firearm or ammunition.

Note of warning: it is also an offence to supply firearms and shotguns to minors.

Other weapons

Crossbows

Under 17

It is an offence for anyone under 17 to buy or possess a crossbow.

It is a crime to carry an offensive weapon which is 'any article made or adapted' to cause injury. Among the categories are:
- a weapon which is made for that purpose e.g. a knuckle-duster or sword-stick
- a weapon 'adapted' for the purpose (e.g. a broken bottle).

Knives

It is an offence to have a an article with a blade or point in a public place. This applies to a folding pocket-knife if the blade is longer than three inches.

Under the Offensive Weapons Act 1996 it is an offence to have an article with a blade or point on school premises.

It is an offence to sell knives to persons under 16.

Marketing of knives – Knives Act 1997

An Act was passed in 1997 which makes it unlawful to market a knife in any way so as to indicate either that it is suitable for combat or that it might encourage violent behaviour. The Act applies to advertising, packaging, retail sales etc.

E. LIABILITY OF PARENTS

It has already been noted that under existing law the parents of offenders under 16 must generally be ordered to pay their children's fines, and any compensation and costs orders made against their children. The court has the option to order parents of children between 16 and 18 to make such payments.

In the government Green Paper produced just before the election in March 1997, proposals to 'make parents face up to their responsibilities' were put forward. The Paper stated that parents have a primary responsibility for ensuring that children know the difference between right and wrong and are brought up to respect the law.

PARENTING ORDERS

For parents who fail to carry out their responsibilities, the Crime and Disorder Bill proposes to give the courts a new power to make a 'parenting order' to add to or be imposed instead of a binding-over order. The order would be available in respect of parents of children under 16. It would require parents to exercise proper care over their children in cases where the court was satisfied that the child had demonstrated behaviour which

- was likely to lead to offending or
- resulted in the conviction of an offence

and that
- this behaviour had resulted from a lack of parental care and control and

- the order would be effective in tackling that lack of care and control.

If the child is convicted of an offence, it is proposed that the court can decide whether to make a parenting order.

Where a child is at risk of offending but has not yet come before a court, either the police or the social services department could apply to the court for an order. The intention behind the order is to ensure that the parents exercise control to prevent any further offences or anti-social behaviour.

The court must obtain information on the family circumstances and the stipulations in the order must avoid conflict with the parents' religious beliefs or their working times. An order would run for 12 months and could include a three-month weekly guidance or counselling session for parents. Failure to comply with the order could result in a fine.

Appeals against the imposition of a parenting order can be made to the High Court.

PROPOSED CHANGES TO THE LAW

The changes proposed in a consultation document, *Tackling Youth Crime*, by the Home Office are now to be found in the Crime and Disorder Bill which was published in December 1997. The following changes have been proposed:

Anti-social behaviour order

Where children aged 10 or over act in a manner that causes harassment, alarm or distress outside their own home either the police or officers from the local authority can apply to a magistrates' court for an anti-social behaviour order. Failure to comply with the order can result in imprisonment.

Child safety order

This is an order which would apply to children under 10 who, had they been over 10, could have been charged with a criminal offence. It can also be used to protect children under 10 who are at risk of becoming involved in crime.

Local curfew

Local authorities will be able to operate a local child-curfew scheme which would ban children under 10 from being in a public place during specified hours unless they are under the control of a person aged 18 or over.

Local authorities would have powers to impose a child safety order to protect children under 10 who are at risk of becoming involved in crime; and to impose local child-curfews on children under 10 so as to deal with the real nuisance that they can cause.

New structures to deal with youth crime

A Youth Justice Board is to be set up to monitor the operation of the youth justice system and the provision of youth justice services. A duty is imposed on local authorities to set up 'youth offending teams' in their area including a probation officer, social worker and a police officer, as well as education and health nominees. They are to formulate and implement, on an annual basis, a youth justice plan which is to be submitted to the Board.

Timetables are to be imposed on the courts to speed up juvenile justice.

Orders to deal with children convicted of crime (non-custodial)

Reparation orders

A 'reparation order' will require young offenders to make some form of reparation to their victims or to the community at large.

Action plan orders

A three-month order will require the offender to comply with an action plan which will lay down requirements with regard to his activities and whereabouts during that period.

Multi-agency approach

The Crime and Disorder Bill, which contains some of these provisions, also proposes a multi-agency approach to juvenile offenders through 'youth offending teams' which are to consist of a number of specialists including a police officer. Some pilot schemes which have been mainly police-driven have apparently yielded encouraging results and it is hoped that the expense of the organization required will be offset by the reduction in the amount of juvenile crime and the costs of dealing with it.

The Bill thus evinces a clear intention to seek to involve parents, as well as community and other workers, in the necessary and on-going attempt to deal with the problem of juvenile crime.

CHAPTER 15
CHILDREN AS VICTIMS OF CRIME

All the crimes which may be committed against adults may also be committed against children. They may be assaulted, robbed or murdered. We therefore comment on some general crimes but with specific reference to children. However there are a number of crimes which specifically relate to children which we also cover.

As we shall see, children are much more likely to be the victims of crimes of violence than to perpetrate crimes themselves (according to NSPCC statistics, only about four young people in a thousand are found guilty of violent crimes).

In this chapter we examine the following:

- the death of a child
- cruelty
- sexual offences
- child abuse
- abduction
- compensation
- evidence of children.

Section A deals with *crimes committed against children*; section B provides information on *compensating child victims of crime*; and Section C outlines the situation of *the child witness*.

A. CRIMES COMMITTED AGAINST CHILDREN

Causing Death

Children under one year old are at greater risk than any other part of the population of being murdered. Murder requires either an intention to kill or a high degree of recklessness on the part of the perpetrator. If there was no intent or significant recklessness but behaviour where the causing of harm was foreseeable and if death results, the conviction is likely to be of manslaughter rather than murder.

The au pair who shakes a child violently and causes it brain damage from which it subsequently dies is likely to be found guilty of manslaughter. However, if she were to throw the child onto a hard floor causing a fractured skull which led to the child's death, a murder conviction would be probable.

Death caused by couples

There have been a number of reported cases in which a child has died as a result of ill treatment at the hands of one or other of the couple who had care and control of it. Neither man nor woman confessed to the act causing the child's death and in the absence of evidence as to which one of them actually caused the death, both were acquitted of the murder charge. In order to convict them it would have been necessary to prove that they had jointly behaved in a manner which caused the child's death.

Chapter 15 — Children as victims of crime

Infanticide

It was recognized in the late nineteenth century that depression following childbirth might lead the mentally disturbed mother to kill her child. Rather than finding her guilty of murder, the crime of infanticide was created. It is defined as the causing of the death of a child under 12 months old where the balance of the mother's mind is disturbed because she has not recovered from childbirth or because she is suffering from depression caused by lactation. However, there must have been a live birth, even if premature.

Sentences

The maximum sentence for murder, manslaughter and infanticide is life imprisonment. In the case of murder this is a compulsory [mandatory] sentence. The sentence actually imposed for manslaughter or infanticide will depend on the circumstances but in the case of infanticide a sentence of imprisonment is improbable and indeed there is unlikely to be any significant penalty.

For the sentencing of children who have been convicted of murder, see Chapter 14, p.174.

Child Destruction

As well as infanticide, which requires a live birth, child destruction is also a crime. While the purpose of abortion is to bring a pregnancy to an end, the purpose of child destruction is to get rid of a child before it has an existence independent of its mother. Child destruction is thus an act committed at the time a child is being born in the ordinary course of nature. There must be an intent to destroy the life of a child 'capable of being born alive'. A pregnancy which has lasted 28 weeks would be apparent proof that the child was capable of being born alive.

Abortion was considered a crime until 1967 when the Abortion Act was passed. It permits legal abortions under certain conditions. In fact, since the Abortion Act, though it is not intended that abortion should be provided on demand it has become relatively easy to persuade the medical authorities to abort. This topic is dealt with in Chapter 1, *Expecting a baby*, p.9.

Prosecutions for abortion and child destruction are now extremely rare.

Cruelty

Section 1 of the Children and Young Persons Act 1933 specifically provides that it is an offence for any person over the age of 16, who looks after a child who is under that age, to assault, ill-treat, or neglect the child. The Act has been treated as creating a general offence of cruelty of which this list merely provides instances. The maximum sentence for an offence under the Act is now 10 years. It is anticipated that this increase in sentence, which was originally only two years, will lead to greater use of the Act.

The general law relating to assault occasioning actual bodily harm and causing grievous bodily harm is also used in relation to assaults on children.

'Moderate and reasonable chastisement' by parents is permitted, but corporal punishment by teachers of pupils whose education is wholly or partially state-funded is no longer allowed.

Sexual Offences

The law is concerned to protect young persons against sexual advances of those adults, including close family members, who would seek to take advantage of their youth and inexperience. Indeed most cases of child abuse take place in the child's own home. Moreover, persistent child abusers have also been able to infiltrate child welfare services and move from children's home to children's home, taking advantage of the young and vulnerable.

On the other hand, in their endeavour to protect children thought to be at risk, social workers have committed errors of judgment in removing children from their families because of alleged abuse. Interviews have not always been properly conducted, evidence has not been properly checked, and the social workers themselves have been accused of being credulous in accepting children's accounts of alleged abuse.

Further, because of the publicity given to recent cases of indecent assault, there is a danger that accidental contact, for instance in a swimming pool, or what are intended as gestures of affection may be misconstrued. Thus all those dealing with or in contact with children must be constantly aware of the danger of allegations of indecency against which defence may be difficult. Conviction – and even caution – now entails notification on the newly-instituted register of sex offenders. See *Public protection*, p.183.

Unlawful sexual intercourse

It is unlawful for a man to have sexual intercourse with a girl under 16. Her consent is immaterial.

It is also unlawful for a man to have sex with a boy under 18. Again consent is not material. However, the present government intends to lower the age of consent to 16 for consensual homosexual sex in private.

A doctor may give contraceptive advice to a girl under 16 when he thinks it appropriate (see Chapter 10, *Your child's health*, p.96, for a detailed discussion on this topic).

Incest

(a) For a man

It is an offence for a man to have sexual intercourse with a woman whom he knows to be his daughter, granddaughter, mother or sister.

(b) For a woman

It is an offence for a woman, aged 16 or over, to permit a man to have sexual intercourse with her when she knows that he is her father, grandfather, grandson, son, or brother.

The rules of incest apply notwithstanding that the relationship is not traced through lawful wedlock. In other words, the crime of incest is committed where a man has sex with his own daughter although he has never been married to her mother. It also applies to adopted children.

Indecent assault

A child under the age of 16 cannot in law give any consent which would prevent an act from being an indecent assault. For example, a 15-year-old boy might welcome sexual advances from an older woman but his consent would not prevent her acts from being indecent assault.

Both boys and girls over 16 can give consent to sexual acts (except for consensual homosexual sex where the age limit at present is 18).

It is an offence to take an unmarried girl under 16 'out of the possession' of her parent or guardian whether or not she has consented. For example, if a 15-year-old girl goes to live with a man, he could be prosecuted for taking her out of the possession of her parent or guardian without the necessity of prosecuting him for, and then having to prove that he had, sexual intercourse with a minor.

Chapter 15 — Children as victims of crime

Indecent photographs

The taking of indecent photographs of children is also an offence, as is distributing such photographs. It is also an offence to have an indecent photograph of a child aged under 16 in one's possession. There is no definition of 'indecent' in this context.

The Photo Marketing Association has formulated guidelines to assist photoprocessors and retailers who could commit a criminal offence by processing and printing indecent photos of children from film received from customers and returned to them. They are advised to speak to the Child Protection Unit of the nearest police station if the material is potentially indecent according to indicators laid out in guidelines.

Legal capacity

Until 1993, the legal view prevailed that a boy of under 14 could not have sexual intercourse notwithstanding any evidence to the contrary. That view was abolished by the Sexual Offences Act 1993. Therefore a boy under the age of 14 is regarded in law as capable of sexual intercourse, and provided all the other elements of the offence are present, he can be found guilty of rape.

Child Abuse

Allegations of child abuse can result in

(a) prosecution in criminal proceedings and/or
(b) civil proceedings where children are taken into care by the local authority for their own protection.

In this chapter, we are concerned on the whole with prosecutions in criminal proceedings. Care proceedings are dealt with in Chapter 9, *When parenting fails*.

Child abuse in the home

Most sexual abuse takes place within the family environment and the abuser may be well known to the child, i.e. a parent, relative, or friend.

> *You notice that your child appears fearful whenever the regular baby-sitter arrives. You are struck by your child's reserve as the babysitter always brings with him elaborate computer games which are normally a great family favourite.*

You must check the background of anyone having contact with your child while you are not in the house to supervise them. If you suspect that a child is being abused, you must report it to the local authority social services department, the police, or the NSPCC.

All these bodies have powers to investigate alleged criminal offences against children. The NSPCC runs a Child Protection Helpline, 0800 800 500, which operates 24 hours per day and offers counselling, information and advice.

Note of warning: You are strenuously advised never to confront a suspected abuser yourself.

Police protection

Under the Children Act 1989 the police are empowered to take children into police protection. They cooperate closely with the social services or other agencies and will enter the family home for that purpose. Even when prosecution does not ensue because of either lack of evidence or the likely harmful consequences, their intervention protects the child at risk. They are instructed to liaise with the appropriate authorities and to make evidence they have collected available for civil proceedings.

Removing the abuser from the home

If the suspected abuser is a family member, he may be removed from the home while the investigation is proceeding. Surveys show that only about five per cent of abuse is carried out by adult females.

Under the domestic violence provisions of the Family Law Act 1996, which came into force on 1 October 1997, a person may apply for a 'non-molestation' order against someone in their household with whom they live in close association. The Act refers to a 'person who is associated with the respondent'. An order may also be made on behalf of a 'relevant child' (these terms are explained below).

(a) What is molestation?

This term is not defined. However, the court must pay regard to all the circumstances before it exercises its powers, including the need to secure the health, safety and well-being of those involved.

If it appears to the court that the person against whom the order is sought has threatened violence against the applicant or a relevant child, a power of arrest can be attached to the order.

(b) Who is an 'associated person'?

A person is 'associated with the respondent' if

- he or she is the present, or ex-, husband and wife, or they are partners who have lived together as man or wife
- they have lived together in the same household sharing the household chores
- they are relatives, which include children, stepchildren, and grandchildren (as well as brothers, sisters, uncles, aunts, nieces or nephews).

Do note: commercial household arrangements are excluded, so a lodger, for example, could not be an associated person.

(c) Who is a 'relevant' child?

The relevant child is

- any child living with either party
- any child to whom an order under the Children Act or Adoption Act relates
- any other child whose interests the court considers relevant.

(d) When can a child make an application for a non-molestation order?

A child is defined as being under 18 years of age.

A child aged 16–18 may apply as of right for a non-molestation order. A child under 16 may make application with permission of the court, which has to be satisfied that he or she has 'sufficient understanding' to make the proposed application.

The legislation provides that police officers may also be able to apply for an order although this provision has not yet come into effect.

Child abuse by strangers

In order to protect children from abuse, parents are increasingly concerned about and feel the need to warn children against, attention from strangers. At the same time, there are concerns that both parents and children are becoming increasingly confined, both physically and mentally, by fear of real or perceived threats.

Public protection

In the wake of convictions of child molesters who have clearly found it relatively easy to move from job to job which involved child care, public demand grew for greater protection from them. The new Sexual Offences Act and the National Register of Paedophiles are intended to meet these demands and to assuage some of the public anxiety.

(a) National Register of Paedophiles

The Register came into effect on 1 September 1997. Under the Act, sex offenders are required to notify the police of their names and addresses, as well as any changes to them, which will be kept by the police on their national computer. The length of the sentence determines the period for which notification is necessary. For 30 months' or more imprisonment, the duration is indefinite; for a non-custodial sentence or caution the period is five years.

The Home Office guidelines specify that the information on the computer should not be handed out freely by the police but should be made available, on a case-by-case basis, to identified individuals in local agencies such as social services, schools or playgroups. It would only be made available to the general public in the most exceptional circumstances.

The guidelines stress that the police will have to make judgment on a careful assessment of risk between protecting the public and the protection of the offender's legal rights.

Abuse carried out by another child

Where abuse is carried out by another child, the child protection procedures have to be observed for both the victim and the abuser (see Chapter 14, *In trouble with the law*).

For those young offenders under 18, who are convicted of sex abuse, the period of notification on the Paedophile Register will be halved. The notification will also be halved for an under-18-year-old offender who is being cautioned (see Chapter 14, *In trouble with the law*, p.168).

Thus for an adult who is cautioned, the period is five years' notification. For an under-18-year-old similarly cautioned, the notification period is halved to two-and-a-half years.

Sex offender orders

Under the Crime and Disorder Bill a chief officer of police can apply to a magistrates' court for a 'sex offender order' for the purpose of protecting the public from serious harm from a person who has been convicted of a sexual offence. The order is to last for not less than five years.

Abduction

It is an offence for a person connected with a child to take the child out of the United Kingdom without the appropriate consent (see below). Where there is 'a real and imminent' threat of removal it is possible to obtain an order for a stop to be put on the exit of the child through any port or airport.

With the number of failed marriages and the present general state of flux in family relationships, the abduction of children by estranged parents is a growing and grave issue. About 200 children a year are abducted within the UK and about the same number are taken abroad. About 90 per cent of abductions are carried out by fathers, of whom about one in five is British.

Newspaper and other reports testify to the heartbreak of the parents involved. The traumatic effects on the children involved can only be guessed at. The headlines refer to child abduction as 'tug-of-love' but the end result is human misery.

There are complex legal issues involved, particularly in view of the fact that the problem of child abduction often crosses international borders. If you are fearful of a possible abduction, legal advice should be taken as a pre-emptive measure whenever possible.

There are organizations to advise and assist at every stage. The National Council for the Abducted Child (Reunite) is on hand to give advice and has a network of lawyers who have had experience in this field. The Official Solicitor's Office has a special child-abduction unit and issues a booklet entitled *Child Abduction* (see DIRECTORY). Two international agreements have been drawn up to facilitate co-operation in the search for missing children.

Appropriate consent

Where a child is living with someone under a residence order [i.e. an order of the court which determines with whom the child is to live], the child cannot be taken abroad for longer than a month without permission of the court or without the consent of the other parent, a guardian, or any other person who has parental responsibility for that child.

You do not have to wait for the worst to happen before you can act. If you have proper grounds to fear that your child might be abducted, there are immediate steps which you can take.

You are divorced from your American husband who has regular access to your three-year-old son. Both your ex-husband and yourself live in London and he has never indicated in any way to you that he is thinking of taking the child away from you. However, you learn from mutual friends that he has been making threats to that effect. You wonder if there are any steps that you can take to forestall any such eventuality. The child is registered on your passport.

You should proceed as follows:

(a) You must consult a solicitor.
(b) Try to ensure that there is a third party present at all meetings between your child and his father. This could be made a condition of his visits by court order.
(c) You must keep all documents concerning your son (such as birth certificate) so that they cannot be used to enable his father to have his son's name placed on his passport. Also keep a photo of your ex-husband, details of his passport if you have them, and any other information which could assist in tracing him if such a need arose.

Under the Children Act you are allowed to take a child abroad for less than a month without written consent of the other parent.

The UK Passport Agency has issued guidelines on the issue of passports to children. (See also Chapter 4, *Parental responsibilities*, p.40.)

B. COMPENSATION

COMPENSATION AND THE CRIMINAL INJURIES COMPENSATION BOARD

A person who has injured a child and been convicted of the offence could be sued for damages for the injury in a civil court but most such persons would have no money to meet the damages claimed. The State therefore has set up a scheme to compensate victims for injuries caused by crimes – The Criminal Injuries Compensation Board administers the scheme on behalf of the Criminal Injuries Compensation Authority.

Compensation and Child Victims

Your 12-year-old daughter was punched in the face by a gang of bullies in the school playground. One of her front teeth was broken. The incident was reported immediately to the headmaster. The other children involved were disciplined by the school. You want to apply for compensation on behalf of your child.

Application in a prescribed form must usually be made to the Criminal Injuries Compensation Board within two years of the date of the incident. To obtain an award, the victim must have suffered 'personal injury' which was caused by the 'crime of violence.'

Information and claim forms may be obtained from the Criminal Injuries Compensation Board, Morley House, 24-30 Holborn Viaduct, London EC1A 2JQ, telephone 0171 842 6800.

When an application is made on behalf of someone under 18, it must be made by an adult or someone with parental responsibility for the child, i.e. the natural or adoptive parent or another person with legal parental responsibility. A copy of the birth certificate must also be enclosed.

In certain circumstances, the Board accepts that it is appropriate to report an incident to an authority other than the police. It applies particularly in the case of a school pupil, assaulted at school, who reports the incident to the school authorities. On the form you must give details of the school and the person to whom the incident was reported, i.e. the headteacher.

There is a 'tariff' for injuries suffered. For example, someone who has had teeth broken could receive compensation set at £1,000.

Note: Where a child is in care, application should be made by the local authority.

Children playing dangerous games

The Board will not make an award where children play dangerous games and there is little to choose between the perpetrator of the injury and the victim with regard to conduct. It cites as an example a case of two boys firing catapults at each other, using stones, and one boy suffers a serious eye injury. Both would seem to be equally at fault.

However, where children of different age groups are involved or take unequal shares in a game, then there may be an award depending on the degree of involvement and how fully the children understood the risks they ran.

Compensation and victims of child abuse

To obtain an award, the victim must have suffered 'personal injury' which was caused by a 'crime of violence'. Sexual abuse, indecent assault, rape and incest would be considered crimes of violence for this purpose. Personal injury would include mental injury such as shock or psychological disturbance.

There need not be an actual conviction but the Board would have to be satisfied that the events actually occurred. Generally an applicant, on behalf of a child, would have taken steps to inform the police or other authorities without delay.

Sexual abuse within the family

Where both the abuser and the child victim live in the same household, compensation will only be paid if there has been a prosecution or there is good reason why the abuser has not been prosecuted.

Moreover compensation will not be paid where it could benefit the offender, particularly if he is still living under the same roof as the child.

Compensation will also not be awarded if, in the view of the Board, it is in the child's interests that the incident should be treated as over and done with rather than involving a lengthy process such as investing the award until the child reaches 18.

Time limits

Application in a prescribed form must usually be made to the Criminal Injuries Compensation Board within two years of the date of the incident causing injury. However, in the case of child abuse, the time limit may be put to one side if 'it is reasonable and in the interests of justice to do so.'

The Board's leaflet on *Child Abuse* states that it adopts a sympathetic attitude towards late claims put in on behalf of children, or by children themselves when made within a reasonable time of reaching 18 years of age.

It is not necessary that the offender should have been convicted. However, compensation may not be forthcoming if the police or some other authority was not promptly informed.

2.4 Administering awards on behalf of children

Awards may be invested and managed by the Criminal Injuries Compensation Authority until the child reaches 18 years of age.

C. GIVING EVIDENCE

EVIDENCE OF CHILDREN

There is an increasing tendency to accept the evidence of children which recent research has shown is not more inaccurate than that of adults.

The judge can decide whether or not a young child should be permitted to give evidence.

Taking an oath

The evidence of a child under 14 must be given unsworn, and over that age the judge must ascertain whether or not the child really understands the meaning of the taking of an oath.

Committal proceedings

Serious criminal cases which are tried in the Crown Courts must in general be preceded by a hearing in a Magistrates' Court to establish that there is a 'case to answer.' These are known as 'committal proceedings'. This means that witnesses may have to be called twice.

In certain cases there is a procedure for arranging for cases involving children to be transferred immediately to the Crown Court without this intermediate stage.

In committal proceedings, unless the defence objects, the evidence of children may be taken by written statement. A videotape can also be used. Strict guidelines for the preparation of video evidence are laid down which stress the great importance of adequate training for those conducting the interviews.

Assisting the child witness

The judge has power to clear the court when a child is to give evidence and may permit the evidence to be given from behind a screen. A child can also give evidence by means of a live television link.

Child witnesses can find the experience of giving evidence very stressful. Cases generally involve children who have themselves been victims of crime or who have witnessed crimes of violence committed against others. Children can be called as witnesses for either the prosecution or the defence.

Chapter 15 — Children as victims of crime

The judge may also allow a social worker or relative to sit by the child to assist him or her in not becoming too nervous while giving evidence. The role of the 'adult supporter' can involve liaising with both the prosecution and the defence before the trial, as well as with the police, local authorities and the Crown Prosecution Service, in order to try to minimize the trauma for the child witness.

The NSPCC has produced a *Child Witness Pack* which is intended for children, parents and their carers to assist in understanding trial procedures. The Children's Legal Centre has available a leaflet, *Being a Witness*, which tells children what to expect at court. It is intended for children of eight and over, but should be read together with an adult familiar with court procedure (see DIRECTORY).

Directory

PART 1 – STARTING A FAMILY

Pregnancy and Childbirth

Association for Improvements in the Maternity Services (AIMS) 40 Kingswood Avenue
London NW6 6LS
TEL:0181 960 5585

Association for Post-Natal Illness (APNI)
25 Jerdan Place
London SW6 1BE
TEL:0171 386 0868

British Pregnancy Advice Service (BPAS)
Austy Manor
Wootton Wawen, Solihull
West Midlands B95 6BX
TEL:01564 793225
Actionline:0345 30 40 30

Brook Advisory Centres
165 Gray's Inn Road
London WC1X 8UD
Helplines:0171 713 9000
(Young People's Information Line),
0171 617 8000 (recorded information line)

Serene
BM Cry-sis
London WC1N 3XX
TEL:0171 404 5011

Family Planning Association
27-35 Mortimer Street
London W1N 7RT
TEL:0171 636 7866

Family Planning Association
2-12 Pentonville Road
London N1 9FP
TEL:0171 837 5432
Helpline 0171 837 4044

Family Welfare Association
501-505 Kingsland Road
London E8 4AU
TEL:0171 254 6251

La Leche League
(Breastfeeding help and information)
BM 3424
London WC1N 3XX
TEL:0171 242 1278 (24 hours)

LIFE
(Pregnancy, birth, adoption, DSS benefits, facilities for disabled parents or children)
LIFE House
Newbold Terrace
Leamington Spa
Warwickshire CV32 4EA
TEL:01926 421587

Lifeline Pregnancy Care
Cae Bach
4 Pant Y Wennol
Bodafon, Llandudno, Gwynedd LL30 3DS
TEL:01492 543 741

MAMA (Meet-a-Mum Association)
26 Avenue Road
South Norwood London SE25 4DX
TEL:0181 771 5595
Post Natal Illness helpline: 0181 768 0123

Marie Stopes Internationl
Marie Stopes House
108 Whitfield Street
London W1P 6BE
TEL:0171 388 0662
Advice Sister:0171 388 8090

Maternity Alliance
45 Beech Street 5th Floor
London EC2P 2LX
TEL:0171 588 8582

National Association for Maternal and Child Welfare
1st Floor
40-42 Osnaburgh Street
London NW1 3ND
TEL:0171 383 4115

The National Childbirth Trust
Alexandra House, Oldham Terrace
London W3 6NH
TEL:0181 992 8637

The National Childbirth Trust – ParentAbility
Address as above

Parentline
Endway House
Endway, Hadleigh
Essex SS7 2AN
TEL:01702 554782
Helpline:01702 559900

Directory

Parents Anonymous
6-9 Manor Gardens
London N7 6LA
TEL:0171 263 8918

United Kingdom Central Council for Nursing,
Midwifery and Health Visiting
23 Portland Place
London W1N 4JT
TEL:0171 333 6557

WellBeing
27 Sussex Place, Regent's Park
London NW1 4SP
TEL:0171 262 5337

Benefits

Child Benefit Centre
Benefits Agency
DSS
Washington
Newcastle upon Tyne
NE88 1AA

Child Support Agency (CSA)
DSS
PO Box 55
Brierley Hill, West Midlands
DY5 1YL
TEL:0345 133 133

Family Credit
Government Buildings
Cop Lane
Penwortham
Preston
PR1 0SA
Family Credit Helpline: 01253 500050

Guardian's Allowance Unit
Child Benefit Centre
The Benefits Agency
PO Box 1
Newcastle upon Tyne NE88 1AA
TEL:0191 225 2286/2151/2283

Health Benefits Division
Sandyford House
Newcastle upon Tyne
NE2 1DB
TEL:0191 203 5555

Infant Death

The Cot Death Society
1 Browning Close
Thatcham, Berkshire
RG18 3EF
TEL:01635 861771

Cruse Bereavement Care
Cruse House
126 Sheen Road, Richmond
Surrey TW9 1UR
TEL:0181 940 4818
National Helpline:0181 332 7227

The Foundation for the Study of Infant Deaths
14 Halkin Street
London SW1X 7DP
TEL:0171 235 0965 (General Enquiries)
0171 235 1721 (24 Hour Cot Death Helpline)

Miscarriage Association
Head Office
c/o Clayton Hospital
Northgate, Wakefield
West Yorkshire WF1 3JS
TEL:01924 200 799

SATFA (Support around Termination for Abnormality)
73-75 Charlotte Street
London W1P 1LB
Helpline: 0171 631 0285

Stillbirth and Neonatal Death Society
28 Portland Place
London W1N 4DE
TEL:0171 436 7940
Helpline: 0171 436 5881

Infertility

CHILD
(Charity for Infertility, Education and Counselling)
Charter House
43 St Leonards Road, Bexhill on Sea
East Sussex TN40 1JA
TEL:01424 732 361

The Human Fertilisation and Embryology Authority
Paxton House
30 Artillery Lane London E1 7LS
TEL:0171 377 5077

Directory

ISSUE (National Fertility Association)
114 Lichfield Street
Walsall West Midlands WS1 1SZ
TEL:01922 722 888

WellBeing
27 Sussex Place
Regents Park, London NW1 4SP
TEL:0171 723 9296

PART 2 – WHOSE RIGHTS? – WHOSE RESPONSIBILITIES?

Boys and Girls Welfare Society (BGWS)
BGWS Centre
Schools Hill
Cheadle
Cheshire SK8 1JE
TEL:0161 283 4848

The Brandon Centre (formerly London Youth Advisory Centre)
26 Prince of Wales Road
Kentish Town
London NW5 3LG
TEL:0171 267 4792

British Association for Counselling
1 Regent Place
RugbyCV21 2PJ
TEL:01788 578 328

Centrepoint
Bewley House
2 Swallow Place
London W1R 7AA
TEL:0171 629 2229

Child Support Agency (CSA)
Quay House
The Waterfront
Brierley Hill
West Midlands DY5 1XZ
TEL:01345 133 133 (Enquiry Line)

Childline
2nd Floor
Royal Mail Building
50 Strudd Street
London N1 0QW
TEL:0171 239 1000 (admin)
or
Childline Freepost 1111
London N1 0BR

(Freephone) 0800 1111
For children in care:
Tel. 0800 844 4444
Minicom Tel: 0800 400 222

Children's Legal Centre
University of Essex
Wivenhoe Park
Colchester
Essex CO4 3SQ
TEL:01206 873 820 (advice line)

The Children Panel
Professional Accreditation
The Law Society
Ipsley Court
Redditch
Worcestershire
B98 0TD
TEL:0171 242 1222

The Children's Rights Development Unit
England   235 Shaftesbury Avenue
              London WC2H 8EL
Wales Children in Wales/Plant yng Nghymru
              25 Windsor Place
              Cardiff CF1 3BZ

Children's Society
Edward Rudolf House
Margery Street
London WC1X 0JL
TEL:0171 837 4299

The Children's Society (Advocacy Unit)
14 Cathedral Road
Cardiff, South Glamorgan
CF1 9LJ
TEL:01222 396974

Citizens' Advice Bureau
National Association
115-123 Pentonville Road
London N1 8LZ
TEL:0171 833 2181

Citizenship Foundation
15 St Swithin's Lane, London EC4N 8AL
TEL:0171 929 3344

The Early Childhood Unit
National Children's Bureau
8 Wakley Street, London EC1V 7QE
TEL:0171 843 6000

Directory

Exploring Parenthood
4 Ivory Place
Treadgold Street
London W11 8BP
TEL: 0171 221 4471

Family Conciliation Service
(Northumberland and Tyneside)
MEA House, Ellison Place
Newcastle upon Tyne NE1 8XS
TEL:0191 261 9212

The Family Law Bar Association
2nd Floor
Queen Elizabeth Building
Temple
London EC4Y 9BS
TEL:0171 797 7837

Family Mediators Association
The Old House
Rectory Gardens
Henbury
Bristol BS10 7AQ
TEL:01179 500 140

Family Rights Group
The Print House
18 Ashwin Street
London E8 3DL
TEL:0171 923 2628
Advice line freephone: 0800 731 1696

Family Service Units (offices nationwide)
207 Old Marylebone Road
London NW1 5QP
TEL:0171 402 5175

Family and Youth Concern
Wicken
Milton Keynes MK19 6BU
TEL:01908 571 234

Human Rights Information Centre
Council of Europe
F – 67075 Strasbourg Cedex
France
TEL:00 33 3 88 41 20 24

Immigration Advisory Service
County House
190 Great Dover Street
London SE1 4YB
TEL:0181 814 1559

Independent Representation
for Children in Need (IRCHIN)
1 Downham Road South
Heswall
Merseyside
L60 5RG
TEL:0151 342 7852

Kids' Clubs Network
Bellerive House
3 Muirfield Crescent
London E14 9SZ
TEL:0171 512 2100

Kidscape Helpline
152 Buckingham Palace Road
London SW1W 9TR
TEL:0171 730 3300

National Early Years Network
77 Holloway Road
London N7 8JZ
TEL:0171 607 9573

National Family Conciliation Council
Shaftesbury Centre
Percy Street
Swindon SN2 2AZ
TEL:01793 514 055

National Family Mediation
9 Tavistock Place
London
WC1H 9SN
TEL:0171 383 5993

National Youth Agency
17-23 Albion Street
Leicester LE1 6GD
TEL:01162 856789

Network of Access and
Child Contact Centres
St Andrews with Castle Gate URC
Goldsmith Street
Nottingham
NG1 5JT

National Association of
Councils for Voluntary Service (NACVS)
3rd Floor Arundel Court
177 Arundel Street
Sheffield S1 2NU
TEL:0114 278 6636

National Childcare Campaign (NCCC)
Wesley House
4 Wild Court
London WC2B 5AU
TEL:0171 405 5617/8

National Children's Bureau
8 Wakley Street
London EC1V 7QE
Tel: 0171 843 6000

National Children's Centre
Brian Jackson House
New North Parade, Huddersfield
West Yorkshire HD1 5JP
TEL:01484 519988

Parents Against Injustice (PAIN)
10 Water Lane
Bishop's Stortford
Herts CM23 2JZ
TEL:01279 656 564

Parents' Lifeline
73d Stapleton Hall Road
London N4 3QF
TEL:0171 263 8918 (24 hr 840 7000)

Relate
Herbert Gray College
Little Church Street
Rugby CV21 3AP
TEL:01788 573241
(see local telephone directories also)

Solicitors' Family Law Association
PO Box 302
Orpington
Kent BR6 8QX
TEL:01689 850 227

Tavistock Centre
120 Belsize Lane
London NW3 5BA
TEL:0171 435 7111

Teen Challenge UK
52 Penygroes Road
Gorslas
Llanelli
Dyfed
SA14 7LA
South Wales
TEL:01269 842718

Trust for the Study of Adolescence
23 New Road
Brighton
East Sussex BN1 1WZ
TEL:01273 693 311

Young Homelessness Group (YHG)
2nd Floor
10 Livonia Street
London W1V 3PH
TEL:0171 494 0333

Youth Access (formerly NAYPCAS)
1-2 Taylors Yard
67 Alderbrook Road
London SW12 8AF
TEL:01533 558 763

Children and Work

Health and Safety Executive
Public Enquiry Point
Information Centre
Broad Lane
Sheffield S3 7HQ
TEL:0541 545 500

West Midlands Low Pay Unit
(WMLPU)
Wolverley House
18 Digbeth
Birmingham B5 6BJ
TEL:0121 643 3972

PART 3 – OTHER CARERS

British Agencies for Adoption and Fostering
(BAAF)
Skyline House
200 Union Street, London SE1 0LX
TEL:0171 593 2000

Carers National Association
20/25 Glasshouse Yard
London EC1A 4JS
TEL:0171 490 8818
CarersLine0171 490 8898

Children Need Grandparents
2 Surrey Way
Laindon West, Basildon
Essex SS15 6PS
(include SAE)

Directory

Daycare Trust
4 Wild Court,
London WC2B 4AU
TEL:0171 405 5617

Families Need Fathers
134 Curtain Road
London EC2A 3AR
TEL:0171 613 5060 or 0990 502506

Grandparent Support Organisation (GSO)
57 Lyon Street, Newtown
Southampton
Hants SO14 0LW
TEL:01703 632 387

Grandparents' Federation
Moot House
The Stow, Harlow
Essex CM20 3AG
TEL:01279 444964

Guardians Allowance Unit
Child Benefit Centre
The Benefits Agency
PO Box 1
Newcastle upon Tyne
NE88 1AA
TEL: 0191 225 2286/2151/2283

Independent Adoption Service (IAS)
121-123 Camberwell Road
London SE5 0HB
TEL:0171 703 1088

National Childcare Campaign
4 Wild Court
London WC2B 5AU
TEL:0171 405 5617

National Childminding Association
8 Masons Hill
Bromley, BR2 9EY
TEL:0181 464 6164

National Children's Home
85 Highbury Park
London N5 1UD
TEL:0171 226 2033

National Foster Care Association (NFCA)
Leonard House
5-7 Marshalsea Road
London SE1 1EP
TEL:0171 828 6266

National Organisation for the Counselling of Adoptees and Parents
(NORCAP)
112 Church Road
Wheatley
Oxford OX33 1LU

National Stepfamily Association
Chapel House
18 Hatton Place
London EC1N 8RU
TEL:0171 209 2460
Counselling Service 0990 168 388

Parent to Parent Information on Adoption Services
Lower Boddington, Daventry
Northamptonshire NN11 6YB
TEL:013272 60295

Parents at Work
77 Holloway Road
London N7 8JZ
TEL:0171 700 5771/2

Parents for Children
41 Southgate Road
London N1 3JD
TEL:0171 359 7530

Post-Adoption Centre
5 Torriano Mews
Torriano Avenue
London NW5 2RZ
TEL:0171 284 0555

Professional Association of Nursery Nurses
2 St James's Court
Friar Gate
Derby DE1 1BT
TEL:0332 343029

Step Family Publications
Chapel House
18 Hatton Place
London EC1N 8RU
TEL:0171 209 2460
Helpline 0990 168 388

Voice for the Child in Care
Suite G15 Redlands
3/5 Tapton House Road
Sheffield S10 5BY
TEL:0114 267 9389
or

Unit 4, Pride Court
80-82 White Lion Street
London N1 9PS
Tel: 0171 209 2460
Helpline: 0990 168 388

Lone Parents

Gingerbread
16-17 Clerkenwell Close
London EC1R 0AA
TEL:0171 336 8183

National Council for One Parent Families
255 Kentish Town Road
London NW5 2LX
TEL:0171 267 1361

Single Parent Action Network (SPAN)
Millpond, Baptist Street, Easton
Bristol BS5 0YW
TEL:0117 951 4231

PART 4 – MINIMIZING RISKS

Health

Action for Sick Children
(National Association for the Welfare of Children in Hospital)
Argyle House
29-31 Euston Road
London NW1 2SD
TEL:0171 833 2041

Action for Victims of Medical Accidents
Bank Chambers
1 London Road
Forest Hill
London SE23 3TP
Tel: 0181 291 2793

Boys' and Girls' Welfare Society
Central Offices
Schools Hill
Cheadle
Cheshire SK8 1JE
TEL:0161 283 4848

British Medical Association
BMA House
Tavistock Square
London WC1H 9JP
TEL:0171 387 4499

Department of Health
Richmond House
79 Whitehall
London SW1A 2NS
TEL:0171 210 3000

Health Education Authority
Hamilton House
Mabledon Place
London WC1H 9TX
Health Information Service
TEL:0800 665 544

Health Publications Unit
(for Guides produced in conjunction with the Children Act)
Heywood Stores
No 2 Site
Manchester Road
Heywood
Lancashire OL10 2PZ

Mental Health Act Commission
Maid Marian House
56 Hounds Gate
Nottingham NG1 6BG
TEL:0115 943 7100

National Association for the Education of Sick Children
Open School
18 Victoria Park Square
Bethnal Green
London E2 9PF
TEL:0181 980 6263/8523

National Autistic Society
393 City Road
London EC1V 1NE
TEL:0171 903 3599

National Society for the Prevention of Cruelty to Children
(NSPCC)
4 Curtain Road
London EC2A 3NH
TEL:0171 825 2500

National Schizophrenia Fellowship (NSF)
28 Castle Street
Kingston upon Thames
Surrey KT1 1SS
TEL:0181 547 3937
Advice Service:0181 974 6814

Directory

The Samaritans
10 The Grove
Slough
SL1 1QP
TEL:01753 532713
National Helpline:0345 90 90 90

Safety

British Association of Toy Retailers
24 Baldwyn Gardens
London W3 6HL
Helpline:0181 993 2894

British Toy & Hobby Association
80 Camberwell Road
London
SE5 0EG
TEL:0171 701 7271

Child Accident Prevention Trust
18-20 Farringdon Lane
London
EC1R 3AU
TEL:0171 608 3828

Kidscape (campaign for children's safety)
152 Buckingham Palace Road
London
SW1W 9TR
TEL:0171 730 3300

National Toy Council
1 Chelsea Manor Gardens
London SW3 5PN

Royal Society for the Prevention of Accidents
(RoSPA)
Edgbaston Park
353 Bristol Road
Birmingham B5 7ST
TEL:0121 248 2000

PART 5 – PARENTAL CONTROL AND GUIDANCE

Alcohol

Alcohol Concern
Waterbridge House
32-36 Loman Street
London
SE1 0EE
TEL:0171 928 7377

Alcohol & Health Research Centre
Top Floor
New Medical Block, City Hospital
Greenbank Drive
Edinburgh EH10 5SB
TEL:0131 536 6217

Health Education Authority
Trevelyan House
30 Great Peter Street
London SW1P 2HW
TEL:0171 222 5300

Hybu Lechyd Cymru
Health Promotion Wales
Ffynnon-las
Ty Glas Avenue Llanishen
Cardiff CF4 5DZ
TEL:01222 752 222

The Portman Group
2d Wimpole Street
London W1M 7AA
TEL:0171 499 1010
(to order 'Proof of Age' application forms)
TEL:01787 882 009

The United Kingdom Alliance
Action Against Alcohol and Drug Abuse
176 Blackfriars Road
London SE1 8ET
TEL:0171 928 1538 or 01923 221348

Drugs

ADFAM National
(for families and friends of drug users)
Waterbridge House
32-36 Loman Street
London SE1 0EE
TEL:0171 928 8900

Healthwise (for sex and drug education)
1st Floor
Cavern Walks
8 Mathew Street
Liverpool L2 6RE
TEL:0151 227 4415

The Institute for the Study of Drug Dependence
(ISDD)
1 Hatton Place, Hatton Garden
London EC1N 8ND
TEL:0171 430 1993

National Association of Young People's
Counselling and Advice Services
11 Newarke Street
Leicester LE1 5SS
TEL:01533 558 763

The National Drugs Helpline - 0800 77 66 00

RELEASE (information about drugs and the law) -
0171 603 8654

Release (Drugs in School Helpline)
TEL:0345 36 66 66

SCODA (Standing Conference on Drug Abuse)
32-36 Loman Street
London SE1 0EE
TEL:0171 928 9500

Trust for the Study of Adolescence
23 New Road
Brighton
East Sussex, BN1 1WZ
TEL:01273 693311

Smoking

ASH (Action of Smoking and Health)
16 Fitzhardinge Street
London W1H 9PL
TEL:0171 224 0743

QUIT - 0800 002200

Respect
Brewer Blackler
The Little Green
Richmond
Surrey TW9 1QH
TEL:0181 296 1919

Solvents

Re-Solv
30A High Street
Stone, Staffs ST15 8AW
TEL:01785 817 885

Gambling

BACTA
(Representing Britain's Pay-to-Play Leisure
Machine Industry)
BACTA House
Regents Wharf
6 All Saints Street,
London N1 9RQ
0171 713 7144

BACTA Helpline - 0845 6000133

Camelot Group plc
The National Lottery
PO Box 1010
Liverpool L70 1NL
TEL: 0645 100000

Telephone Helpline 0541 56 16 16
(when someone under 16 has purchased a ticket)

GAM-ANON (for partners and families of
compulsive gamblers)
PO Box 88
London SW10 0EU
TEL:0171 384 3040

GamCare
Suite 1
25-27 Catherine Place
Westminster
London SW1E 6DU
TEL:0171 233 8988

UK Forum on Young People & Gambling
PO Box 5
Chichester
West Sussex
PO19 3RB
TEL:01243 538 635

Media

The Advertising Association
Ashford House
15 Wilton Road
London SW1V 1NJ
TEL:0171 828 2771

Advertising Standards Authority
Brook House
Torrington Place
London WC1
TEL: 0171 580 5555

Press Complaints Commission
1 Salisbury Square
London EC4Y 8AE
TEL:0171 353 1248

Directory

Photo Marketing Association
 International (UK) Ltd
Peel Place
50 Carver Street
Birmingham B1 3AS
TEL:0121 212 0299

TeenAge Magazine Arbitration Panel
c/o Periodical Publishers Association
28 Kingsway
London WC2B 6JR
TEL:0171 405 0819

Chatlines

Independent Committee for the Supervision of
Standards of Telephone
Information Services (ICSTIS)
3rd Floor, Alton House
177 High Holborn
London WC1V 7AA
Chatline:0171 240 5511

Film

British Board of Film Classification
3 Soho Square
London W1V 6HD
TEL: 0171 439 7961

Video Standards Council
Kinetic Business Centre
Theobald Street
Borehamwood
Hertfordshire WD6 4SE
TEL:0181 387 4020

Internet

NCH Action for Children (Internet)
85 Highbury Park
London N5 1UD
TEL:0171 226 2033

Television and Radio

Broadcasting Standards Commission
TEL:0171 233 0544

Independent Television Commission
33 Foley Street
London W1P 7LB
TEL: 0171 255 3000

National Viewers' and Listeners' Association
All Saints House
High Street
Colchester CO1 1UG
TEL:01206 561155

Radio Authority
Holbrook House
14 Great Queen Street
London WC2B 5DG
TEL:0171 430 2724

PART 6 – EDUCATION

Advisory Centre for Education (ACE)
Unit 1B
Aberdeen Studios
22-24 Highbury Grove
London N5 2DQ
TEL:0171 354 8321 (advice line)

Anti-Bullying Campaign
185 Tower Bridge Road
London
SE1 2UF
TEL:0171 378 1446

Boarding Schools Association
Ysgol Nant
Valley Road
Llanfairfechan
Gwynedd
LL33 0ES
TEL:01248 680542

Boarding School Survivors (BSS)
128a Northview Road
London
N8 7LP
TEL:0181 341 4885

Campaign for Real Education
18 Westlands Grove
Stockton Lane
York
YO3 0EF
TEL:0171 937 2122

Campaign for State Education (CASE)
158 Durham Road
London SW20 0DG
TEL:0181 944 8206

Careers Research and Advisory Centre (CRAC)
2nd Floor
Sheraton House
Castle Park
Cambridge CB3 0AX
TEL:01223 460 277

Centre for Studies on Inclusive Education
1 Redland Close
Elm Lane
Redland
Bristol BS6 6UE
TEL:0117 923 8450

The Children's Society
Edward Rudolf House
Margery Street
London WC1X 0JL
TEL:0171 837 4299

School Admissions Team
Department for Education & Employment
3F Sanctuary Buildings
Great Smith Street
London SW1P 3BT
TEL:0171 925 5525

School Liaisons Manager
Technology Colleges Trust
9 Whitehall
London SW1A 2DD
TEL:0171 839 9339

Education Otherwise
General Enquiries:
PO Box 7420
London N9 9SG
TEL:0891 518 303

End Physical Punishment of Children (EPOCH)
77 Holloway Road
London N7 8JZ
TEL:0171 700 0627

English Schools' Athletics Association
26 Newborough Green
New Malden
Surrey KT3 5HS
TEL:0181 949 1506

Grant Maintained Schools Centre
36 Great Smith Street
London SW1P 3BU
TEL:0171 233 4666

Independent Schools Careers Organisation
12A Princess Way
Camberley
Surrey GU15 3SP
TEL:01276 21188

Independent Schools Information Service (ISIS)
56 Buckingham Gate
London SW1E 6AG
TEL:0171 630 8793/4

Local Government Ombudsman
(Greater London, Kent, Surrey, East and West Sussex)
21 Queen Anne's Gate
London
SW1H 9BU
TEL:0171 915 3210

(East Anglia, the South, the South West and Central England)
The Oaks
Westwood Way
Westwood Business Park
Coventry CV4 8JB
TEL:01203 695 999

(East Midlands and North of England)
Beverley House
17 Shipton Road
York YO3 6FZ
TEL:01904 630 151

National Association of Governors & Managers (NAGM)
Suite 36-38
21 Bennetts Hill
Birmingham B2 5QP
TEL:0121 643 5787

National Confederation of
Parent-Teacher Associations (NCPTA)
2 Ebbsfleet Estate
Stonebridge Road
Gravesend
Kent DA11 9DZ
TEL:01474 560 618

Parliamentary Commissioner for Administration
Church House
Great Smith Street
London SW1P 3BW
TEL:0171 276 3000

Directory

Pre-School Learning Alliance
69 Kings Cross Road
London WC1X 9LL
TEL: 0171 833 0991
Childcare helpline: 0171 837 5513

Pre-School Playgroups Association
69 Kings Cross Road
London
WC1X 9LL
TEL:0171 833 0991

Pupils, Parents and Youth Group
Department for Education
and Employment
Sanctuary Buildings
Great Smith Street
London
SW1P 3BT

Qualifications, Curriculum
and Assessment Authority for Wales
Castle Buildings
Womanby Street
Cardiff
CF1 9SX
TEL:01222 375400

Qualifications Curriculum and
Assessment Authority
Newcombe House
45 Notting Hill Gate
London
W11 3JB
TEL:0171 229 1234

Schools Need Governors
Department of Education
Room 3E1
Sanctuary Buildings
Great Smith Street
London
SW1P 3BT
TEL:0171 925 5000

Welsh Office Education Department
Schools Administration
 Division 3
4th Floor
Welsh Office
Cathays Park
Cardiff
CF1 3NQ
TEL:01222 825 111

Special Needs

Contact a Family
170 Tottenham Court Road
London W1P 0HA
Helpline:0171 383 3555

Council for Disabled Children
c/oNational Children's Bureau
8 Wakley Street, London EC1V 7QE
TEL:0171 843 6061

DIAL UK
Park Lodge
St Catherine's Hospital
Tickhill Road
Doncaster DN4 8QN
TEL:01302 310 123

Disability Law Service
Room 241, 2nd Floor
49-51 Bedford Row
London WC1R 4LR
TEL: 0171 831 8031

Down's Syndrome Association
155 Mitcham Road
London SW17 9PG
TEL:0181 682 4001

Genetic Interest Group (GIG)
Farringdon Point
29-35 Farringdon Road
London EC1M 3JB
TEL:0171 430 0090

I CAN
Barbican Citygate
1-3 Dufferin Street
London EC1Y 8NA
TEL:0171 374 4422

Mencap (London Division)
Early Years Project
115 Golden Lane
London EC1Y 0TJ
TEL:0171 454 0454

MIND (National Association for Mental Health)
Granta House
15-19 Broadway
Stratford
London E15 4BQ
TEL:0181 519 2122

ParentAbility (provides support for
disabled parents)
c/o National Childbirth Trust
Alexander House
Oldham Terrace
London W3 6NH
TEL:0181 992 8637

Parentline
The Endway House
Hadley
Benfleet
Essex SS7 2AN
TEL:01702 559 900 (for local group)

Royal Society for Mentally Handicapped Children
& Adults (MENCAP)
123 Golden Lane
London EC1Y 0RT
TEL:0171 454 0454

SKILL
National Bureau for Students with Disabilities
336 Brixton Road
London SW9 7AA
TEL:0171 274 0565

Supportive Parents
c/o HFT
Merchants House
Wapping Road
Bristol BS1 4RW
TEL:0117 977 2225

PART 7 – CRIME

Child Abduction Unit
Official Solicitor's Office
81 Chancery Lane
London WC2A 1DD
TEL:0171 911 7047/7140

ChildLine
Royal Mail Building
Studd Street
London N1 0QW
TEL: 0171 239 1000
or address for children:
Childline
Freepost 1111
London N1 0BR
Freephone: 0800 1111
Freephone for children in care: 0800 884444
Minicom: 0800 400222

The Children's Legal Centre
PO Box 3314
London N1 2WA
TEL:0171 359 9392
TEL: (Advice Line) 0171 359 6251
(open 2pm - 5pm weekdays)

Criminal Injuries Compensation Board
Tay House, 300 Bath Street
Glasgow G2 4JR
TEL:0141 331 2726

Foreign and Commonwealth Office
Consular Division
1 Palace Street
London SW1E 5HE
TEL:0171 270 1500

Law Society Children Panel
The Law Society
113 Chancery Lane
London WC2A 1PL
TEL:0171 242 1222

Legal Aid Head Office (England and Wales)
85 Gray's Inn Road
London WC1X 8AA
TEL: 0171 813 1000

Metropolitan Police Service
New Scotland Yard
Broadway
London SW1H 0BG
TEL:0171 230 1212

National Association for the Care and Resettlement
of Offenders, (NACRO)
169 Clapham Road,
London SW9 0PU
TEL:0171 582 6500

NSPCC
42 Curtain Road
London EC2A 3NH
TEL:0171 825 2500
Helpline:0800 800 500

Reunite
National Council for
Abducted Children
PO Box 4
London WC1X 3DX
TEL:0171 404 8356 (Advice Line)
TEL:0171 404 8357 (Admin Line)

Directory

The United Kingdom Passport Agency
Clive House
Petty France
London SW1H 9HD
TEL:0990 210 410

Victim Support
National Office
Cranmer House
39 Brixton Road
London SW9 6DZ
TEL:0171 735 9166

GENERAL

Family Policy Studies Centre
231 Baker Street
London NW1 6XE
TEL:0171 486 8211

Federation of Independent Advice Centres (FIAC)
4 Deans Court
St Paul's Churchyard
London EC4V 5AA
TEL:0171 489 1800

General Register Office
(Births, Deaths & Marriages)
St Catherine's House
10 Kingsway
London WC2B 6JB
TEL:0171 242 0262
or
Office for National Statistics
General Register Office
Smedley Hydro
Trafalgar Road
Birkdale
Southport PR8 2HH
TEL:01704 569824

Immigration and Nationality Department
Lunar House
40 Wellesley Road
Croydon
Surrey CR9 2BY
Tel: 0181 686 0688

Law Centres Federation (offices nationwide)
Duchess House
18-19 Warren Street
London W1P 5DB
TEL:0171 387 8570

The Law Society
113 Chancery Lane
London WC2A 1PL
TEL:0171 242 1222

Legal Aid Head Office
85 Gray's Inn Road
London WC1X 8AA
TEL:0171 813 1000

Principal Registry of the Family Division
First Avenue House
High Holborn
London WC1
TEL:0171 936 6976

The Prince's Trust
18 Park Square East
London NW1 4LH
TEL:0171 543 1234

The Samaritans
10 The Grove
Slough SL1 1QP
TEL:01753 532 713

The United Kingdom Passport Agency
Clive House
70-78 Petty France
London SW1H 9HD
TEL:0990 210 410

Wales Advocacy Unit
The Children's Society
14 Cathedral Road
Cardiff
South Glamorgan
CF1 9LJ
TEL:01222 668956
Advice line: 0800 581862

INDEX

Abandonment of child, 41, 69, 106
Abduction, 40, 183-4, 201
Abortion
    fathers and, 11
    lawful, conditions for, 10-11, 179
    prosecution for, 179
    time limit for, 10-11
Abuse. *See* Child abuse
Accidents
    caused by children, 107-8
    compensation. *See* Compensation
    dangerous games, involving, 185
    insurance, 108, 109
    negligence. *See* Negligence
    road. *See* Road safety
    safety measures, 111-14, 196
    to a child, 105-7
Action plan orders, 172, 177
Activity holidays, safety of, 110
Adopted child
    family unit, as part of, 49
    intestacy, succession under, 81
    stepfamily and, 71
Adoption
    abroad, from, 24
    adopting parents, 22-5
    advice, 22, 24, 193-4
    age limit, 24
    changing patterns of, 17, 24
    child
        contact with natural parents, 24
        passing on information to, 25
    definition, 22
    gay couple, by, 25
    grandparent, by, 74, 75
    guardian, court-appointed, role of, 89
    inspection reports, 17
    natural parents, role of, 22-4
    post-adoption services, 25
    procedures, 23-4
    religion and, 43
    review, 25
Advertising
    children, protection of, 55
    cigarettes, 124
    television, on, 130-1
Age
    compulsory school age, 55-6, 140-1
    duration of childhood, 164
    majority, of, 31
Alcohol
    abuse of
        generally, 124
        pregnancy, during, 6
    alcopops, 124, 127
    consumption over 18, 120
    drunk in charge of child, 126-7
    employment of minor in bar, 127
    helplines etc, 196
    licensing controls, 124-7
    police powers, 126, 166
    rules as to, 124-6
    under-age drinking, 119, 124-7, 166
Amniocentesis test, 7-8
Anabolic steroids, 122

Anorexia nervosa, treatment of, 99-100
Antenatal care
    medical negligence, 6
    screening, 7-9
    time off work for, 2-3
Anti-social behaviour order, 164, 176
Apprenticeship, contract of, 53
Arcade machines, 137
Armed forces, service in, 31
Assault
    child, on, 69, 106, 179, 180

Baby
    clothing, safety of, 111, 113-14
    handicapped, 7-8
    injury to, 6-7
    NHS card for, 16, 92
    nursery equipment for, 111, 113
Baby-sitters, 69, 105
Back-to-work schemes, 69
Bail, 172
BBC, 129
Bereavement
    counselling, 190
    fostering and, 76
    parenting and, 79-81
Betting, licensing of, 136-7
Binding over, 173
Birth of child
    advisory services, 189
    'attendance at', 12
    birth certificate, 16, 23
    Caesarean section, by, 13
    home, at, 12
    hospital, in, 12-14
    infanticide following, 15, 179
    medical examination of baby, 92
    mother's rights, 12-13
    multiple birth, 11
    name of child, registration of, 38
    notice of, 15
    post-natal care, 14-15
    premature, 14
    registration of
        married parents, by 15
        surrogate mother, by, 16, 26-7
        unmarried parents, in case of, 15-16, 30, 38, 39
    stillborn, 14, 81, 190
Blood test
    paternity, to determine, 32-4
    pregnant woman, 7
Bookmakers, 136
British Board of Film Classification, 132, 133
Broadcasting standards, 129-30, 198
Bullying, 155, 158, 159, 198
Burial, 81

Car
    insurance, 55
    learner-driver, 116
    seatbelts, 114-15
Care order
    application for, 86, 89
    factors to be considered, 83, 85

204 Index

grandparents, in favour of, 74, 75
scope of, 85-6
Careers information and advice, 154, 199
Chaperones, 59
Chatlines, 135, 198
Child abuse
  carried out by another child, 183
  child in care, 88, 181
  compensation for victim, 185-6
  generally, 106, 179-80
  home, in, 179, 181-2
  internet and, 134
  police protection, 181
  prosecution, 181
  public protection, 183
  reporting, 87
  stranger, by, 182
Child assessment order
  application for, 86
  challenging, 87-8
  scope of, 84-6
Child at risk, 29, 81-9
Child benefit, 190
Child destruction, 179
Child in care
  abuse of, 88, 181
  care order. *See* Care order
  helpline, 86
  medical examination of, 98
Child in danger, 85-7
Child in need
  'carers', protection from, 88
Child Protection Registers, 83-4
  court orders
    application for, 86-7
    challenging, 87-8
    factors to be considered, 84
    types of, 84-6
  definition, 84
  duties etc of local authority, 83, 84
  independent representation, 192
  young carer as, 81
Child of family: definition, 47, 49, 81
Child Protection Registers, 83-4
Child safety order, 176
Child support (*See also* Maintenance of child)
  application for, 33
  Child Support Agency, role of, 34-6, 72, 190-1
  Child Support Appeal Tribunal, 36, 37, 38
  Child Support Commissioner, 37-8
  DNA testing and, 33
Childbirth. *See* Birth of child
Childminder
  accident report form, 65
  choice of, 62
  contract, 62-5
  criminal liability, 106
  disciplining child, 65, 69
  duty of care, 108
  informal, 61
  legal requirements, 61, 107
   search for, 61-2
  tax, 65
Children's homes, 76, 179, 194
Cigarettes, 123-4
Cinema
  films, classification of, 132, 133, 198
  licensing, 133
Clothing, flammability of, 111 113-14

Coach seatbelts, 115
Committal proceedings, 186
Community care legislation, 81
Community sentences, 172, 173
Compensation
  administration of award for child, 186
  child victims, 184-6, 201
  death of child, 81
Computer games, 133
Consent to medical treatment. *See* Healthcare
Contact centres, 51
Contact order
  application for, 46, 49, 89
  challenging, 87-8
  grandparent, for, 74, 75
  nature of, 46, 47, 86
  suitability of, 47
Contraceptive advice, 96
Contract
  childminder and parents, 62-5
  minor, of
    exceptions to general rule, 52-3
    general rule, 52
    guaranteeing child's debt, 54
    insurance, 55
    parent-child agreement, 54
    parents' liability, 53-4
    return of goods, 54
    review of law, 52
  private nanny, 66
Contributory negligence, 116
Co-parenting, 22
Corporal punishment, 42-3, 65, 155-6, 179
Cot deaths, 190
Counselling
  adoption, as to, 24, 25, 193-4
  drug addiction, 97, 122, 196-7
  fertility treatment, as to, 18, 21, 190-1
  gambling, as to, 136, 197
  marriage, 49
  school nurse, by, 92
  smoking, 197
  surrogacy arrangements, where, 27
County schools, 141, 143-5, 146, 157
Courts
  criminal proceedings, 164-5, 171
  evidence of children, 164, 186-7
  publicity, constraints on, 171-2
Creches, 68, 69
Cremation, 81
Criminal Injuries Compensation Board, 184-6, 201
Crime
  anti-social behaviour, 164, 176
  child victims of, 178-87
  children and, generally, 164-5
  compensation, 184-6
  courts system. *See* Youth courts
  evidence of children, 164, 186-7
  'guilty intention', 165
  legal advice, 164, 167
  offensive weapons, 165, 174-5
  parents' liability, 106, 175-6
  penalties. *See* Youth justice
  police procedure. *See* Police
  proposed changes to law, 164-5, 176-7
  right to silence, 167
  youth justice. *See* Youth justice
  See also under name of particular crime
Crossbow, offences as to, 175

Index

Cruelty to child, 179
Curfew schemes, 176
Custodial sentences, 165
Cyclists, safety of, 115-16

Dangerous games, 185
Day nursery
  equipment, safety of, 111, 113
  local authority nursery, 67, 108
  private nursery, 67
  registration of, 67-8
  types of, 67
Death of child
  burial/cremation, 81
  compensation, 81
  crimes involving, 178-9
  support organisations, 81, 190
Dental treatment
  child, for, 43, 92
  pregnancy, during, 2
Dietary supplements, 2
Directory, 189-203
Disabled adult, young carer for, 81-2
Disabled child
  born disabled, 6-7
  fostering, 76
  trust for, 81
See also Special educational needs
Discipline
  childminder, by, 65, 69
  parental, 42-3
  school, 155-7
Divorce
  care order and, 86
  child of the family: definition, 47, 49
  delay, 48
  financial provision, 50
  mediation services, 45, 49, 192
  new legislation, 28
  orders relating to children
    most suitable, 47-9
    orders available, 46
    scope of, 47
    who can obtain, 46
  procedure, 49-50
  reconciliation, 49
  welfare of children, 45-6, 48-9
DNA testing, 32-3
Doctor
  complaints about, 102, 104
  confidentiality, duty of, 96-7
  negligence. *See* Medical negligence
  refusal of treatment by, 100
  role of, 92
Domestic violence
  contact centres, 51
  generally, 28
  non-molestation order, 50-1, 73, 182
  occupation order, 50-1
Donor insemination, 19-21
Drinking
  drunk in charge of child, 126-7
  generally. *See* Alcohol
Drugs
  abuse, preventative measures, 120, 122
  addiction, counselling, 97, 122, 196-7
  anabolic steroids, 122
  controlled, 121
  'drugs czar', 120
  education as to, in school, 122

'herbal high' drugs, 123
licensed medicines, 120-1
offences, 121-3
pregnancy, taking during, 6-7
public entertainment licences and, 123
'soft drugs', legalization of, 120
solvent abuse, 123, 197
videos and, 131
Drunk in charge of child, 126-7
Duration of childhood, 164

Eating disorders, 99-100
Education (*See also* School)
  child performers etc, 58-9
  duty to educate, 139-43
  education supervision order, 84, 160
  free State education, 139
  further education, 150
  home-based education, 141-2
  legislation
    existing, scope of, 139
    proposed, 140, 161-2
  litigation, 139
  National Curriculum, 147, 151-4, 200
  nursery education, 141
  parental responsibilities, 29, 140, 160
  political education, 154
  private sector, 139, 155-6, 199
  pupil referral units, 157-8
  religious, 43, 152-3
  school leaving age, 55-6, 140-1
  sex education, 154
  sick child, 92, 101, 150-1, 159
  special educational needs. *See* Special educational needs
  work experience, 57
  young carer and, 82
  young offender institution, in, 174
Emergency protection order, 85-8, 97
Emigration, 28, 39-40
Employment
  bars, in, 127
  child: meaning, 56
  child models, 58-9
  child performers, 58-9
  childcare facilities, 61
  contract of, 53
  directory services, 193
  employment card, 56-7
  health and safety requirements, 57-8
  pregnancy, during, 2-5
  private nanny. *See* Nanny
  taxation of earned income, 54
  under-18s, restrictions as to, 56-7, 59
  unfair dismissal, 4-5
  welfare of child, 57
  work permit, 57
Evidence of children, 164, 186-7
Eyesight tests, 92-3

Family assistance orders, 47
Family centres, 68, 69
Family credit, 37, 190
Family home
  occupation order, 50-1
  transfer of property order, 50
Family planning, 189
Fatal Accidents Acts, claims under, 81
Father
  abortion and, 11

donor insemination, in case of, 19-20
father-to-be, time off work, 5
genetic screening, 9
maintenance of child. *See* Maintenance of child
Fertility treatment
   age restrictions, 17, 22
   child's right to know parental background, 21
   clinics available for, 18, 190-1
   confidentiality of donors, 21
   counselling, 18, 22, 190-1
   donor insemination, 19-21
   gender restrictions, 22
   genetic material, supply of, 18-19
   IVF treatment, 19
   legal consequences of, on parenthood, 20-1
   legislation as to, 17-18
   procedures, 18
   relationships, 18-22
Films
   classification, 132, 133, 198
   television, on, 130
Firearms offences, 174-5
Fireworks
   criminal offences, 113
   safety of, 112-13
Forms
   FEW 8, 2
   FP 58, 16
   MAT B1, 4
   See also Police
Fostering
   advisory services, 193-4
   carer
      assessment of, 77-8
      complaint by, 87
      consent to medical treatment of child, 98
      duties of, 78
      negligence, 78, 107
   involuntary, 76
   local authority, 77-9, 85
   offences, 77
   private, 76-7
   religion and, 43
   Utting Report, 79, 88
   voluntary, 76-7
Fruit machines, 136-7

Gambling
   addiction, 136, 197
   licensing, 136-7
   restrictions on, 119, 135-6
Gay couples, adoption by, 25
Genetic testing, 8-9
Gifted child, education of, 150
Gifts, taxation of, 54-5
Grandparents
   guardian, appointment of, 79
   local authorities and, 75
   orders available to, 74
   rights of, 73-4
Grant-maintained schools, 141, 143-6, 157, 199
Guarantee of child's debts, 54
Guardian
   allowance, 80, 190
   appointment of, 79, 80
   court-appointed, 88-9
   granchild, for, 74, 75
   legal aid, 81

refusal to act, 80
stepchild, for, 72

Handicapped baby, life of, 9-10
Healthcare
   antenatal. *See* Antenatal care
   complaints about treatment
      NHS, 102-4
      private treatment, 104
   consent to treatment
      child, by, 95-6
      dental treatment, 92
      eating disorders, 99-100
      emergency, 97-9
      foster carer, by, 98
      grandparent, by, 73
      local authority, by, 97-8
      parents, by, 95
      relatives and friends, by, 98
   continuity of, importance of, 97
   contraceptive advice, 96
   dental treatment, 2, 43, 92
   directory, 195-6
   doctors. *See* Doctor
   entitlements, 92-5
   eyesight, 92-3
   free prescriptions, 2, 93
   generally, 91
   health visitors, 92
   hospitalization, 12-14, 100-1, 104
   immunizations, 93-4
   mental health, 101-2
   negligence. *See* Medical negligence
   refusal of treatment, 99-100
   school health, 92
   special needs. *See* Special educational needs
'Herbal high' drugs, 123
HIV test, 7, 21
Holidays, school and, 160
Hospitalization
   birth of child, for, 12-14
   children, of, generally, 100-1, 104
   education during, 101
   mental health and, 101-2
Human Fertilization and Embryology Authority, 17-18, 190
Human Rights
   European Convention, 42, 88, 153
   European Court of, 88
   information centre, 192

Ill-treatment of child, 41, 69, 71, 87, 179
Immigration, 40, 202
Immunizations
   consent to, 94
   range available, 93-4
Incest, 172, 180
Income support
   availability of, 57
   reduced benefit direction, 37
Indecent assault, 180
Indecent photographs, 181
Independent Television Commission, 129-30, 198
Infanticide, 15, 179
Infertile couples
   adoption by. *See* Adoption
   fertility treatment. *See* Fertility treatment
Inheritance, 30, 70, 72, 80-5
Insurance
   accident, 108, 109

Index

childminder, 62
contracts of, 55
life, 55
nanny, 66-7
travel, 55
International Treaties, 8
Internet and children, 134-5, 198
Intestacy
illegitimate child's position, 30
rules, 72, 80-1
Intoxicating liquor
definition, 124-5
generally. *See* alcohol
IVF treatment, 19

Jobseeker's allowance, 57
Judicial reviews, 87-8

Knives, offences as to, 174, 175

Learner-drivers, 116
Learning difficulties. *See* Special educational needs
Legal aid
child, for, 48, 103, 169, 171
child support cases, 38
grandparents, for, 73
guardian, for, 81
mediation services, for, 49
medical negligence cases, 103-4
offices, 201, 202
parent, available to, 88
Legitimacy, 30
Legitimation of child, 16
Lesbian relationships, 22
Life insurance, 55
Local authority
child in care of. *See* Child in care
child in need. *See* Child in need
childminders and, 61-2
day nurseries and, 67-8
education. *See* Education
family centres, 68
grandparents and, 75
negligence, 106-8
parental responsibilities and, 83, 97
police and, 164
private fostering, notice of, 76
special educational needs. *See* Special educational needs
young carers, support for, 81
Local Government Ombudsman, 88
Lone parents
back-to-work scheme, 69
maintenance of child, 28
organizations regarding, 195

Maintenance of child
abroad, 35
appeals, 36-7
assessment of maintenance, 34-5
child support legislation, 34-6
confidential issues, 36
departure direction, 36
disabled child, 36
divorce and, 50
duty to maintain, 28
educational expenses, 31, 36
father's duty, 33, 34
private arrangements, 35

reduced benefit direction, 37
review of, 37
single parent family, 28
step-child, 36, 70, 72
Manslaughter
conviction of, 178
sentence, 179
Marriage
breakdown. *See* Divorce
cessation of parental responsibility, 31
minor, of, consent to, 41-2
preservation of, 45
stepfamily, within, 72
Married parents
child's passport, 40
donor insemination, 19
fertility treatment. *See* Fertility treatment
naming of child, 38-9
parental responsibilities. *See* Parental responsibilities
registration of birth of child, 15
Maternity
allowances, 2, 4
leave
return to work after, 5
right to, 4
statutory maternity pay, 4
Media entertainment, rules as to, 119, 127-35
Medical negligence
access to records, 103
assisted conception, in case of, 19
birth of child, 14
legal costs, 103-4
pregnancy, during, 6-7
proof of, 102-3
suing on child's behalf, 103
time limit for claim, 103
Medical treatment
child, for, 43
generally. *See* Healthcare
prolonging life, 9-10, 99
Mental illness, treatment of, 100-1, 195
Mentally handicapped person, legal aid for, 81
Minibus seatbelts, 115
Miscarriage, 81
Mopeds, safety of, 116
Motor cycles, 116
Motor insurance, 55
Murder
conviction of, 178
sentence for, 174, 179
trial for, 171

Name of child
change of, 38-9, 73
registration, 38
unmarried mother, of, 38-9
Nanny
choice of, 66
insurance, 66-7
nanny-share, 67
regulations as to, 66
tax, 67
National Curriculum, 147, 151-4, 200
National Health Service (*See also* Healthcare)
complaints about treatment, 102-4
NHS card, 16, 92
pregnancy
dental treatment during, 2

Index

free prescriptions, 2
National insurance, 57
National Lottery, 119, 135-7
National Register of Paedophiles, 180, 183
National Society for the Prevention of Cruelty to Children, 85, 86, 195, 201
Nationality of child, 28, 40
Natural parents
  adoption and, 22-4
  fostering and, 78, 79
Necessaries, contracts for, 52-3, 55
Neglect of child, 71, 87, 106, 179
Negligence
  childminder, of, 62
  contributory negligence, 116
  criminal liability distinguished, 106
  local authority, 106-8
  parents' liability, 105-8
  schools, 108 -11, 155
Next friend of child, 14
Non-molestation order, 50-1, 73, 182
Nursery
  day nursery. *See* Day nursery
  equipment, safety of, 111, 113
  schools, 141

Oath, taking of, 186
Occupier's liability
  children and, 116-7
  schools and, 108, 109
Offensive weapons, children and, 165, 174-5
Outdoor activity centres, 110
Overseas school trips, 111

Parental contact order. *See* Contact order
Parental order, 26
Parental responsibilities
  appointment of guardian and, 29
  criminal liability, and, 106, 165, 175-6
  definition, 28, 29, 41
  discipline, keeping, 42-3
  education and, 140, 160
  fostering and, 77-8, 140
  grandparents and, 74
  local authorities and, 83, 97
  marriage of minor, as to, 41-2
  married parents, 29
  medical tretment of child, 43
  naming of child and, 38-9
  parental duties and, 28, 41
  Parental Responsibility Agreement, 30-1
  Parental Responsibility Order, 31
  protection of child, 41
  religious upbringing of child, 43-4
  residence order and. *See* Residence order
  sharing of, 31
  step-parents and, 71-2
  termination of, 31
  unmarried parents
    child's position, 30
    father's position, 30
    mother's position, 29-30
Parenting orders, 84, 160, 164, 175-6
Parents
  adoption and. *See* Adoption
  lone. *See* Lone parent
  married. *See* Married parents
  Step-parents. *See* Step-parents
  unmarried. *See* Unmarried parents
Passport for child, 28, 40-1, 184, 202

Paternity
  blood tests, 32, 34
  declaration of, 15
  DNA testing, 32-3
  issue as to, 28
  presumption as to, 32
Pedestrians, safety of, 115
Photographs, indecent, 181
Playground equipment, 117
Playgroups, 68, 69, 200
Police
  caution by, 168-70
  children and, 164-5, 181
  laying a charge, 169
  police station, procedure at, 166-70
  procedure, 165-70
  raves, powers as to, 166
  stop and search powers, 165-6
  under-age drinking and, 126, 166
  youth and community sections, 165
  warning by, 168-9
Political education, 154
Pre-school care, 60-9, 200
Pregnancy
  antenatal care. *See* Antenatal care
  dental treatment during, 2
  dietary supplements during, 2
  directory services, 189
  employment, during, 2-5
  free healthcare, 2, 6
  miscarriage, 14
  school, absence from, 157
  taking care during, 6-7
  teenage, 154, 158
  termination of, 9-11
Press Complaints Commission, 119, 198
Presumption of paternity, 32
Private nanny. *See* Nanny
Prohibited steps order
  application for, 46, 49
  scope of, 41, 43, 46
  suitability of, 47
Psychological injury to child, 105
Psychotic state after childbirth, 15
Pupil referral units, 157-8

Racial origins, fostering and, 77
Radio
  broadcasting standards, 129, 198
  parental control, 128-9
Rape, 181, 185
Raves, 166
Reckless driving, 6
Religion
  adoption and, 23, 43
  blood test, and refusal of, 33
  edcuation and, 152-3
  fostering and, 43, 77
Reparation order, 172, 176-7
Residence order
  application for, 31-2, 46, 49
  divorce proceedings, 46-7, 49
  effect of, 38
  grandparent, for, 74
  guardian, to displace, 80
  parental responsibilities and, 46
  step-parents, for, 71
  suitability, 47
  taking child out of jurisdiction, 39-41
  termination of, 85

Index

Road safety
  child seatbelts, 114-15
  contributory negligence, 116
  cyclists, 115-16
  learner-drivers, 116
  mopeds, 116
  motor cycles, 116
  pedestrians, 115
  prevention of accidents, 196
Rubella
  immunization, 94
  screening for, 9

Safety
  accidents and, *See* Accidents
  adventure activities, of, 110
  clothing, of 111, 113-14
  fireworks, measures as to, 112-13
  nursery equipment, of, 113
  occupier's liability, 108, 109, 116-17
  playground equipment, of, 117
  school, at. *See* School
  toys, requirements for, 111-12, 196
  work, at, 57-8
School (*See also* Education)
  admission procedures, 142-3, 161-2
  annual parents' meeting, 140, 145
  anti-smoking education, 122, 124
  assisted places, 150
  attendance order, 141
  bullying, 155, 158, 159, 198
  careers information and advice, 154, 199
  categories of, 141, 161
  child with special educational needs. *See* Special educational needs
  choice of, 140, 124-5
  class sizes, 162
  compulsory school age, 55-6, 140-1
  county, 141, 143-5, 146, 157
  detention, 156
  discipline, 155-7
  drug education in, 122
  failing schools, 162
  grant-maintained, 141, 143-6, 152, 157
  healthcare, 92
  holidays during term, 160
  home-school agreements, 162
  justifiable absence from, 159-60
  negligence, 108-11, 155
  nursery school, 141
  parent governors, 140, 146
  poor progress in class, 158-9
  premises, safety of, 108
  primary school, 142
  pupil exclusion, 156-7, 162
  registration of child, 141
  secondary, 143-5
  security, 160-1, 174
  staff claim against pupil, 11
  supervision of pupils
    break times, at, 109
    out of school hours, 110
    sports, during, 109-1
  trips, safety of, 110, 111
  truancy, 155, 159, 161
  voluntary, 141, 143-5, 146, 157
  walking distance, 142-3, 159
Scratch cards, 136
Screening
  pre-pregnancy, 8-9
  pregnancy, during, 7-9
Secretary of State, role of, 87
Sex education, 154
Sexual offences
  child abuse. *See* Child abuse
  compensation for victim, 185-6
  generally, 179-80
  incest, 172, 180
  indecent assault, 180, 185
  indecent photographs, 181
  legal capacity, 181
  publicity, 172
  rape, 181, 185
  sex offender orders, 183
  unlawful sexual intercourse, 180
Shotgun offences, 165, 174-5
Sick children
  directory services, 195
  education of, 92, 101, 150-1, 159
Smoking (*See also* Tobacco)
  anti-smoking education, 122, 124
  changes in attitude to, 123
  counselling, 197
  pregnancy, during, 6
Solvent abuse, 122, 123, 197
Special educational needs
  child over 16, 150
  child under 5, 95
  Code of Practice, 147-8
  definition, 147
  directory services, 200-1
  disagreement as to provision of help, 151
  generally, 95, 140, 146-7
  gifted children, 150
  National Curriculum and, 152
  statement of, 148-50
  statutory assessment, 147, 148-9
Specific issue order
  application for, 40, 46, 49
  nature of, 43, 46, 47
Spectacles, vouchers for, 92-3
Sperm donation. 19-21
Stepchild
  contact order, 47
  family unit, part of, 47, 49
  intestacy rules and, 81
  maintenance of, 36, 72
Stepfamily
  associations regarding, 194
  inheritance, 70, 72
Step-parents
  adoption and, 71
  domestic violence, 73
  duties of, 70-1
  guardian, appointment of, 72
  natural parents and, 70
  parental responsibilities, 71-2, 140
  wills, 72
Stillbirths, 14, 190
Stress, counselling, 42
Supervision order
  application for, 86, 89
  challenging, 87-8
  education supervision order, 84, 160
  fostering and, 77
  scope of, 84, 85
Surrogacy arrangements
  commercial surrogacy, 26
  definition of surrogacy, 25
  enforcement of, 26

government review, 17
legal private arrangements, 26
obtaining records by child involved, 27
parental order, 26
registration of birth, 16, 26-7

Taxation
  childminder, 66
  gifts, 54-5
  guardian's allowance, 80
  nanny, 67
Teenage magazines, 133-4, 198
Teenage mothers, 158
Television
  advertisements, 130-1
  broadcasting standards, 129-30, 198
  evidence of child by TV link, 186
  films on 130
  parental control, 128-9
Theatre, child performers in, 58-9
Tobacco
  advertisements, 124
  sale of, 120, 123-4
  smoking, 120, 122-4
Toys
  safety requirements, 111-12, 196
Travel insurance, 55
Travelling alone, 116
Trespassers, children as, 117
Truancy, 155, 159, 161
Trust for disabled child, 81

Under-age drinking. See Alcohol
Unfair dismissal, 4-5
Unmarried father, orders available to, 46
Unmarried mother
  registration of child's birth, 38, 39
  surname of child, 39
Unmarried parents
  birth of child, registration of, 15-16
  child's passport, 40-1
  donor insemination, 19-21
  fertility treatment, 19-21

Victims of crime
  children as, 178-87
  generally, 165

Video
  classification process, 132
  consumer advice, 132
  evidence of child, 186
  games, 133
  offences, 132, 133
  parental control, 131
  standards control, 195
Violence
  domestic. See Domestic violence
  pregnant mother, to, 7
  screen, 129
  video, on, 131
Voluntary schools, 141, 143-5, 146, 157

Wardship
  definition, 89
  grandparents' application for, 74, 75
  procedure, 87, 89
  use of, 89, 100
Whooping cough vaccination, 94
Will
  need to make, 79, 80
  step-parent, 72
Work. See Employment

Young carer
  education, 82
  support services, 81
Youth courts (See also Youth justice)
  criminal proceedings, 164-5, 171
  evidence, 164, 186-7
  publicity, constraints on, 171- 2
Youth justice
  absolute discharge, 172
  bail, 172
  binding over, 173
  care orders, 86
  community sentence, 172, 173
  conditional discharge, 172
  courts. See Youth courts
  custodial sentence, 172, 173-4
  financial penalties, 172-3, 175
  murder cases, 171, 174
  penalties available, 172-4
  sex cases, 171, 172